Citizen Speak

Morality and Society Series

EDITED BY ALAN WOLFE

Citizen Speak

The Democratic Imagination in American Life

ANDREW J. PERRIN

THE UNIVERSITY OF CHICAGO PRESS   CHICAGO AND LONDON

ANDREW J. PERRIN is assistant professor of sociology at the University of North Carolina, Chapel Hill.

The University of Chicago Press, Chicago 60637
The University of Chicago Press, Ltd., London
© 2006 by The University of Chicago
All rights reserved. Published 2006
Printed in the United States of America

15 14 13 12 11 10 09 08 07 06   1 2 3 4 5

ISBN: 0-226-66079-6 (cloth)
ISBN: 0-226-66081-8 (paper)

Image credits: "Listening" in figures 1.1 and 1.2 courtesy of the Connecticut Department of Labor. "Talking" in figures 2.1 and 3.1 copyright © 2000 New Vision Technologies Inc. (NVTech.com). "Thinking" and "Practicing" in figures 2.1 and 3.1 © 2005 JupiterImages Corporation.

Library of Congress Cataloging-in-Publication Data

Perrin, Andrew J., 1971–
    Citizen speak : the democratic imagination in American life / Andrew J. Perrin.
        p.   cm.—(Morality and society series)
    Includes bibliographical references and index.
    ISBN 0-226-66079-6 (cloth : alk. paper)—ISBN 0-226-66081-8 (pbk. : alk. paper)
        1. Citizenship—United States.   2. Political participation—United States.   3. Political culture—United States.   4. United States—Politics and government—21st century—Public opinion.   5. Public opinion—United States.   I. Title.   II. Morality and society.
JK1759.P47   2006
323.6′50973—dc22

2005031373

⊗ The paper used in this publication meets the minimum requirements of the American National Standard for Information Sciences—Permanence of Paper for Printed Library Materials, ANSI Z39.48-1992.

Contents

Acknowledgments

This book found its genesis as I wrestled with ideas I first encountered as a student in Rick Valelly's seminar on American politics at Swarthmore College. When and why do people participate in politics? How do they understand and justify those decisions? I came to see that complete answers to these questions need the insights of sociology, not just those of political science proper, for the simple reason that sociology's intensely theoretical lens allows us to interpret anew problems whose study has become routine. Sociologists benefit from theoretical heterogeneity, which allows us to ask about the sociality of behaviors from voting to social movement participation and everything in between. Nevertheless, the lessons of that terrific seminar (along with the cynicism) have stuck with me. I came to the class with an appreciation for social theory and an activist bent, each of which made me cynical about the state of American democracy. I gained respect for the delicate balances among the myriad formal and informal institutions of that democracy, and for the importance of approaching big questions with empirical investigation.

In fact, it is a tribute to the extraordinary intellectual atmosphere at Swarthmore that the questions I started thinking about there have perplexed and motivated me for so many years. It was at Swarthmore that I had the good fortune to work with Robin Wagner-Pacifici on a senior thesis on the democratic transition in Namibia. My thinking about the representational and even aesthetic character of democracy began during that project. Robin's mentorship has continued to be helpful and gratifying. At Swarthmore I also met John Krinsky, my friend, comrade, and colleague, whose interest, challenge, and engagement suffuse this project. Robin and John both discussed this project in its early stages and offered incisive ideas and comments on drafts along the way.

Becoming immersed in the intellectual climate at Berkeley was a very nurturing way to enter professional sociology. My mentors there—my dissertation chair, Kim Voss, along with committee members Ann Swidler, Margaret Weir, and Henry Brady—offered academic rigor along with encouragement to be creative and imaginative along the way. Every doctoral student should enjoy the mixture of freedom and support they offered. My fellow students were a great bunch, and, in particular, Eric Klinenberg, Anna Korteweg, Laurie Schaffner, and Rachel Sherman have been close friends and colleagues. Each has helped with this project and provided constructive critique in different ways. Eric, in particular, has helped to guide this project from idea to book.

In Chapel Hill I've found another richly creative atmosphere in which to think about urgent issues of citizenship and engagement. Judith Blau, Charlie Kurzman, Felicia Mebane, Chris Smith, Meenu Tewari, and Wendy Wolford offered helpful comments on the book as well as friendship, advice, and support. Guang Guo was patient and helpful with statistical advice for chapter 2. Sharon Christ (who helped write chapter 2) did great work implementing the analysis there. Students Sarah MacCarthy and Sondra Smolek provided expert research assistance.

Doug Mitchell has been the ideal champion of the book. He is the consummate intellectual, having far surpassed his role of shepherding the book through review and publication. Our initial conversation ranged from Plato to the aesthetics of gourmet food, all the while remaining relevant to the project. His mind found connections to far-flung fields and sociological niches. He has improved the book immeasurably. Series editor Alan Wolfe has been excited about the project, challenging, and intellectually stimulating. Nick Murray's careful editing has made the book's arguments far clearer.

Without the 143 focus group participants, as well as the organizations and people around Alameda County who agreed to help recruit participants and organize the focus groups, the research would have been impossible. Unfortunately, I cannot acknowledge them by name without violating guarantees of anonymity, so this generic statement of gratitude must suffice. You know who you are.

Portions of the research for this book were funded by the National Science Foundation (Doctoral Dissertation Improvement Grant number SBR-9900805); a Charlotte W. Newcombe Fellowship from the Woodrow Wilson Fellowship Foundation; and two Humanities Research Grants from the University of California, Berkeley. Diane Beeson, at California

State University, Hayward, provided meeting space for some of the focus groups, as did the UC Berkeley Extension Center at Fremont. A version of chapter 7 appears as "Political Microcultures," *Social Forces* 84 (2005): 1049–82 (copyright © 2005 by the University of North Carolina Press; used by permission of the publisher).

While friends, colleagues, and institutional contexts have contributed much to my sociological life, that life has been influenced immeasurably by its connection to the past. My grandmother, Rose Laub Coser, died before I began the project in earnest, but her creative, restless spirit motivates much of it. My grandfather, Lewis Coser, discussed the project with me many times and remains a personal and intellectual inspiration to me even after his death.

My parents, Jim and Ellen Perrin, have been interested and supportive on the long road leading to this book, and I owe much to them. My parents-in-law, Norman and Andrea Miller, have also been interested and helpful throughout. They discussed, read, edited, and commented in detail on many of the chapters—some of them several times. All four, in varying ways, are exemplars of engaged citizenship. My two amazing sons, Jonah and Daniel, underscore the urgency of invigorating a new kind of citizenship we can be proud of, as well as of valuing everyday talk and discovery.

Most important, though, is the emotional, intellectual, and creative input of my wife, Eliana, who has both kept me grounded and encouraged me to take off, as appropriate, throughout the work. She helped me come up with the idea for the research on our honeymoon, as we walked among olive groves in Tuscany, and she has patiently endured much time spent writing, thinking, talking, and agonizing. She has read every word and offered insights and suggestions on literally every step of this project. She is a personal and professional inspiration, and it is to her that the book is dedicated.

The successes of this research are due, at least in part, to these people and more. The failures remain my responsibility alone.

CHAPTER ONE

Citizenship, Creativity, and the Democratic Imagination

Imagine that you are reading your hometown paper one morning and come across a short item, buried on page 4A:

> Since Mayor Jones's election three years ago, crime rates in our area have been cut almost in half. Jones credits his get-tough approach to crime along with the license he has granted to the police department to cut crime however it sees fit.
>
> One controversial step the police department has taken is so-called "profile stops": pulling cars over for minor infractions in the hope that they will yield arrests for more serious crimes. Critics have called the practice punishment for "driving while black," noting that black drivers are three times as likely to be pulled over under the program as are white drivers.

You've heard about "racial profiling" before, on television and in the newspaper. You have some thoughts and feelings on the subject, but you have never become actively involved with it. But now things are different: the issue has come to your town. Decreasing crime is certainly a good thing for your community, but racial fairness is an important principle too. What if friends, neighbors, or colleagues are victimized by the police? What if they benefit from what seems like a real reduction in crime?

Suddenly, the debates are not so distant or abstract. Would you do anything about it? What would you do? Write a letter? Call a friend? Talk to a religious mentor? A work colleague? Worry about it silently all day? Just wait and see what others do? The answers to those questions are many and varied. Many citizens regard the problem of what to do as so complicated, daunting, or conflict-ridden that they ignore it altogether or treat it as if it remained a distant problem. The responses of others (whether supporting or opposing the policy) range from quietly assuming an opinion to becoming a leading voice for a particular position.

The premise of this book is that what you decide to do (or not do) is based largely on what you can imagine doing: what is possible, important, right, and feasible. These concerns, and others like them, are the stuff of what I call the *democratic imagination*. The democratic imagination is born in conversation with others at work, at home, in schools, organizations, associations, and neighborhoods, and through media like newspapers, television, movies, books, and the Internet.

I asked twenty groups of ordinary citizens to imagine being confronted with this scenario and three others, and to talk about them as groups. To understand how Americans' democratic imaginations work, I wanted to get a snapshot of democratic imaginations in action. This book uses those twenty conversations—their ideas, emotions, concerns, and conclusions— to develop an account of problems in the democratic imagination itself. It then provides a "diagnosis" of the contemporary American democratic imagination and, finally, a consideration of public policies that might "cure" it.

Citizenship in the United States

How do we learn good citizenship? This question is as difficult to answer as it is crucial to assessing the current health of American democracy. In this book, I propose that we fabricate a *democratic imagination* from our experiences in civic life, along with those in other domains such as work, family, and neighborhood. We use this democratic imagination to tell us when and why to get involved in politics, how to do so, and when and how to stay away. We use it to justify (to ourselves and others) decisions we have made. And we use it to decide when we can expect to convince fellow citizens of our political positions.

Since the design of the American republic, academics, commentators, politicians, and pundits have worried about the fragile state of American democracy (Schudson 1998). At various points in the nation's history, they have criticized citizens for the way they combine private and public concerns. In the 1950s, a raft of popular books worried about the disappearance of the individual in the urban, modern crowd (e.g., Riesman, Glazer, and Denney 1950; Vidich 1958; Whyte 1956). Looking back, recent commentators (e.g., Putnam 2000; Ehrenhalt 1995) bemoan Americans' overly individualistic attitudes and look to the same collective behavior of the 1950s as a time of great civic engagement. Political parties have been vilified for insufficient strength and for too much strength (Shefter 1994; Valelly 1990). News media, communication technologies, public deliberation, social movements—each of these has come under fire for threatening American democracy by being either too strong or too weak.

One reason for this persistent democratic anxiety, as sociologist Michael Schudson suggests in his pathbreaking history of American citizenship, is that a string of necessary evils has plagued the American democratic experiment since its beginning (Schudson 1998). These included compromises and corruptions that allowed the republic to function by glossing over important philosophical differences. Political scientist James Morone, for example, explains that American democracy has been characterized over the years by a compromise between communal sentiments and fierce individualism (Morone 1990). Lawyer and legal theorist Lani Guinier points out that the mechanics of American electoral systems only approximate the Founders' ideals of democratic representation—and often fail even to approximate them (Guinier 1994).

Another, more optimistic, interpretation is that angst itself is *good* for democracy, the constant vigilance of a thinking public being a check on state power (Havel 1987; Marcus, Neuman, and MacKuen 2000). Indeed, in seeking to understand when representatives will pay attention to citizens who fail to vote, political scientist R. Douglas Arnold introduced the concept of *attentive publics* (Arnold 1990, 64–65). These are, essentially, groups of nonvoting citizens who pay attention, raising the possibility that they will choose to vote if they become sufficiently concerned about a problem. The idea of voters lying in wait, ready to become engaged when things go awry, conjures up an image of an anxious voter (not to mention an anxious legislator). I suspect that a large proportion of the country's citizens are parts of such attentive publics: reading, talking, complaining, following, thinking, but not actively engaging. One important implication of Arnold's idea, which I develop later, is that we should not consider attentive publics idle. Rather, the very process of remaining attentive ought to be understood as a practice of citizenship.

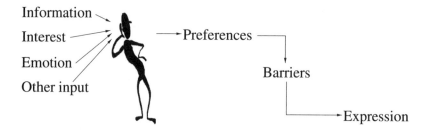

FIGURE 1.1. Citizenship involves processing information, interests, and emotions.

In this book, I suggest a third explanation for the seemingly contradictory diagnoses of democratic malaise. As the saying goes, "Stop, stop, you're both right!" The periodic hand-wringing over the health of democracy expresses an abiding, if hidden, concern about citizens' ability to think, deliberate, and act democratically. Sometimes this concern is about the information available to citizens; sometimes, about their ability to discuss, deliberate, and debate the issues; and sometimes, about whether electoral processes and representative structures adequately bring the outcomes of these discussions to the public agenda.

All of these worries, I argue, are rooted in questions about citizens' ability to think democratically. Democracy, as I argue in chapter 3, is a communication system involving information, interest, and emotion (see fig. 1.1). With its faith rooted in the *demos*—the people—as the source of authority and legitimacy, democratic theory is justifiably afraid of a public that can be misled or tricked by powerful interests or, perhaps worse, may become too distracted or poorly informed to develop meaningful preferences.

As citizens, we constantly seek ways to process new and changing information about politics and the social world around us. To do so, we turn to interpretive filters: collections of ideas, experiences, stories, narratives, and preferences that tell us how to understand what is going on around us (fig. 1.2). The democratic imagination is one such filter we use to interpret these inputs.

Although I argue that citizens—indeed, beyond the realm of politics, all humans—spend much of their time processing information, interests, and emotions, they do not do so in mechanical, predictable ways. The work of interpreting information and forming responses to it is fundamentally a creative, iterative, social, and imaginative task. We use creative faculties to respond to new situations with tools and ideas that spring from a wide variety of past experiences.

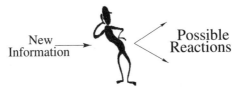

Thin Democratic Imagination

Thick Democratic Imagination

FIGURE 1.2. Thicker democratic imaginations offer more possible reactions to new political information.

The Democratic Crisis and the Deliberative Solution

Are we in a democratic crisis? Cooler heads suggest we are not, at least in comparison to the compromises and concerns raised by American political practice at other times. Patronage, corruption, and party machines in years past—not to mention slavery, Jim Crow, the disenfranchisement of women, and more—certainly compete with today's poor information, media manipulation, and voter apathy as challenges to democracy. But comparing our current political system with its historical precedents is not our only option. We can (and should) compare it with the ideal of what democratic politics could be. With a formally open system, the legal enfranchisement of most groups in society, and better access to information, we ought to be able to build a closer approximation of deliberative democracy than we have had in the past.

One popular approach to this ideal has been developing programs to encourage rational, open citizen deliberation around elections and issues (Leib 2004; Gutmann and Thompson 1996). The most ambitious of these is the "Deliberation Day" proposed by political scientists Bruce Ackerman and James S. Fishkin (Ackerman and Fishkin 2004). Noting the success of experiments that brought citizens together in small groups for concentrated periods of discussion, Ackerman and Fishkin propose expanding the practice nationwide: changing the Presidents' Day holiday

into Deliberation Day and offering time off work and a small deliberation stipend to citizens who participate in local discussions.

As a model for democracy in general, though, such deliberation is insufficient at best. The outcomes of such discussions always depend on the
inputs: which citizens are placed in which groups, how the groups interact,
and so on. Ignoring the group dynamics and social psychology that would
underlie such an exercise would render it at least as suspect as our current
mechanisms of democratic engagement. Removing citizenship talk from
the everyday contexts in which it naturally arises may even make it *less*
democratic.

Furthermore, American politics involves many institutional and organizational actors, ranging from the Sierra Club to the NRA (Walker 1991;
Schlozman 1994). Presumably, these groups would—and *should*—seek to
engage in the deliberation process as well. That is not, in itself, a problem,
but a plan for nationwide deliberation should recognize that individual
citizens are less likely to be doing the deliberating than are the *groups* to
which they belong.

The way we have thought about deliberation, to sum up, is all too deliberate, in both senses of the word. It is deliberate in the sense of "on purpose": deliberation theorists look for opportunities when citizens come
together with the express purpose of political discussions. It is also deliberate in the sense of "with care and dignity": deliberators are to be
measured, cautious, and above all rational. But each of these qualities
excludes normative speech that ought to be included in a democratic dialogue. Citizens routinely think, talk, and practice citizenship in ways that
are anything but deliberate.

Citizens think with a complex and ever-changing array of tools: information and reason, to be sure, but also emotion, solidarity, taste, aesthetics, friendship, empathy, and animosity, to name a few. Generations
of feminist theory have demonstrated that privileging abstract, rational
thought over other ways of thinking serves to silence important, often
marginal, constituencies (Gilligan 1982; Belenky et al. 1996). Propo-
nents of isolated, pure deliberation claim that these nonrational modes
of thought should be excluded from the democratic process and that
carefully designed deliberative forums will help keep them out. But,
as political theorist Danielle S. Allen has pointed out, "[If] . . . speakers
enter the deliberative forum already mutually well-minded toward one
another, . . . the battle to achieve a reasonable policy outcome is already
75 percent won" (Allen 2004, 56). Political scientist Jason Barabas carried

out a series of experiments showing, eventually, that real deliberation resulted in an enlightened consensus (Barabas 2004). But since he required
that his participants have open minds before the study began, it remains
unclear whether the consensus emerged because of the deliberation or
because of the unusual mental state in which his subjects began the experiments.

Later I present evidence and a theory of citizenship to demonstrate
that seeking to eliminate these elements from citizenship talk is futile.
And it is also the wrong goal. The point of a political regime is to rec-
oncile divergent views that are potentially deeply divided, and they may
be—indeed, they often are—divided precisely along the kinds of nonrational lines that current theories of deliberation seek to write out of politics (Walzer 2004).

Scholars who see social movements (or, more broadly, "contentious
politics," [McAdam, Tarrow, and Tilly 2001]) as an avenue for renewal
(e.g., Polletta 2002; M. R. Warren 2001; Wood 2002) offer a different
approach to resolving the democratic crisis. Since politics is essentially
about conflicts between groups, they reason, social movements arise from
the democratic potential of these groups to make their needs and preferences known. Social movement scholars have successfully shown how,
in specific circumstances, less-powerful groups may enter the democratic
arena. A plethora of groups designed to further causes may also provide
"political education" (Walzer 2004, 92) for citizens beyond their actual
effectiveness in the political arena.

Social movements have inspired a lot of good research that examines
their recruitment, mobilization, development, and success. But if the deliberative ideal is an artificially thin vision of democracy, social movements are such a rare kind of politics that they cannot provide a general
democratic solution. Successful, popular social movements are the exception rather than the rule. Most social problems never lead to the formation of collective grievances (McAdam 1982; Schlozman and Verba 1979),
and most collective grievances die quiet deaths, failing to spawn noticeable, let alone successful, social movements.

In everyday political life, though, citizens *do* have the opportunity
to deliberate, though not in the laboratory conditions of Ackerman and
Fishman, nor in the dramatic street battles of social movements. They can
deliberate with friends, colleagues, fellow students, neighbors, members
of organizations they belong to, anonymous others through letters to the
editor, talk radio, Internet chat, and more (Clayman 2004; Warner 2002).

When they choose to do so, how often, with whom, and within what parameters, helps define their democratic imaginations. I have called these contexts *political microcultures* (Perrin 2005b). Bounded and incomplete as they may be, they are a more realistic starting point for deliberative democracy than are either social movements or formal deliberation.

Bounded Imaginations

The sociological study of culture and political psychology gives us an important basis for understanding the democratic imagination. Perhaps most important, sociologists of culture and cognition have shown persuasively that the cultures people are part of endow them with specific ways of understanding and approaching social tasks—what sociologist Ann Swidler (1986) calls "styles, skills, and habits."

This collection of styles, skills, and habits—the elements of the democratic imagination—is not fixed, comprehensive, or uniform, either for a given person or throughout a culture. It is not fixed, meaning that groups and individuals can learn and forget cultural elements over time.[1] It is not comprehensive: the collection of cultural elements *excludes* some potential elements just as it includes others. And it is not uniform, since individuals and cultures may have better or worse command of different elements, and may combine and deploy them in different ways. This last point—the variability in the use and command of cultural elements—is best captured by using the term *repertoire* to describe the collection (Swidler 2001; Tilly 1992; Silber 2003). Citizens make choices—sometimes conscious, sometimes not; sometimes "rational," sometimes "emotional"; sometimes wise, sometimes not. In navigating these options, they draw upon and construct cultural repertoires to provide themselves with tools not only to respond to new situations (Swidler 1986) but also, crucially, to determine what they want to happen, both morally and in terms of their own self-interest (Eliasoph 1998; Smith 2003).

Following these cultural insights, I portray the democratic imagination as both a creative and a restraining force in relation to citizenship. Mapping the democratic imagination gives us the ability to understand both why citizens sometimes act as they do, and why they sometimes *fail* to act when we might expect or want them to.

---

1. This idea is explored in detail in Charles Tilly's (1995) work on contentious repertoires.

The Importance of Creativity

The fact that citizens draw on repertoires does not mean that citizenship is routine, or that new ways of doing citizenship are not possible. Citizenship (like, perhaps, other kinds of cultural work) is a creative act. Like other forms of creativity (see, e.g., Becker 1974), it is set in a social context, and it borrows ideas and methods from scores of prior citizens. And like other forms of creativity, it cannot be reduced to simply selecting from a list of others' work.

Sociology's understanding of creativity comes mostly from its consideration of art: an area that has captured sociologists' imaginations for generations. Political sociologists would do well to borrow from colleagues in the sociology of art to understand what creativity is, how it works, and where it comes from. To be sure, some social theorists have begun this project (Joas 1996; Misztal 2000). The creative, imaginative nature of citizenship—which I establish and defend here—should provide a good place to start in studying how creativity might explain people's cultural behavior, both in politics and in other realms of social life.

An enduring and thorny problem for sociologists of culture and politics has been the so-called structure/agency debate. Sociologists engaged in this debate seek to understand to what extent social, institutional, and cultural rules (called "structure") constrain people's behavior, and to what extent people freely choose actions for strategic, emotional, or personal reasons (called "agency"). The most interesting recent entries in this debate point out that structure and agency do not necessarily stand in opposition to one another. Several authors suggest, instead, that patterns, rules, and systems—the things we call "structure"—help define the meaning of acts of agency. At the same time, apparently "agentic" acts help reproduce and change structures over time. This is the idea behind French sociologist Pierre Bourdieu's much-maligned definition of *habitus*: "structured structures predisposed to function as structuring structures" (Bourdieu 1990, 53). It also animates American ideas, such as those of "repertoires" (Tilly 1992; see Swidler 2001, 30, for an excellent defense of the concept) and historian William Sewell's well-known statement that "[a]gency arises from the actor's knowledge of schemas [structure], which means the ability to apply them to new contexts.... Agency is implied by the existence of structures" (Sewell 1992, 20).

What these (admittedly divergent) literatures share is the idea that people can innovate—that is, they have agency—when their access to several different structures lets them combine or employ patterned actions in new ways. This idea predates and reaches well beyond contemporary cultural sociology; see, for example, Coser (1991) and Rothbell (1991) for feminist approaches to the same basic issue.

Consider, for example, the case of ballet versus modern dance.[2] Ballet is characterized by a highly structured set of moves, each of which has an accepted correct practice and a well-defined technique. Choreographers and dancers exhibit creativity by combining these moves in different ways or by introducing changes to these accepted practices. Importantly, *such changes need not be large to be innovative.* A change in the angle of a toe or the position of the arm constitutes enough deviation from expectations to be noticeable. By contrast, modern dance is characterized by ever-changing moves and statements; it is less structured, aiming to promote freedom (i.e., agency) for its practitioners (Cohen 1966). Because of the relative lack of rules, though, *each innovation must be substantial in order to approach the ideal of agency.* This points up an apparent paradox: structures designed to encourage freedom may actually reduce the meaning of the freedom they provide. To return to our example, a modern dancer must do more than a ballet dancer to convey the same sense of innovation, since it is harder to break rules when there are few rules to break.

This paradox points out the poverty of assuming that innovation must be no more than recombining or mobilizing elements of an existing repertoire. The solution, I believe, lies in understanding cultural work as neither entirely structured nor entirely agentic, but *creative.* Much like artistic, musical, or literary creativity, cultural actions (including citizenship) are patterned by, *but not reducible to,* the constraints of structure and past innovation. Democratic citizenship need not be limited to borrowing from and combining elements of political action gone by, although these recombinations can be innovative in themselves, as sociologists Mustafa Emirbayer and Ann Mische have shown (Emirbayer and Mische 1998). Citizenship can also be creatively shaped anew. Creativity, like (as I argue below) citizenship, need not be aimed at a specific, successful outcome; indeed, artistic creativity may even be harmed by artists' attention to commercial concerns. Similarly, citizenship may be more creative when it is *not* concentrating on a particular policy outcome.[3]

2. This example is from Swidler and Jepperson (1995). See Meyer (1956) for more on the argument.

3. David Meyer has made a similar argument about social movements' successes (Meyer 2000).

The psychologist Mihaly Csikszentmihalyi, probably the best known scholar of creativity, distinguishes between "big-C" creativity and "small-c" creativity. Big-C creativity characterizes people we might call "creative geniuses": the poets, scientists, artists, and so on who become widely known for their brilliance. These are the subjects of his famous study, entitled *Creativity* (Csikszentmihalyi 1996). He points out, though, that small-c creativity—creative responses to everyday situations—is carried out regularly by most people.

According to Csikszentmihalyi, creativity of either kind occurs when an individual injects novelty into a "symbolic domain." A symbolic domain is what others, such as the French sociologist Pierre Bourdieu, have called a *field*: "a social arena within which struggles or manoeuvres take place over specific resources or stakes and access to them" (Jenkins 1992, 84). In other words, it is a group of individuals and institutions who speak the same language well enough to evaluate each other's contributions. Innovations introduced outside a symbolic domain capable of evaluating them will die silent deaths, much like the sound made by a tree falling in the woods with no one around to hear it. Creativity is, therefore, the product of a "complex system" (Csikszentmihalyi 1996, 56). It involves generating new ideas in response to existing concerns and approaches, and validating those ideas in a symbolic community. Creativity is, almost by definition, unpredictable, since novelty is at its core, but it can be fostered by a rich symbolic community and the right conditions for developing novel ideas.

Creativity also requires favorable emotional conditions to develop. As sociologist Barbara Misztal has written (building on the work of psychologist Howard E. Gruber [1989]),

> human projects can be dehumanizing and alienating when they are done without emotions. In contrast, the love of one's work, the passion for works of art, the enthusiasm for scientific and technological achievements would shape the nature of one's achievements in such a way as to help people to become more human (Passmore 2000).
>
> The role of emotions in the process of creativity is appreciated in a variety of works trying to grasp what is the essence of creativity.... There is some shared understanding that a creator should be seen as having "emotions and aesthetic feelings as well as social awareness of the relation of his or her work to the world's work, its needs, and feelings" (Gruber 1989, 5). Creative works, because of being innovative, can be risky and disruptive of the existing

arrangements. Thus, in order for "wild" ideas to become effective, "the creator must be in good touch with the norms and feelings of some others so that the product will be one that they can assimilate and enjoy" (Gruber 1989, 14). This means that emotions are an important component of the process of creativity in more than one way. (Misztal 2000, 163–64)

The "right conditions" for the creativity of citizenship include structural concerns such as the freedom to create without fear of retribution. Analysts of civil society and culture in authoritarian regimes as diverse as Syria (Wedeen 1999) and pre-transition Czechoslovakia (Havel 1987), for example, have noted that such regimes seek to saturate the cultural lives of their subjects with "monotonous slogans and empty gestures, draining citizens' political energies" (Wedeen 2002, 723).

Citizenship may involve creativity (now in the small-c sense) in many ways. Citizens can creatively combine ideas and practices from their non-political lives to enhance their citizenship activities. They can generate novel ideas for thinking and doing citizenship, thinking strategically about how to interpret and address a new political situation. And they can be creative in choosing the other groups and individuals with whom they discuss situations and concerns. All of these are potentially creative moments: opportunities for citizens, given the right conditions, to approach a political problem creatively and contribute new ideas to the symbolic domain of citizenship.

A Case in Point

As an example, recall the "Freedom Rides" during the civil rights movement of the 1950s and 1960s. In 1961, a group of activists decided to challenge the common southern practice of segregating interstate buses and bus terminals. Drawing on previous attempts to bring attention to segregation in transportation, the activists rode buses from Washington, D.C., to Alabama before being stopped by segregationist mobs. The Freedom Rides that followed brought national attention to segregation and racism in the deep South, and helped bring an end to segregated transportation (Branch 1988, 412–90). They were a creative response to a political situation.

Forty-two years later, a group of activists concerned with Latino workers' rights held several "Freedom Ride" bus trips throughout the United States. According to the group that sponsored the events, "The road to citizenship needs a new map. The Immigrant Workers Freedom Ride intends to help draw that map. The destination? Policies that work for immigrants and for all Americans. Policies consistent with our most noble principles and sacred values" (Immigrant Workers Freedom Ride 2003). As the group itself claimed, "We draw our inspiration from the Freedom Riders of the early 1960s."

How did the form of an interstate bus ride enter the movement's repertoire—its collective democratic imagination? The 1960s Freedom Rides were similar in form, but quite different in content. The original Freedom Riders sought to desegregate interstate public transportation. Thus their choice of a bus ride emerged directly, yet creatively, from their situation. In the process, they invented a method of citizenship that had never been tried before. That form entered the repertoire of countless movements and would-be movements that followed. The 2003 riders' democratic imaginations were enriched by the 1960s riders' innovation, but they were also constrained by the available repertoire. In the final analysis, it is always easier for an actor, whether an individual, group, movement, or government, to adapt an existing mode of citizenship than to invent a new one.

This, of course, is an example from the extreme end of democratic citizenship: tactics and ideas from the high-commitment world of social movements. More common, less costly, kinds of citizenship work in the same way, borrowing ideas and practices from prior citizenship while molding and changing them to address the problem at hand. In the focus group discussions that form the backbone of this book, participants often went through a similar process, choosing from a long list of political tactics they already knew or had heard about. For example, in a white-collar union group that had already decided to take action on the hypothetical issue of a local factory violating environmental regulations, I asked them to decide what they wanted to do. They responded by presenting a laundry list of possible actions:[4]

MODERATOR: Do you feel there's anything you could or would want to do to try to push them in this direction?

VICTOR TRUJILLO: To do that I would probably write a congressman, you know, my assemblyman in that area. Let him know that, hey, you have this company, it's sending all this ozone-depleting stuff up in the air and we have these two other

---

4. I have changed the names of all the participants to protect their privacy. Where possible, I have preserved the speakers' gender and the ethnicity of their names to keep them as similar to the originals as possible.

companies that are competitors at the same time they're not using it. And these guys are saying, well we can get away with it 'cause we have the money to keep doing it.

MARVIN WIMMERS: Petition to people to write to Congress, especially those in the affected area, because their health is going to be affected quicker than us.

...

MODERATOR: So you'd write letters to Congress.

JAVIER ROMERO: Do you want to go as far as to, I don't know, have a rally in front of the dangerous [factory]?

PAULO DOMINGUEZ: Bring attention, media attention.

VICTOR TRUJILLO: Make the company feel the pressure, the more the community knows about it.

MARVIN WIMMERS: The wider spread it is, the . . .

PAULO DOMINGUEZ: Yeah, I mean, more people start doing something about it.

MARVIN WIMMERS: You could always boycott their products. There's a lot that the people can do with a company. . . . (U4)[5]

Although the scenario they are discussing is fictional, the methods they consider to address it are real and have been tried elsewhere. Much like the immigrant workers' coalition that used the "Freedom Ride" tactic, this group brings up tried and true political tactics, perhaps mobilized creatively, to address a new problem.

This tension between new information and ideas—and the creative responses they seem to require—and the limited, yet varied, repertoire of political tactics that citizens know about appears throughout the book. I argue that citizens' capacity for creative thought makes citizenship more interesting, more difficult—and in less of a crisis—than others have claimed.

Is Citizenship in Decline?

Recent observers (e.g., Putnam 2000; Ehrenhalt 1995) have argued that American democracy is threatened by a recent decline in involvement in

---

5. Throughout the book, excerpts from focus group discussions are referenced by their group number. The letter refers to the group type (B: business group; C: Catholic church; P: Protestant church; S: sports group; U: labor union). A list of the groups and some characteristics of the people in them appears in appendix B, table B.1.

civic organizations. Participating in these organizations (everything from bowling leagues to Elks Clubs, PTAs, and more) often gives people the concerns, connections, skills, and ideas to approach political participation. Furthermore, such organizations provide a space where citizens can discuss their needs and concerns outside the control of government.

This resurgence of concern with civic participation returns attention to a persistent question for democratic theory: How are citizens' commitments to civic and community involvement related to the level and form of their political engagement? For Alexis de Tocqueville and those who have followed in his footsteps, participation in the civic life of the community and in the political debates of the time are inextricably tied. The democratic citizen participates in both political issues and nonpolitical life, bringing preferences and ideas formed in the course of everyday practice and sociability to bear on the public agenda.

But existing explanations of civic contributions to democracy are inadequate to explain such a wide-reaching phenomenon. Neither social networks (Putnam 2000; Lin 2001) nor civic skills (Verba, Schlozman, and Brady 1995)—useful explanatory concepts offered by other researchers—is sufficient for understanding why civic life is so important to citizenship. Keeping these two areas in mind, I turn to culture as an explanatory mechanism.

Understanding what goes on inside civic contexts is a crucial task. As political theorist Mark E. Warren (2001, 11) points out, associations may affect democracy in several distinct ways.[6] And, as sociologist Nina Eliasoph (1998, 231) has shown, Americans' likelihood of behaving as citizens has as much to do with their social environments as with the beliefs and ideals they hold privately. This book seeks to take these ideas seriously, delineating the influences of different civic contexts on the culture of citizenship—in Eliasoph's language, what "hats" different civic contexts ask their participants to wear.

The broader point of this study is that citizens' democratic imaginations are rooted in a complex set of social, organizational, and media experiences. Civic life matters for citizenship, but it matters most as a rich source of such experiences, from which citizens can construct their imaginations. Different kinds of civic life provide different kinds of experiences—some enriching, others impoverishing.

6. They may also actually *impede* democracy (Fiorina 1999; Guttmann 1998), an important political effect of civic culture that we should not ignore.

Political Participation and Civic Engagement

Political Participation

Two main approaches characterize the study of political participation (Valelly 1990):[7] one concerned primarily with individual characteristics (age, education, and income, for example) and one concerned with structural and institutional factors such as the complexity of elections, registration requirements, and citizens' connectedness with organized political groups (Powell 1986; Piven and Cloward 1988; Rosenstone and Hansen 1993).

Political scientists Raymond Wolfinger and Steven Rosenstone's (1980) classic treatment of voting behavior set the standard for individual-level analysis, finding that, in most ways, political analyst E. E. Schattschneider's indictment of the class bias in American political enfranchisement was correct ("the flaw in the pluralist heaven is that the heavenly chorus sings with a strong upper-class accent" [Schattschneider 1960, 35]). Demographic factors such as age and income affected voter participation, as did the "overriding" influence of education. Ruy Teixeira (1987) expanded this line of research to include a discussion of changing attitudes toward voting, arguing that a combination of individual-level characteristics and attitudes conspired to depress voter turnout.

Frances Fox Piven and Richard Cloward (1988) and G. Bingham Powell (1986) took a structural-institutional approach, claiming that the American structure of voter registration and the complexity of elections in the United States discouraged voting. Rosenstone and John Mark Hansen (1993) introduced a relatively new strain in structuralist approaches, arguing that it was *mobilization*—organized groups motivating individuals to vote—that best explained differences in voting behavior. They argued that basic inequalities (principally income, education, and race) affected voter turnout partly because the institutions that facilitate voting (such as parties, groups, and movements) tend to mobilize citizens with existing political resources. Thus the potentially equalizing force of political mobilization was muted because mobilizing organizations tend to concentrate efforts on people who are already likely to vote.

The most thoroughgoing examination of mobilization and voting in recent decades, *Voice and Equality*, by political scientist Sidney Verba and his colleagues (Verba, Schlozman, and Brady 1995) followed this

---

7. Throughout this chapter, I use *participation*, *involvement*, and *engagement* interchangeably to refer to participation in organizations or activities.

discussion of the organizational environment of voting behavior, offering the most complete treatment of the civic institutional environments that encourage Americans to participate in political life. Using some of the same data that I use in chapter 2, they found that education was a strong predictor of participation, and that two types of institutions—labor unions and churches—were strong additional predictors of political engagement. Unions had a greater effect on their members' likelihood of participating, but the sheer number of Americans involved in churches made them a greater contributor to overall participation.

For political scientists Norman Nie, Jane Junn, and Kenneth Stehlik-Barry (1996), however, the data's strongest message was different. They found that education was the prime predictor of political activity. Their central argument is that political activity has two faces: what they call "political engagement" and "democratic citizenship." Political engagement consists of pursuing individual goals in the public sphere, while democratic citizenship (their central concern) is being involved "for the public good" (2). They find that education predicts both kinds of involvement, but in different ways. Political engagement is a function of "*relative* education"; that is, increasing the general level of education in society should not increase the amount of goal-directed political activity. On the other hand, democratic citizenship is a function of "*absolute* education." Since there is no competition for "slots" in the field of democratic citizenship, increasing the general level of education should increase the prevalence of democratic citizenship (Tenn 2005).

Interestingly, they find that even participation in nonpolitical civic organizations—those that participants said took no political stands—was a significant predictor of "political engagement" (Nie, Junn, and Stehlik-Barry 1996, 87) as well as several other types of political participation (74, 76, 77). I build on these findings to understand how and in what circumstances citizens choose to participate in each level of political activity.

Civic Engagement

Recent years have seen a resurgence of interest in—and concern about—the civic sector, largely the result of political scientist Robert Putnam's influential 1995 article, "Bowling Alone" (Putnam 1995a). Americans remain more likely to join associations than citizens of most other countries (Dekker and van den Broek 1998, 24; Persell, Green, and Seidel 1998; Persell et al. 1998), and volunteering is an especially significant activity for Americans (Wilson and Musick 1997, 703). But Putnam showed that involvement in organized, face-to-face organizations was in decline. For Putnam, this decline indicated a reduction in the availability of "social capital" (1995a, 67),[8] since the kinds of ties that arise in face-to-face associations were being replaced by impersonal connections to large, anonymous "check-writing" organizations on the national level and by private, family- and entertainment-oriented activities on the individual level (see also Putnam 1995b). Although some authors (e.g., Samuelson 1996; Ladd 1999) have argued that Putnam's data are suspect, most other studies have largely confirmed his findings (Persell, Green, and Seidel 1998; Persell et al. 1998; Wuthnow 1998a). Others have pointed out that the civic activity Putnam highlighted was the exception to the rule: in general, Americans have not been so heavily involved in civic activities as they were in the 1950s (Skocpol 1996, 1999; Schudson 1996, 1998). Indeed, Putnam's similarly titled, book-length exploration of the civic decline thesis calls that era the "great civic generation," pointing out its unusually high level of civic engagement (Putnam 2000; see also Fischer 2005).

Other critics have noted that the kinds of associations Americans take part in may have changed (Ladd 1999), and in particular that less-formal kinds of associations like support groups, spiritual gatherings, and neighborhood gatherings may have taken the place of clubs like the Elks, PTAs, and—yes—bowling leagues (Wuthnow 1998b).[9] These studies of civic and volunteering activities, however, do not generally address the implications of these patterns for social capital or political involvement.

Sociologists Sarah Sobieraj and Deborah White discovered another important point: associations are important for the access they provide to political talk, not just for the "social capital" they instill (Sobieraj and White 2004). So the debate on whether associational life has declined or not may be misplaced—perhaps what is most important is to determine how citizens gain access to the richest sources of democratic discourse.

Thinking and Talking Citizenship

To evaluate citizenship activities, we first need to know what we're looking for. Political scientists who study political thought and discussion have

---

8. The concept of social capital has a long and interesting history, which is beyond the scope of this chapter. See Portes (1998) and Lin (2000) for discussions.

9. Writing in the *Nation*, columnist Katha Pollitt pointed out that bowling with family and friends is not, in fact, "alone" (Pollitt 1996).

typically held that thought and talk may *lead to* citizenship activities like voting, running for office, demonstrating, or signing petitions. Departing from this view, I hold that thinking and talking *are* citizenship activities. They are, of course, different from one another—thinking has no immediate audience, while talking nearly always has one, for example. But each is a crucial piece of citizenship in its own right, not only because it may lead to a citizenship practice. My position is that rich, varied ways of thinking and talking politically are citizenship goods, *independent* of any particular activities they may inspire. We should care about the health of our collective democratic imaginations for their own sake.

Strictly speaking, thinking may take place in isolation, but in practice, learning new ideas and new ways of thinking requires interaction with others. This interaction may be mediated—say, by a newspaper, telephone, television, or Internet chat room—or it may be direct, in face-to-face discussions with others. *The fundamental unit of citizenship is, therefore, the group*. We think and talk politics in groups (even if the group consists of only one other person). In addition, we think and talk citizenship using the memories of groups distant in space or time. Individual citizens carry ideas and messages from these groups to other social and political contexts.

The democratic imagination, then, is both social and situational. It is social because it is, at its core, the product of interaction among citizens. It is situational because a given citizenship opportunity is both produced and shaped by a particular configuration of citizens and mediators with their idiosyncratic civic histories. Some contexts and some narrative styles make it easier for people to formulate their arguments in terms of morality; others lend themselves better to the logic of self-interest, cynicism, or disempowerment. Sociology, with its focus on social and situational behavior, is uniquely qualified to understand the democratic imagination.

My conception of the democratic imagination has important implications for how we understand political behavior—voting, "public opinion," deliberation, and attitudes—as well as other kinds of evaluation. By insisting on the fundamentally *public* character of evaluation, orders of worth (Boltanski and Thévenot 1991), and political behavior, this framework takes seriously the idea that politics is, to paraphrase Émile Durkheim, an eminently social thing (Durkheim 1995; Fields 1995). How, exactly, do these social configurations give rise to democratic imaginations? And how does a structured, constrained democratic imagination work to influence the issues and methods citizens select? The road map to the democratic imagination offered here is intended to answer those questions.

We can understand the repertoire of political logics that constitutes the democratic imagination as the set of resources and experiences that Americans "think with," to use Schudson's (1992b) term—the experiences and understandings that structure and inform their political ideas. These political logics involve ways of thinking and arguing about social issues that determine (1) the range and scope of the public sphere; (2) the range of possible outcomes from public-sphere activities; and (3) the menu of actions that are legitimate and useful in pursuing these outcomes. Together, they constitute the democratic imagination.

Current research in political culture has shied away from linking specific cultural elements with political engagement or behavior. Most comparative research has concentrated on demonstrating the impact of culture by showing differences between national cultures (e.g., Dobbin 1994; Lamont 2000a; Biernacki 1995). At the same time, research on American political culture has been concerned with documenting the cultural elements in political life but has made little attempt to attach causal significance to these elements (Berezin 1997; Kane 2000). Also, since the very definition of political culture has been under substantial debate, there remains little agreement even as to the object of study in the field.

Eliasoph (1997, 1998) suggests that the noted American distaste for political discourse is the product of active work by citizens, who seek to define as many concerns as possible as being outside the boundaries of the public sphere. Similarly, Clemens's (1997) work on the development of interest-group politics shows that much of the early discussion in interest groups was about how to promote their interests without being tainted by the language of politics. These findings portray an overly constrained cultural idea of the public realm. Citizens who mistrust "political" methods and ideas contribute to the idea that the public sphere is limited, both in its capacity for social improvement and in its legitimate substantive reach.

The Path from Here

The research for this book took place in two distinct stages. In the first stage, I used existing survey data to explore links between civic engagement and political participation. I used my findings to structure the second stage of research, in which targeted focus groups explored issues of political involvement.

I started by looking for information on the two areas I investigate: Americans' participation in civic associations and in citizenship activities. The best data I found were from the 1990 American Civic Participation Survey and the combined 1972–92 General Social Survey. (For my analyses using those data, see chapter 2 and appendix A.) That research gave me a guide to the kinds of organizations that would be most likely to foster different kinds of democratic imaginations. Ultimately, I was interested in searching for the varieties of imaginations that Americans in different civic groups would display. I used the results of my survey analysis to target recruitment of twenty groups of citizens that held discussions under my direction, providing the "laboratory" data that I analyze in the rest of the book.

During the spring of 2000, I organized and directed these discussions with members of different civic associations in Alameda County, California. Each group consisted of members of a single association. The twenty associations were made up of four of each type: Protestant churches, Catholic churches, business organizations, labor unions, and sports clubs. Each group began with refreshments (pizza, cookies, coffee, soda) and a questionnaire before the discussion began. I asked the groups to consider four fictional but realistic scenarios that might come up in their communities: one about racial profiling, one about a scandal involving "their" senator, one about a local factory violating pollution laws, and one about increased airport noise in their neighborhoods. For roughly two hours, the groups discussed these scenarios, deciding whether to get involved, what (if anything) to do, and why. They sometimes agreed with one another from the outset, but, more often, some had to convince others that their way of viewing the situation was correct. Out of these conversations comes a uniquely rich view of how citizens think about and decide on political matters. (More detail about the focus groups appears in chapter 3 and in appendix B.)

My analysis of the focus groups explores the cognitive structure of participants' political decision making in three main dimensions. The first dimension is the size and landscape of the "public sphere": What issues and problems are appropriate for public debate and why? What kinds of concerns can public activity address? The second might be called *policy imagination*: what kinds of outcomes can people imagine as potential solutions to social problems? The third dimension is tactical: What is the menu of actions that may be taken in the public sphere, and how do people select from this menu? These three dimensions belong to the realm of political culture; they deal not so much with political *behavior* as with the ideas, perceptions, and resources that are brought to bear on public problems. The focus groups were, therefore, designed to "measure" these logical and ideological toolkits (see Swidler 1986)—the cognitive repertoires participants bring to the process of making political choices.

Having laid out the terms and bases of the argument in this chapter, I turn next to laying the empirical groundwork. In chapter 2, I outline the results of the analysis of survey data to examine the relationship between organizational memberships and citizenship. That provides a broad overview of the landscape to help us decide where best to zoom in on the democratic imagination. (Additional information about the methodology in that chapter appears in appendix A.) Having outlined where to look, I turn next to the question of what to look for and how to look for it. What kinds of settings and discussions should we target in mapping the democratic imagination? Chapter 3 introduces the focus group discussions at the heart of the study, and proposes a schema for classifying and evaluating citizenship talk. The next three chapters demonstrate three crucial axes of citizenship talk. These axes—mistrust, information, and legitimation (chapter 4); morality, ideology, and interest (chapter 5); and methods of involvement (chapter 6)—use the theoretical tools from the first three chapters to show the democratic imagination in formation and action. Chapter 7 builds on the prior chapters and adds an analysis to argue that the principal building block of the democratic imagination is *political microcultures*: spaces of citizenship talk that enrich or impoverish political thought. Chapter 8 argues that social policies aiming to rebuild democratic citizenship should pay attention to "citizen speak," not just organizational membership, as a principal contributor to democracy.

In sum, this book shows a strong link between everyday life and democratic citizenship. In one sense, it is optimistic: I insist that we look for, and find, citizenship activities in a much wider swath of everyday life than most analysts have considered. In another, though, it is pessimistic: As widely as we cast the net, we find an increasingly narrow democratic imagination. Citizens spend more energy deciding what *not* to do than what to do, arguing *against* engagement rather than for it. If I have done my job, this book will change the way we think about citizenship. No longer will we concentrate only on the ritualized, visible acts of citizenship, from registering and voting to writing letters to the editor and participating in demonstrations. Instead, we will understand citizenship as the political dimension of our social imagination. My general aim is to show that American citizenship is about thinking, talking, and acting, and about the relationships among the three. Citizenship is about creativity and imagination: using skills, ideas, and expectations gleaned from the social world to engage with political questions. Beyond those abstract ideas, though, the book explores where the democratic imagination comes from and how it is structured.

What to do about it is another matter. To the extent that American democratic practice needs to be improved—and I believe it does—the widely diffuse set of influences on citizenship activities that I describe does not easily admit to change. Change would be simpler (but probably less lasting) if we learned and practiced citizenship only during elections, or only in town meetings, or only when talking about national policy. But we do not. Since citizenship comes from influences all around us, change is a more complicated task. The final chapter offers some pointers to get us started.

CHAPTER TWO

How Do Civic Organizations Mobilize?

To begin the search for the democratic imagination, we need to think strategically. Where should we look for citizens who, though they appear to be similar, think and behave differently from one another when it comes to politics? Where, that is, can we find a diverse collection of democratic imaginations to examine and catalog? To assemble groups for political discussions—the central method behind this book—we need some clues about where to find them. This chapter takes stock of what we know about the settings for democratic discourse before we set out in search of the democratic imagination.

Before I start that process, though, we need to recognize a difference between *thinking* citizenship and *practicing* citizenship. When we ask, as many have, who is likely to take particular political actions—voting, marching in a demonstration, telephoning or writing a representative—we are asking about citizenship *practices*. By contrast, when we ask about people's attitudes toward political issues or principles—or even toward ways of practicing citizenship—we are talking about *thinking* citizenship. Somewhere between these two kinds of citizenship falls a third: *talking* citizenship.

There is good reason to believe that these three are closely connected, but *how* they are connected is not at all clear (see fig. 2.1). Through thinking citizenship, people often begin to talk citizenship and then to practice it. As they practice citizenship, people may begin to think and talk differently about it (Leighly 1991; Smith and Ingram 1993; Landy 1993; Valelly 1993). And talking about citizenship can encourage people to think and act differently (Eliasoph 1998; Walsh 2004). My investigation

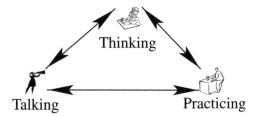

Thinking

Talking   Practicing

FIGURE 2.1. The citizenship triangle: thinking, talking, and practicing citizenship

of the democratic imagination focuses on talking citizenship as one corner of this triangle.

Political scientists have been asking similar questions for years: Who votes? Why do people choose to vote, write letters, demonstrate, and more? Early discussions of these questions—for example, Raymond Wolfinger and Stephen Rosenstone's classic book, *Who Votes?* (1980)— answered that question by discussing the kinds of people who tended to vote. Many of the discipline's most enduring findings come from that research. Whites, men, and relatively wealthy and well-educated citizens are more likely to vote than are others.

Later, another important set of studies noted that citizens are more likely to participate when they are *mobilized*: that is, when someone specifically asks them to do so. Political scientists Stephen Rosenstone and John Mark Hansen showed this in their groundbreaking book, *Mobilization, Participation, and Democracy in America* (1993). Similarly, political scientists Philip Pollock (1982) and Jack L. Walker (1991) found that citizen organizations have grown in size and importance, and that they serve important mobilizing functions in inspiring their members to engage in political activities. Involvement in the political system, these works showed, is not just about who you *are*: it is also about whom you *know*.

The most far-reaching recent studies of associations and political participation are *Voice and Equality*, by Sidney Verba, Kay Lehman Schlozman, and Henry E. Brady (1995) and *The Private Roots of Public Action*, by Nancy Burns, Schlozman, and Verba (2001). These studies confirm that civic associations are a good place to find Americans "practicing citizenship." Specifically, they suggest that churches and labor unions—for different reasons—are likely to be good political mobilizers.

What Organizations Mobilize Their Members?

Given that background, I began looking for information about what kinds of groups were likely to have theoretically interesting democratic imaginations, and which were likely to have democratic imaginations that differed from one another. I wanted to know what kinds of civic organizations contribute more and less to their members' political activity, and how they influence that activity. (More technical detail on this process, and the complete statistical analysis, appears in appendix A.)

Of the various large-scale surveys of Americans' attitudes and behaviors, two lend themselves to investigating these questions. The most appropriate is the American Citizen Participation Survey (Verba et al. 1995), which contains the results of 2,517 interviews done in the spring of 1990. Respondents were asked for detailed information about civic and religious involvement as well as about participation in political activities ranging from voting to participating in demonstrations. Secondarily, the combined 1972–1996 General Social Survey (Davis and Smith 1998) provides less complete individual information for a larger number of respondents.

I began the process by looking for information on what kinds of organizations seem to have more politically active members than others and than the general population. Here, I wanted to answer the following questions: (1) Does being a member of an association make a person more likely to "practice citizenship"? (2) What kinds of associations excel at mobilizing their members? (3) Are there differences among mobilizing associations in how their members "think citizenship"?

In the past, researchers have tended to focus on voting as a sign of good citizenship. Voting—whether in general, in the most recent election, or in the most recent presidential election—does seem to embody one popular image of the good citizen. Students taking my first-year seminar on citizenship and society in the United States consistently speak of citizenship and voting in the same breath. Implicitly, a good citizen is one who votes, and someone who votes is a good citizen. But a second glance reveals deficiencies. Voting is, nearly always, an artificially private activity, performed in a private booth, sometimes even hidden by an imposing black curtain (fig. 2.2).[1] Other voting systems use different sorts of barriers to

---

1. Michael Schudson (1998, 169–70) points out that it was not always thus—the physical isolation of voting is a product of the "Australian ballot" (see also Fredman 1968), instituted in the late nineteenth and early twentieth centuries.

FIGURE 2.2. A voting machine, 1928

protect voters from interference by others. Candidates and their repre-sentatives are barred from engaging voters in or near polling stations. In short, while designed to mirror *public* opinion, voting in the United States is an extremely *private* activity. The entire experience is designed to iso-late the individual voter from social influence: precisely the opposite of most other kinds of citizenship activity (Adorno 2005; Perrin et al. 2006). We might therefore expect that voting, unlike other ways of practicing citizenship, would be less susceptible (although far from immune) to the influence of social life than more public forms of participation.

Voting is also relatively easy. Even though the American electoral system is more complicated and difficult to navigate than those of most democracies (Piven and Cloward 1988; Powell 1986),[2] it still takes much less effort to vote than to write letters, demonstrate, or run for office. Because voting is quite ritualized and happens on a set schedule, it is arguably even less of a hardship than signing a petition, another "low-cost" citizenship practice. Concentrating on voting therefore misses the commitment of citizens who go above and beyond the routine. We need to understand not just an "on-off" question (whether a person is a good citizen or not) but a "more-less" question: *How much* citizenship does a person do?

I continue to consider voting, but I add an additional way of thinking about citizenship, first proposed by political scientists Norman Nie, Jane

2. In some states, such as California, voters may be asked to decide on a bewildering array of ballot questions, referenda, and local officials about which they have little information.

Junn, and Kenneth Stehlik-Barry (1996). Their measure, based on the same survey I use here, includes information on whether citizens contact public officials (by writing a letter, making a telephone call, etc.); whether they work for one or more political campaigns; whether they are actively involved in local issues through a local board; and whether they engage in other kinds of informal political activity. This is called *difficult political activity* because participating in such citizenship practices is relatively difficult.[3] Because this scale offers a more complete picture of political participation than does mere voting, I spend more time on that part of the analysis than on the part predicting voting.[4]

Other researchers have suggested two additional ways, aside from mobilizing them directly, that organizations may encourage their members to participate. They may instill *political efficacy*, and they may foster the development of *civic skills*. Political efficacy is citizens' belief that they can make a difference in politics; civic skills are the practical abilities to accomplish the necessary tasks of political activity, such as writing letters or leading meetings. In looking for organizational mobilization, I include each of these three pathways (fig. 2.3), estimating the importance of each to the mobilizing process. I use those results to separate organization types into categories according to whether, and how, they mobilize their members.

In addition to information about citizens' organizational involvement, I include information about their personal characteristics and civic lives, in order to make sure that any differences I find are not simply differences in the kinds of people who join organizations. Complete details about the statistical models and the results appear in appendix A.

Like other researchers, I found that the most important route to political efficacy—believing that one has the capacity to make a difference—is education. Family income also bolsters efficacy: citizens with higher incomes are more likely to think they can make a difference in politics.

---

3. More information on this scale appears in appendix A (see the discussion of table A.1) and in Nie, Junn, and Stehlik-Barry (1996, 208).

4. I also constructed my own measure of difficult political activity, based on my idea of active citizenship. It included one point for being among the top 25 percent of citizens in terms of number of weeks or hours spent on campaign work, one point for contacting an official about a problem, one point for attending more than one protest in the past two years, and up to three points for effort devoted to solving community problems, including participating in activities, leading a group, and working informally for a large number of hours. However, this measure proved too restrictive to be useful: 57 percent of the sample scored 0 and fully 85 percent had zero or one.

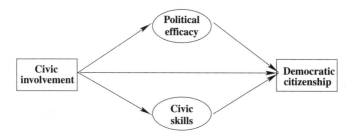

FIGURE 2.3. The mobilization diamond: pathways from civic involvement to democratic citizenship

In the following analysis, results are therefore adjusted for these demographic characteristics.

In general, most types of civic organizations do not build political efficacy in their members. Those that do include churches and synagogues, educational organizations, groups interested in women's issues, and youth organizations (for complete results, see table A.2 in appendix A). Civic skills, however, are fostered by several organization types. As with political efficacy, education builds civic skills, as does family income. The types of organizations that build small, but significant, amounts of civic skills include women's issue organizations, service groups and fraternities, literary, art, and discussion groups, educational institutions, health services organizations, and youth groups. In addition, religious organizations and business and professional groups have particularly large effects on their members' civic skills (for complete results see table A.3). Older citizens and women had, on average, fewer civic skills than their younger, male counterparts.

As I suspected, deciding to *vote*—as opposed to engaging in difficult citizenship practices—appears to be a largely individual process. Membership in two kinds of organizations—churches and synagogues and neighborhood and homeowner associations—increased people's likelihood of voting, but no other memberships showed a discernible impact on voting patterns. Most of the differences in the likelihood of voting are explained by individual characteristics, such as age, education, and income. Political efficacy and civic skills do matter; thus, civic memberships may indirectly increase the likelihood that citizens will vote.

Both efficacy and civic skills are also significant predictors of difficult political activity. Citizens with more efficacy or more civic skills are more likely, on average, to participate in such activities than citizens with less of these. Therefore, the pathways illustrated in figure 2.3 are all theoretically possible ways for citizens to become politically mobilized by membership in organizations. The next step is to investigate which kinds of organizations actually activate these pathways.

The results of my analyses confirm the popular idea that organizational membership increases political participation. Of the eighteen nonpolitical civic organization types in my data, only four do *not* significantly influence participation in difficult political activity. These four types of organizations are nationality/ethnic groups, senior citizens' organizations, labor unions, and cultural organizations. Furthermore, no kind of organization *depresses* its members' political activity below the average level of the general population. The mobilizing organizations run the gamut from such seemingly apolitical organizations as youth groups, literary discussion groups, and sports clubs to those more directly oriented to the public sphere, such as social service organizations and neighborhood associations.

Surprisingly, the four nonmobilizing organization types include two that other theories suggest should prompt political activity. Labor unions have often been seen as political mobilizers, encouraging their otherwise-passive members to lobby for worker-friendly measures. In these data, however, controlling for demographic factors as well as memberships in other organizations erases any effect of labor union membership. Also, given recent strident debates about the promotion of "identity politics" by ethnic and racial groups, we might expect involvement in organizations based on nationality or ethnic origin to be related to political activity, but it is not.

The difference in findings between this analysis and that of Verba, Schlozman, and Brady (1995, see esp. 385–87) on the effects of labor union membership can be explained by the different measurements of membership and contribution to political participation. Verba, Schlozman, and Brady use data only for those respondents who classify a labor union as their *main* organization—that is, they are involved only in a union or they consider it their most important organizational affiliation. By contrast, in this chapter I investigate the relationship between simple union *membership* and participation. The average union member also belongs to 4.7 other civic organizations, suggesting that some union members spend some of their civic energies elsewhere. Union members to whom the union is more important may gain more civic skills or efficacy and, therefore, participate more in political activities than do members to whom it is relatively unimportant. Such active members may

TABLE 2.1 **Mobilizing organization types**

Mobilizing type	Schematic path[a]	Group types matching
General mobilizers		Youth organizations Educational groups Health/service organizations Churches/synagogues

Indirect mobilizers		Business/professional/farm
		    organizations
		Religious organizations
		Women's issue organizations
		Literary/art/discussion
		    groups
		Service clubs/fraternal
		    organizations
		Other organizations

Direct mobilizers		Neighborhood/homeowner's
		    associations
		Nonpartisan/civic
		    organizations
		Hobby/sports clubs
		Veterans' organizations

Nonmobilizers		Nationality/ethnic organizations Senior citizens' organizations Labor unions Cultural organizations

Source: ACPS; author's analysis.
[a]See figure 2.3.

also be more amenable to direct mobilization than their less-involved peers.

The fact that membership in ethnic and nationality-based organizations does not independently predict political participation may be an artifact of the classification scheme used in the survey. The category includes such organizations as Polish-American clubs and German Societies alongside such more likely political organizations as the Mexican-American Legal Defense and Education Fund and the National Association for the Advancement of Colored People. Thus it is difficult to discern the effect of nationality and ethnic organizations. Also, since the analysis controls for racial minority status, the independent effect of ethnic organizational membership may be diminished.

On the basis of the findings in this chapter so far, we can divide the organization types into four categories (see table 2.1): those in which all three pathways to mobilization are active (the *general mobilizers*); those that mobilize members only by increasing their civic skills or political efficacy (the *indirect mobilizers*); those that mobilize their members directly, but do not increase their civic skills or political efficacy (the *direct mobilizers*); and those that do not affect their members' participation rates (the *nonmobilizers*).[5] In order to find the broadest possible representation of political imaginations, it makes sense to draw discussion participants from each of these four kinds of mobilizing organizations. At the end of this chapter I outline the decisions on where to look.

First, though, I need to settle another question. Perhaps organizations' mobilizing capacity is not about imagination at all. Rather, organizations could mobilize their members, partially or entirely, because they simply serve as meeting places where citizens can build networks. If that turns out to be true, it makes no sense to look for differences in political imaginations (the main project of the book), since we have no data to suggest we will find them. I turn next, therefore, to the task of determining whether it is possible to explain differences in political mobilization as a function of the kinds of individuals a citizen is likely to encounter as a member of a particular organization.

How Do Organizations Mobilize?

There are two main ways we could understand the fact that different kinds of organizations mobilize their members differently and to different extents. We could understand it primarily as an effect of the *connections* forged with other citizens through being in the same kind of organization, or as an effect of the *activities* a citizen experiences in that organization. The idea of connections closely follows the views of the sociological field known as "network analysis" (see, for instance, Lin 2001). It also expresses the view of social capital underlying Robert Putnam's work (1995a, 2000): the important thing about organizations is the sociability they foster, not the work they do.

In this section I look for evidence to support the effect of connections. Although I find some weak evidence to support it, I conclude that it is insufficient to uphold the idea that organizational mobilization is only the

5. A fifth hypothetical category, *demobilizers*, does not actually exist; no organizations have a depressive effect on their members' participation.

result of meeting other members through the organization. I therefore close the chapter with a direction for the rest of the book that aims to uncover differences in "thinking citizenship" across different civic organizations.

The logic of this part of the investigation works like this. Since we know that different kinds of organizations are associated with different political-participation profiles in their members, *if the "connections" explanation is right, we should expect differences in the kinds of people a citizen would encounter in these organizations.* In other words, if differences arise because of the different groups of people with whom a member would connect, these groups of people must differ significantly across organizations in order to explain organizational differences in mobilization.

If, for example, education encourages political participation because it gives citizens more resources, a social network should be a useful way of transferring such benefits. To the extent that education is a *resource* citizens use to engage in citizenship, offering citizen A access to people with more education should increase citizen A's likelihood of participation. But if education's effect on citizenship comes more from its role in affecting individuals' political *views*, that effect is less directly transferable through a social network. People may, of course, change their views because they talk to others in their networks, but that process characterizes the "activities" explanation, not the "connections" explanation. So to the extent that education influences participation through changing people's views, we would expect to see little or no confirmation of the connections explanation.

In order to resolve this question, I begin by considering the kinds of people a member of each organization type is likely to encounter through that organization. The idea is straightforward: If organizations have different kinds of people as members, we can see if differences in those kinds of people affect the participation of other members in the group. On a wide variety of measures, I find little evidence for the connection theory.

I use the same data as in the first part of this chapter. Each person who responded to the survey was asked to name the organization to which they volunteered the most time and the one to which they donated the most money. They were then asked which of these two was "most important to you." That organization is called their "main" organization. I looked for effects that could be ascribed to the kinds of people in respondents' main organizations and in all other organizations to which they belonged on the political participation of the respondents.

To investigate these effects, I used two statistical techniques: general linear models (GLM) and hierarchical linear models (HLM). These models allow me to separate the predecessors to political participation. In particular, they allow me to tease individual-level causes apart from group-level causes. These are sophisticated and technical processes; interested readers will find the details of the models and their estimation in the second half of appendix A.

While most of the difference in political participation remains based on individuals (not the organizations to which they belong), the roughly 4 percent explained by their organizations remains important. Its importance is magnified by the imprecision of the data—we have little information about the specific groups to which respondents belonged. Hence, we have probably lost some of the mobilizing effects of their groups by aggregating the groups into broader group types.

Specific information about individuals (their age, sex, education, and income) explains roughly twice that amount of the difference. Considering information about the organizations—the average age of members, for instance—yields little additional information about the source of variation in political participation. Overall, this analysis provides only weak support for the importance of social networks as organizations' way of mobilizing their members.

Looking for the Democratic Imagination

This chapter offers additional support for earlier studies suggesting that individual-level education and income are strong predictors of political participation. Involvement in nonpolitical civic organizations, too, makes people more likely to participate in political activity—particularly the active citizenship represented by the measure of difficult political participation.

However, all civic organizations are not equal mobilizers. Different sorts of civic organizations contribute differently to the degree and kind of people's political involvement. Furthermore, these differences are not simply the result of the collections of people who make up networks and to whom citizens build connections through organizational memberships. The differences among civic groups cannot be explained entirely by reference to who participates in them. This finding strongly suggests that something intrinsic to different kinds of organizational life—resources, ideas, skills, and so forth, arising out of the process of civic participation itself—links civil society to democratic citizenship.

Some research has already begun to consider what citizenship resources Americans gain through involvement in nonpolitical civic associations. Eliasoph (1998), for example, suggests that citizens enact democracy in different ways, and to different degrees, depending on the kinds of associations to which they belong. Other theoretical work (M. E. Warren 2001) and empirical approaches (Perrin 2001a) point to the same conclusion: the civic base of democratic citizenship varies, in part, with the political culture of the organization. Further research should examine more closely the activities and characteristics of specific civic organizations to understand what participation entails and how it is related to citizenship.

The rest of the book pursues that set of questions. This chapter has shown that we cannot explain the impact of associational involvement on democratic citizenship just by looking at the objective characteristics of those associations. Citizenship gets more from associational life than just civic skills and contacts with other people. In what follows, I look for the rest of the story: the imaginative, intangible elements of democratic citizenship that we get from social life. For that, I turn to analyzing citizen speak in civic groups.

CHAPTER THREE

Talking about Politics in Groups: What to Look for in Citizenship Discourse

Having confirmed that membership in associations cannot by itself explain differences in democratic citizenship among citizens, we must now turn to analyzing citizenship talk. The findings in chapter 2 have given us good clues as to where to find the democratic imagination, but how will we know when we have found it? What contours, shapes, and sizes characterize democratic imaginations?

The democratic imagination, as I argued in the first chapter, is best accessed by looking at how people talk. Looking at what people say, how they argue with others, and what they assume reveals how their understanding of politics, citizenship, and democracy is organized. This chapter provides a framework for understanding the democratic imagination. I concentrate on the following question: What kinds of benchmarks should we look for in evaluating political talk? I use the ideas and methods that arise in answer to this question to discuss the specific dimensions of the democratic imagination in later chapters. The rest of the book consists of foraging for the democratic imagination—searching through citizenship talk to find our object. This chapter gives us the tools to know when we have found it.

First I develop a scheme for analyzing specific talk and its relationship to citizenship. The scheme is necessarily abstract, since it is designed to offer a general, broadly applicable way of analyzing citizenship talk, no matter what that talk is or where it takes place. The chapter begins with a discussion of what makes talk *democratic*; that is, What kinds of discourse do the work of structuring political imaginations? Furthermore, among these kinds of talk, what kinds help build a political imagination whose instincts are democratic? I take a cue from political scientists and philosophers who have thought about issues like *deliberation*, but I go beyond those questions in a search for everyday political talk. I offer a process for classifying kinds of political talk based on their *purpose* and their *tone*. Next, I take up the question of what makes talk *imaginative*—what are the clues in citizens' discourse as to the breadth and nuance of their thinking? What repertoires do citizens bring to political talk, and how do they mobilize them? Here, I provide the dimensions we can use to explore citizens' thinking. I conclude by describing the civic contexts I put together in the focus groups—the specific arenas where I found democratic imaginations.

An important difference exists between my project in this chapter and the existing literature on deliberative democracy. In the *normative* approaches that characterize most work on deliberative democracy, theorists investigate what kinds of discussion are to be welcomed and encouraged; in my *empirical* approach, I inquire into what kinds of discussion actually contribute to the democratic imagination. I am not arguing that individuals or groups *should* engage in all forms of political communication, some of which are morally repugnant. But people *do* engage in such activities, and they have important effects on the way others think about politics.

What Makes Talk Democratic?

Political scientists and sociologists have been very interested in *deliberation*, a kind of political talk that many believe is central to a democracy. Generally, deliberation is understood as political talk among two or more participants that is (1) *respectful*: each respects the other's position and legitimacy; (2) *rational*: each participant argues and evaluates others' arguments in terms of a shared standard of reasonableness; (3) *calm*: affective, emotional reactions are unwelcome; and (4) *goal-directed*: participants aim to arrive at a commonly supported outcome. This theory of deliberation is most closely associated with the work of the German sociologist Jürgen Habermas (Habermas 1989, 1998b), although the empirical approaches of political scientists (e.g., Page 1996; Mansbridge 1980; Bryan 2004) have varied in their attention to Habermas.

There are numerous good critiques of this vision of deliberation as an ideal of general political talk. Feminists (e.g., Fraser 1989; Benhabib 1992, 2002; Young 2000) have pointed out that it privileges the "disembodied voice" of pure rationality over feeling, experience, and emotion. Conflict theorists argue that the presumption of a commonly supported outcome is often neither possible nor desirable.

Recent empirical research by political scientists on deliberation typically seeks to determine which citizens are able to gain their political preferences and under what conditions. Schattschneider's (1960, 35) famous demonstration of the class bias in pluralist democracy remains mostly uncontested. Political scientists Benjamin Page and Robert Shapiro (Page and Shapiro 1992) find remarkable consistency among Americans' policy preferences over time, but Page's (1996) later work notes that this consistency may be largely irrelevant, as the range of voices involved in actual policy deliberation is quite narrow. And political scientist Richard Valelly (1993) summarizes a variety of research to show that public policy can and often does affect the extent and content of public deliberation and citizenship (see also Campbell 2003), arguing for a vision of public policy that explicitly aims not just at operational efficiency but also at enhancing citizenship and deliberation.

The political science work on deliberation suffers from a lack of standards to evaluate real deliberation. Does deliberation occur on editorial pages and in other elite discussion forums, as Benjamin Page's (1996) argument suggests? In what publications, broadcasts, or physical locations should we look for evidence of the success or failure of deliberation? The answers to these questions require a theoretical understanding of the concept of the public sphere, its structure, and its boundaries.

The theory of deliberation starts with the commonsense idea that our decisions on matters of public importance will be better if we discuss them with fellow citizens before deciding. The reasons for such improvement vary. Citizens may, for example, gain better *information* about an issue from deliberation; they may learn different ways of viewing an issue by considering other citizens' concerns, as Habermas has recently suggested (1998a). They may simply strengthen their existing ideas, entering the political fray with greater confidence in their convictions (see fig. 3.1).

The weakness of these ideas is that they assume a one-directional process: citizens begin with ideas and interests (thinking citizenship), bring these to a discussion (talking citizenship) and emerge with a consensus or compromise position (practicing citizenship). But since existing research shows that each corner of the citizenship triangle can have important influences on the others (see fig. 2.1), that assumption is untenable. A thorough understanding of the role of talk in democracy needs to expand well beyond what we already think of as deliberation. Deliberation *does*

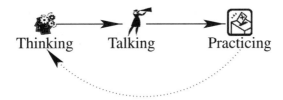

Thinking   Talking   Practicing

FIGURE 3.1. Traditional deliberation theory deals with privately developed preferences that are brought to a public space.

structure the democratic imagination, but it is far from the only kind of talk that does. Furthermore, restricting political talk to its deliberative type robs democracy of important ways of thinking and acting citizenship.[1]

Citizens communicate about politics in countless ways. We talk with friends, neighbors, family members, and co-workers in informal conversations. We have gatherings—at water coolers, lunch tables, conference rooms, even bowling alleys—where we discuss politics itself, or the myriad ideas and issues that inform our political views. These topics emerge as well during formal meetings at work, at school, in organizations and churches.

Beyond such face-to-face talk, we also take part in many *mediated publics*:[2] "places" where we can talk with other citizens (and noncitizens) without ever encountering them in person. We receive political messages from journalists, pundits, politicians, entertainers, advertisers, and more through television, radio, newspapers, and the Internet. Some of us talk back through these forums too: we write letters to the editor, call in to talk shows, and post to Internet "chat rooms." This is also sometimes done by representatives, albeit not elected ones: the professional talkers, questioners, and message-makers who deliberate on our behalf, for example, on shows like *Meet the Press* (Clayman 2004; Page 1996; Lang 2004). All this talk—messages received, messages sent, and memories of how previous messages were received—combines to set our beliefs and expectations of politics.

In 1950–51, a group of German social scientists—members of the Frankfurt School of sociology, reconstituted in Germany after exile in the United States during World War II—conducted a little-known set of experiments called the Groups Experiments (*Gruppenexperiment*;

1. My discussion here has been strongly influenced by Mark E. Warren's work (2001) as well as feminist critiques of deliberation theory.

2. See Clayman (2004) for a discussion of such publics.

Pollock 1955).[3] The experiments were designed to uncover modes of thinking that ran below the surface of German society; the researchers wanted to know how thoroughly the Nazi past had been banished from German opinion.

In writing about the Groups Experiments, Franz Böhm criticized the standard way of researching public opinion, "which expresses itself in elections, referenda, public speeches, groups, parliamentary discussions [and] political assemblies." These private opinions, he wrote, are "only formal expressions we use when we are wearing our Sunday clothes" (Böhm 1955; translation in Olick 2006). The "true" public opinion, the researchers contended, is the product of groups that inspire, inhibit, and shape the kinds of ideas their members hold and express.[4]

The Groups Experiments, although largely unknown in the United States, set off significant criticism and debate in Germany at the time. Regardless of the particulars, though, these researchers were on to a reality that has largely escaped current researchers: People think in social contexts. When a survey researcher reaches a respondent by telephone or in person, that is a particular kind of social context: a specific interaction between the researcher and the respondent. The opinions the subject expresses are not false, but they are also not necessarily the opinions she would express in a conversation with friends, family members, co-workers, political allies, or others. Since it is opinions expressed in public that actually matter, we should pay attention to what kinds of sociability encourage different kinds of public expression.

Think of the last conversation you had with anyone. What did you talk about? Why did you start talking in the first place? How many people were there? How much did you already know about them and their political ideas before you began talking? How did you actually converse—in person, on the telephone, over the Internet?

These questions form the beginning of a schema for understanding political talk. Here are some of the dimensions of talk we should take into account:

· How *political* is it? Some talk is self-evidently political, as when we discuss an upcoming election. Other talk seems entirely nonpolitical: scheduling a

3. See Olick (2006) for an excellent historical and methodological discussion of the *Gruppenexperiment*.
4. One of the researchers, Theodor W. Adorno (2005), reiterates a similar argument.

meeting, for example, or discussing a hobby. There is a continuum here, though; even scheduling a meeting can take on political overtones.

· How *institutional* is it? Political talk can focus on relatively institutional questions such as office holders, elections, and budgets. It can also address more diffuse, cultural questions: fairness, efficiency, even friendliness.

· Is it more *rational* or *symbolic*? Conversation may be governed by terms of strict logic: for example, arguing that a particular policy is more or less effective in promoting a shared ideal. It may also emphasize symbolic representation: simply putting forward a position in discussion without presuming a commonly shared ideal.

· Is its style more *confrontational* or *conciliatory*? We sometimes talk politically in order to maintain and identify differences with others—such talk is confrontational. Sometimes, however, we aim to understand and compromise with others; that is conciliatory talk.

· What is the *expected outcome* of the talk? We expect certain discussions to end in general agreement. In other discussions, we expect a specific outcome but acknowledge that it may be the result of compromise among interests rather than a real agreement. And plenty of political talk does not expect an outcome at all; its goal is to present ideas, positions, and identities *in the service of talk itself.*

Of course, other dimensions may also characterize political talk. My intention here is not to present an exhaustive typology but simply to note that such talk involves many dimensions.

How Political?

As sociologist Nina Eliasoph points out, talk can be political because it is *about* a topic considered political or because it is what Eliasoph calls "public-spirited" in its style (Eliasoph 1998, 14–16). Of course, even nonpolitical talk often informs later political discussions, as people use ideas and experiences drawn from previous interactions to operate within a political context.

Most of our everyday talk is not specifically political. Indeed, aside from relatively few people who are very engaged in political life, many people do not think of themselves as talking "about politics" very often at all. This is particularly true in what we think of as "public" places such as associations and the workplace; citizens seem to talk most about politics with their families and in other "private" settings (Wyatt, Katz, and

Kim 2000, 89–90). Thinking about it further, though, that idea is diffi-cult to sustain. The feminist principle that "the personal is political" has led to an important insight: few, if any, of the things we talk about can be entirely divorced from political questions. We think about politics by bringing experiences from the rest of life to bear on political questions.

Sociologists Bonnie Erickson and T. A. Nosanchuk (1990) studied ex-actly this process by investigating how members of a bridge club (hardly an explicitly political organization) became politically mobilized through their involvement. This happened because they met and discussed issues with other members for whom political issues were relevant. Similarly, political scientist Kay Lehman Schlozman pointed out to me that a bowl-ing league faced with land-use or zoning regulations might be expected to become political, even though its principal mission is nonpolitical.

Political scientist Melissa Victoria Harris-Lacewell, in a groundbreak-ing study, examined the connections between political thought and every-day talk in black communities. After observing overtly nonpolitical talk in a Sunday school, she suggests that

> although none of the individuals engaging in the conversation will be instantly convinced by the arguments of others, all will be affected by their participa-tion in this conversation. Each person who has shared in this interaction will adjust his or her political attitudes to the extent that she or he is convinced by the various arguments being made. It is possible that if this kind of discussion occurred regularly in the Bible study class, and if the advice of the class had a consistent ideological bent, then the individuals who regularly meet in this space are likely to develop similar approaches to addressing discriminatory cir-cumstances. (Harris-Lacewell 2004, 12)

She calls this the "theory of everyday talk." While I do not explicitly adopt her theory, her rich research suggests that my findings may apply across different contexts as well.

To illustrate this principle, I asked the students in my first-year sem-inar on citizenship to form small groups. I told them I had to leave the room for a few minutes, but would be back shortly. When I returned, I gathered the class together and asked each group to report what they had talked about, paying particular attention to the political nature of it. All the groups originally said they had not talked about politics at all (even though the class was on American citizenship!). When we discussed it further, though, most of the groups agreed that there were political implications to their discussions. One, for example, swapped stories of problems they had encountered in seeking academic advising services during their first semester. In a later conversation, this information could provide resources for thinking about education, organizations, and even the state budget, which funds much of the undergraduate education at a public university.

The fact that few discussions are entirely nonpolitical means we should keep asking, *How* political is particular talk? As Nina Eliasoph has shown, talk that seems too political, especially in the U.S. context, may alienate conversational participants (Eliasoph 1998; Eliasoph and Lichterman 2002). At the same time, though, when people experience many conversations that have no explicitly political content, they learn that politics is a taboo subject.[5] Formal and informal rules enforcing politeness may also reinforce inequality, as people of different gender, race, class, and other backgrounds get different messages about whether, how much, and how they may participate in discussions (Mills 2003; Walzer 2004).

Political talk specifically addresses issues of power, resource distribution, or public morality. In general, political talk tends to increase the breadth of citizens' democratic imaginations, but that effect is far from constant. An important example of political talk that *decreases* the breadth of the democratic imagination (and of democratic practice) is negative campaign advertising, which tends to increase cynicism about politics and thereby decrease participation (Ansolabehere and Iyengar 1995).

Because of all this, there is no necessary connection between the degree of political content in discourse and its contribution to the breadth of the democratic imagination. I argue that citizens are more like grazers, moving from context to context, picking up bits of information and social cues as they move. These cues come from all sorts of interactions, not just explicitly political ones. Over the long term, involvement in more and varied conversations with political content serves to shape, expand, and reinforce the democratic imagination.

How Institutional?

Political talk can consider issues at the center of institutional politics, such as voting decisions, public policy issues, and the behavior of elected

---

5. This lesson is often taught overtly, as when parents instruct children never to talk about religion or politics in polite company.

officials. At the other end of the spectrum, talk can be about matters that lie outside institutional politics and still remain political.

Consider, for example, an area of life we don't typically think of as political: exercise and recreation. Whether people's hobbies are bowling, quilting, hiking, NASCAR racing, or jogging, they take part in these activities for fun or for other presumably nonpolitical reasons, such as being with friends or enhancing health. But choosing recreational activities and deciding whether or not to follow through with them may involve important public issues. The U.S. government, for example, has set a goal of increasing neighborhood access to exercise and encouraging people to exercise as a form of recreation (U.S. Department of Health and Human Services 2000b, 2000a). The choice, then, between leisure activities such as watching television or playing video games (which provide little or no exercise) and those such as jogging or hiking becomes a subject of public concern, not just personal preference. Indeed, it has important public policy implications for issues such as health care, land use, taxation, and workplace concerns.

In addition, for both good and bad reasons, people may be afraid to engage in outdoor activities. The 1996 murders of two hiking companions on the Appalachian Trail, for example, scared many would-be hikers off the trail (Hendrix 1997). Women are more likely than men to feel vulnerable to attack (Whyte and Shaw 1994), which means that leisure decisions are also part of gender inequality—very much a political issue. Finally, as sociologist Barry Glassner has shown us, people rarely fear the "right" thing—we are more afraid of misfortunes that are less likely and less afraid of those that are more likely to occur (Glassner 1999). According to Glassner, this happens because the news media cover risk poorly, inflating the likelihood of dramatic problems while ignoring more common, less exciting ones. Thus, the (mis)information we use to make recreation decisions is also the *product* of a political process.[6]

Danielle S. Allen has cogently argued that everyday lessons of childhood also constitute civic education: "One political lesson is inscribed as

6. Indeed, it is difficult to conceive of any talk as nonpolitical in and of itself; rather, we should see political ideas as the application of ideas culled from numerous other contexts to political questions. This idea fits well with the fascinating work of Katherine Cramer Walsh (Walsh 2004, 34): "Much political interaction occurs not among people who make a point to specifically talk about politics but emerges instead from the social processes of people chatting with one another."

deeply as possible into the hearts and minds of all children. 'Don't talk to strangers.'...this admonishment is the central tenet of our current education in citizenship" (Allen 2004, 48). The messages we send and receive about everyday life—safety, hygiene, taste, appearance, and more—become part of our ways of thinking citizenship.

These issues are not what most Americans would consider "politics." Recreation is not generally about elected officials, party preferences, public policy, or even the quality of public works. But especially in the United States, where talking directly about issues labeled "political" is often frowned upon, people may rely on conversations about noninstitutional political issues to make decisions about more institutional questions as well. These experiences and expectations help create the shape and boundaries of the democratic imagination.

Rational versus Symbolic

Theorists of political deliberation often claim that the ticket for admission into political discussions is rationality: participants should be willing to divorce ideas from the people and groups making them, and should be open to being convinced by other participants to change their views. Emotional and poetic approaches, they contend, should be discouraged, since they interfere with true rationality.[7] Otherwise, the reasoning goes, what's the point in holding the discussion at all?

This claim is open to several appropriate objections. Probably the best known is the feminist critique that the spaces for deliberation are unequal (e.g., Fraser 1989); certain groups are more able to make their concerns known and feel more entitled to consideration than others. But more generally, why should a commitment to calm reason be the sine qua non of discussion? Can't people legitimately be angry, sad, upset, afraid, or proud? And shouldn't a forum designated for public speech be able to cope with those feelings?

As Nancy Fraser has argued (Fraser 1997), many political movements—feminism, gay rights, civil rights, and lately right-wing cultural movements as well—are increasingly demanding *recognition* more than

7. This bias dates back to the debate between Plato and his student, Aristotle, about the value of emotional and aesthetic appeals. The debate is the subject of Aristotle's *Poetics* (Aristotle 1961). Recently, Michael Warner has pointed out that the emotional, poetic character of public talk serves an important purpose: it allows citizens to imagine the public as a coherent body (Warner 2002).

redistribution. That shift has an important influence on political talk. Redistribution is largely what political scientists call "zero-sum":[8] for some
participants to be satisfied with the outcome, some others must be dissatisfied. Recognition talk is different. Speakers (groups or individuals) whose
goal is to be recognized as important, different, or oppressed need not try
to diminish other speakers' recognition. That has two significant implications. First, rationality is less important, since partners need not give
up a scarce resource in order to grant recognition; second, compromise
and consensus are devalued, since they involve the failure of a partner to
achieve recognition.

One reason for the shift toward recognition may be the disturbing finding (see Walzer 1983; Guinier 1994) that, on many issues, compromise
solutions consistently favor one group over another. That is, certain participants in deliberations can *never* reasonably expect to achieve satisfac-
tory outcomes. Knowing that, they may reasonably opt for recognition,
which they have a substantially better chance of achieving.[9] Because of
the incentives I outlined above, though, that choice also decreases the
group's chances of achieving compromise or consensus. In addition, some
observers have suggested that the success of recognition struggles pro-
duces a backlash among dominant groups, resulting in further setbacks
for groups seeking recognition.

It is true that to achieve the goal of efficiently decided policy outcomes, participants must come to the table committed to a particular style
of talk, which many theorists have labeled "deliberative." But democracy's primary goal is not efficiency. It involves the recognition of numerous different voices, many of which cannot reasonably be held to
the narrow standard of deliberation. Furthermore, particularly in the
field labeled "contentious politics" (see, e.g., Tilly 2004; McAdam, Tarrow, and Tilly 2001), forms of communication that violate the norms
of deliberation are commonplace. Individuals, groups, and governments
now routinely engage in forms of communication that are explicitly not
deliberative: propaganda, advocacy, demonstration, blockage, intransi-
gence, mystery, identity politics, and violence are some examples. Reasonable arguments exist for the inclusion and exclusion of each of these

8. It is not literally true that redistribution must be technically zero-sum. The important
point for my argument is that in a redistributive situation, one side must "lose" in order for
another to "win."

9. This is essentially the move that Thomas Frank argues working-class Kansans have
made in preferring right-wing cultural politics over left-wing distributive ones (Frank 2004).

communicative forms—but those questions lie beyond the scope of this book.

For my purposes here, we need to take into account the cognitive and emotional effects of political talk. That means that we must treat even forms of communication that are disturbing and patently immoral—such as those involving terrorism (Scarry 1985; Wagner-Pacifici 1986)—as forms of political communication. Terrorism exists in the world, and therefore shapes and changes our political discourse.

Confrontational versus Conciliatory

Political talk may be conciliatory in tone—that is, it may seek to understand other speakers' points of view, search for common ground, and emphasize respect (Habermas 1998a, 49–84). It may also be confrontational; one or more of those involved may be frankly uninterested in apprehending others' points of view (see, e.g., Marcuse 1965).

That possibility reminds us that political talk is often emotional: it is based upon, and appeals to, feelings, relationships, and commitments with emotional importance. Precisely *how* emotional factors play into political discussion is not clear, but common appeals to family, home, morality, virtue, and more make it clear that they do. The idealized, rational citizen—who decides on positions and courses of action based on a dispassionate calculus of cost and benefit—must at least negotiate with a citizen whose thinking is guided by emotions.

Requiring parties to a political forum to be conciliatory (as attractive as it might seem) would effectively bar some citizens and groups from the table (Tannen 1998). If democratic practice is supposed to provide a mechanism to represent citizens' actual ideas, views, and thoughts, requiring them to be strictly rational and conciliatory is simply too constraining. Citizens may be morally committed, emotionally invested, ideologically inflexible, and personally hostile—all characteristics that describe many people in many situations, and all characteristics that impede their ability to engage in conciliatory discourse.

Of course, a sufficiently tolerant political climate might go a long way toward *creating* citizens who are more conciliatory. Beyond relying on tolerance, democratic discourse might help foster it. But while we may hope for that outcome, designing public discourse that *assumes* it is inappropriate.

Some studies of democratic culture argue, in fact, that to be truly political, talk should be invested with moral and emotional overtones (Eliasoph 1998; Lakoff 2002). Truly political discourse is not limited to political scientist Harold Lasswell's famous definition "who gets what, when, how" (Lasswell 1936), but gets at deep conflict over issues of identity, personality, ideology, emotion, and morality (Smith 2003).

Expected Outcomes

Why talk about politics at all? For political scientists who think about deliberation, the answer is clear: to explain and come to agreement upon issues of shared concern. We expect that if two disagreeing groups explain their concerns, positions, ideas, and values, they will arrive at a consensus decision. That decision may be a genuine "meeting of the minds," or a compromise between two positions, or concession by one or more parties in the expectation that, the next time around, the "winning" parties will be more conciliatory (Guinier 1994).

There are two reasons to be suspicious of this story: an ideal reason and a pragmatic one. First, the story assumes that there is a consensus position that groups can reach through deliberation. What if, as many observers believe, the parties are motivated by conflicting interests, values, or even moral orders (Smith 2003)? Maybe the best we can hope for is *compromise*: that one party agrees to surrender its position in the expectation that a future outcome will be in its favor. But some kinds of political talk don't lend themselves to such expectations. Will abortion be legal for a set period of time and then illegal? How about zoning laws? More pragmatically, as should be clear by now, not all parties are interested in policy *outcomes*.

A Conceptual Scheme for Classifying Political Talk

None of these elements should be understood as making talk better or worse. Indeed, normative democratic theory often falters by simply writing off forms of expression that arise from and deserve recognition by democratic practice. But each of the dimensions outlined in this section offers a way to classify political talk. And doing so can help us to understand (1) what kinds of contexts encourage different kinds of political talk and (2) what kinds of political talk encourage active, engaged citizenship.

Combining the elements of political talk, then, we have four important axes for classifying talk:

1. the *domain* of talk, which concerns the degree to which its purpose is understood as part of the public sphere;
2. the *actor* to which talk is directed, which may be, for example, an official agency or individual, a company, or a group;
3. the *target* or rationale for the talk, which may involve expressing a position (voice) or moving toward an outcome; and
4. the *tone* of the talk, which may be, for example, confrontational, conciliatory, calm, or emotional.

Table 3.1 illustrates these axes by placing kinds of political communication on them. Of course, just as we cannot reduce citizenship activities to the cultural repertoires that give rise to them (see the discussion of creativity above), we cannot capture all the elements to talk in these four dimensions. But, complementing political scientist Mark E. Warren's (2001) discussion of the kinds of civic associations, these dimensions give us some basic criteria for categorizing citizenship talk.

What Makes Talk Imaginative?

In mapping the democratic imagination, understanding the political and democratic aspects of discourse is not enough. We also need to know what makes talk *imaginative*. The word *imagination* evokes a mental faculty divorced from, yet in dialogue with, actual observations. We need not imagine something we see or experience; we imagine desires, possibilities, and ideas that fall between what exists and what is impossible.

The early sociologists Émile Durkheim and Marcel Mauss taught us that imaginations reside in cultures, not just in individual minds (Durkheim and Mauss 1963). Cultural ideas, repertoires, and assumptions structure what we can imagine and how we imagine it. An important part of the cultural process that constrains imagination is talk: talk in groups, talk with friends and colleagues, talk in mediated settings.

Unlike investigating what makes talk political, determining what makes talk imaginative is relatively simple. Talk is more imaginative when it (1) contemplates possibilities that have not been observed; and (2) evaluates proposals using evidence and ideas from a wide range of sources.

TABLE 3.1 **Typology of kinds of political talk**

Talk type	Domain		Actor		Target		Tone	
	Apolitical	Political	Institutional	Grassroots	Outcome	Voice	Confrontational	Conciliatory
Town meeting		↑		↔	↔		↔	
"Water cooler" conversation	↔			↑		↑		↑
Recognition march		↑		↑		↑	↓	
Strike for benefits		↑	↓		↓		↓	
Terrorism		↑			↓		↓	
Letter to the editor	↔			↑		↑	↔	
Letter to an official		↑	↓	↑		↑	↔	
Silence	↓		↓	↔	↔			↑
Exit		↑				↑		↑

Talk is unimaginative when speakers discuss only possibilities they have observed before, and when it evaluates the possibility of future developments only in terms of past experience. Sociologist Stephen Hart analyzed something similar to this, pointing out that some associations displayed more "expansive" political dialogue than others (Hart 2001).

We imagine the society we live in through discussion, communication, and observation. As philosopher Charles Taylor puts it, "the way ordinary people 'imagine' their social surroundings...is carried in images, stories, and legends.... The social imaginary is that common understanding that makes possible common practices and a widely shared sense of legitimacy" (Taylor 2002, 106). Michael Warner has applied this idea to publics, in particular, noting that when citizens "speak into the air" (Peters 1999), offering their opinions to others through mediated public spheres, they also succeed in imagining the public to which they are speaking. They use this speech to create an image of those who might be listening (Warner 2002). Imaginative talk is crucial to citizenship because it lets citizens think about the social world they are addressing. It provides the fodder for creativity, leading people to envision modes of citizenship that apply new tools to political problems.

Gendered, Raced Talk

People are taught to engage in particular kinds of political talk by experiences and groups they belong to—including those defined by race and gender. Good research has shown that power in conversations (Gibson 2000) is affected by inequality among conversational participants (see, e.g., Berger et al. 1998). Often, that inequality comes in the door with the people doing the discussing: participants pay more or less respect to others partly on the basis of how they evaluate them.

Such evaluations mean that race, gender, and other apparent social inequalities affect discourse—and therefore the democratic imagination itself. Sometimes this effect is relatively straightforward and predictable (Tannen 1990), but at other times it is complex and hidden. Sensing inequalities in a discussion, some African Americans may "bend over backward" to show white colleagues that they do not represent stereotypes. Some women in conversation may seek to counter expectations that they will be demure, respectful, and conciliatory by being outgoing and confrontational. While I do not seek specifically to understand gender and race in discussions, they figure repeatedly in the discussion because they play significant roles in how citizens talk and listen.

Talk in Settings

What we have at this point is still just a framework. To understand how Americans develop, expand, and constrain their democratic imaginations, we need to fill in the gaps, turning our framework into a specific investigation about how real people actually talk and think citizenship. Doing that, though, requires us to acknowledge that *citizen speak takes place in specific settings* (Mische and Pattison 2000). We cannot understand the democratic imagination without observing actual democratic imaginations at work, deliberating, interpreting, and processing political stimuli.

Sociologists Nina Eliasoph and Paul Lichterman (2002) identified something called "group style." Groups of people in discussion, they found, take on certain ways of talking that are properties of those groups. This implies that the setting in which a citizen finds herself helps structure whether, and how, she talks about important issues. Taking seriously my argument that the democratic imagination is fundamentally about *talk*, we must conclude *the democratic imagination is a social—that is, a group—phenomenon*.

Talk is not political, democratic, or imaginative in the abstract. Its meaning is generated in civic settings: places where citizens can exchange ideas about everything from everyday life to life-and-death political issues. These may be literal meeting spaces of the kind that "social capital" theorists consider (e.g., Putnam 2000), or they may be virtual spaces: discussions through electronic or printed media that let citizens exchange ideas without ever meeting in person. And, crucially, the parameters and group style of a setting can make talk *less* political, less democratic, and less imaginative. Settings are sites that promote *and inhibit* the development and expression of the democratic imagination.

To assess the democratic imagination, I created a unique laboratory. I organized twenty group discussions, each one including members of a single organization. All of them were held in southern Alameda County, California, during the spring of 2000. Comprising between four and ten participants, each group was asked to grapple with four hypothetical political scenarios. I gave the groups wide latitude in their discussions, letting them bring up all kinds of arguments, tangents, preferences, opinions, and emotions. My results are the records of twenty detailed discussions among citizens, inspired by, but not limited to, the same four scenarios.

FIGURE 3.2. Southern Alameda County from the air (photo courtesy of Don Singletary; used by permission)

I intentionally held all the groups in a small geographic area in the hopes of minimizing differences based on the regions they were held in. I chose southern Alameda County, California, for both logistical and demographic reasons. While it is a part of the San Francisco Bay Area, and its residents are therefore significantly wealthier, better educated, and more ethnically diverse than in many other areas of the country, southern Alameda County is less anomalous than other parts of the Bay Area.

From Interstate 880, the first impression is of suburban sprawl (fig. 3.2): industrial, retail, and housing developments nestled between the hills and the eastern edge of the San Francisco Bay. The signs on shopping centers along the freeway recite a litany of national chain stores, alongside more local electronics and Asian food outlets. The major cities of the region are Hayward, Fremont, and Union City. The majority of the focus groups were held in these cities, although a few had to be scheduled in nearby towns like Newark, San Leandro, and Pleasanton. In addition to residential areas for commuters to the nearby cities of Oakland, San Jose, and San Francisco, several important manufacturing facilities are located in the region, including New United Motors Manufacturing Incorporated (NUMMI), the Toyota–General Motors joint venture that assembles Chevrolet and Toyota cars for the U.S. market. There are also smaller "spillover" plants and offices from Silicon Valley, the area of Santa Clara and San Mateo counties teeming with high-tech companies and very high costs of business (Perrin 2002). Alameda County's workforce is roughly 20 percent manufacturing, nearly double the region's 10 percent figure but very similar to the national average.[10]

According to the 2000 Census, Alameda County's African-American population is similar to the national average (14.9 percent as compared to the national 12.3 percent, but only 6.7 percent California-wide). There are more Hispanic and Asian residents in Alameda County than in the country in general. People in Alameda County are well educated, with more high school and college graduates per capita than California and U.S. averages.[11] Alameda County is a very Democratic county in a generally Democratic state—in the 2000 general election, just after the focus groups, Californians voted for Democratic candidate Al Gore over George W. Bush by about 12 percentage points more than did the country as a whole. Alameda County added another 32 percentage points to that, giving Gore a 45-point spread over Bush.

The historical context of the discussions deserves mention as well. In the spring of 2000, as the presidential primary elections were underway, California was an important part of the campaigns. Party front-runners George W. Bush and Al Gore were battling the insurgent campaigns of John McCain and Bill Bradley, respectively. Second-term president Bill Clinton remained relatively popular, even in the wake of the sex scandal and impeachment proceedings over his relationship with White House intern Monica Lewinsky (Sarfatti-Larson and Wagner-Pacifici 2001). Our discussions were all held before some of the most important events of the past few years: the 2000 general election (Perrin et al. 2006), the 2001 terrorist attacks (Perrin 2005a), and the wars in Afghanistan and Iraq. But the approach I use should still stand. Indeed, people are likely to be more tuned in to political discussion now than they were when the study was originally conducted.

10. These statistics are for March 2000, when the focus groups were conducted. Unfortunately, statistics are not available for the southern Alameda County region, so these counts include the northern region as well, which includes the cities of Berkeley and Oakland. The percentages are from the California Employment Development Department, available online at http://www.calmis.ca.gov/htmlfile/subject/indtable.htm, and the U.S. Bureau of Labor Statistics, online at ftp://ftp.bls.gov/pub/suppl/empsit.ceseeb1.txt.

11. Statistics are from the U.S. Census, available online at http://quickfacts.census.gov/qfd/ states/06000.html.

In some ways, then, southern Alameda County in the spring of 2000 was quite similar to other suburban areas of the country (Oliver 2001), with national chain stores, multilane highways, and residential development. In other ways, it is substantially different. I do not claim that the people and groups I examine here are sufficiently similar to stand in for people and groups throughout the country.[12] Rather, like other focus group researchers, I use these discussions to show the power of social context in forming citizenship ideas and practices. I offer this portrait of the context in which the discussions took place to provide a sense of where the participants were coming from.

The Discussions

My survey-based research (chapter 2) led me to look for distinct democratic imaginations in five types of groups: Protestant churches; Catholic churches; labor unions; business organizations; and sports groups. After making contact with such groups, I placed announcements in newsletters, obtained telephone contact lists, or attended meetings to announce the group discussions. Details about the participants are in table B.1 in appendix B.

I presented the following four scenarios to the focus groups.

Profiling. This scenario dealt with alleged racial profiling by local police.

Since Mayor Jones's election three years ago, crime rates in our area have been cut almost in half. Jones credits his get-tough approach to crime along with the license he has granted to the police department to cut crime however it sees fit. One controversial step the police department has taken is so-called "profile stops": pulling cars over for minor infractions in the hope that they will yield arrests for more serious crimes. Critics have called the practice punishment for "driving while black," noting that black drivers are three times as likely as white drivers to be pulled over under the program.

Halfin. In this profile, the groups' U.S. senator, Joan Halfin, took questionable campaign contributions and changed key positions related to the interests of the contributors.

WASHINGTON—Sources close to Senator Joan Halfin confirmed today that rumors of an influence-peddling scheme were at least partly true. Halfin, who

12. See Pitkin (1967) for a discussion of this fallacy.

won reelection two years ago in a close race against businessman Hugh Lankson, was unavailable for comment yesterday.

The charges stem from that reelection campaign, reported to be the most expensive in state history. Lankson, a toy-manufacturing magnate who spent over $20 million of his own money in the race, challenged Halfin to run a campaign "without special-interest money." Halfin, in response, agreed not to accept money from PACs.

However, since the campaign, charges of bribery and influence-peddling have dogged the senator. Halfin, who is known in Washington as a defender of environmental protection and international children's rights, has recently shifted positions on each of these issues, and the latest revelations suggest that the automobile and clothing industries have pressured her to make the changes in exchange for promised support in her next reelection bid.

Furthermore, asked about accepting soft money, she said, "I continue to support legislation to restrict or outlaw soft money. But for now, no candidate can afford to reject soft money unless she's a multi-millionaire. Until the law is changed, I have no choice but to accept soft money contributions."

Chemco. This scenario dealt with a local chemical company's violations of Environmental Protection Agency (EPA) regulations and the possibility of its being shut down.

Chemco, the region's second-largest employer, escalated the dispute between itself and the Environmental Protection Agency yesterday, claiming that Chemco was immune to the agency's regulations.

The dispute arose after the EPA fined Chemco $400,000 for releasing too many ozone-depleting chemicals into the air. The ozone regulations, which have been controversial for years, went into effect two years ago over the objections of the chemical industry.

The EPA local office is threatening to pursue further action in the case, including requiring that Chemco's plant be shut down if it continues violating the regulations.

John Ellis, the chief lobbyist for the Washington, D.C.–based environmental group AirWatch, backs the EPA's finding. "We think Chemco's behavior is scandalous," said Ellis. "They're flouting the health of the earth and the laws of the country." He urged EPA to follow through by shutting down the factory.

Airport. Excessive neighborhood noise from a recent airport expansion is the subject of this scenario.

Since the recent airport expansion, the number of airplanes flying over your home has more than doubled. The airport, which was a small, regional facility, has become a major destination with the construction of a hub for Global Airways here. The planes are loud enough to rattle your windows and make it impossible to have conversations when they fly overhead.

There is no neighborhood association in your area, although you are on friendly terms with most of your neighbors.

Details about the focus group research strategy, including pilot testing, the selection of the scenarios, and the groups, appear in appendix B.

Strengths and Weaknesses of the Focus Group Strategy

The strategy of organizing targeted group discussions with standardized discussion topics to study citizenship allows us to model and observe the process of political deliberation as it happens in civic contexts of varying types, sizes, and dynamics. Constructing the research this way avoids the bias Eliasoph (1998, 231) warns against: assuming that political attitudes and behaviors are considered and engaged in on a purely individual level (see also Adorno 2005). Although the participants express strategies and ideas individually, structuring the investigation as a series of group discussions takes into account the influence of groups on the repertoires from which individuals draw their expressions.

My strategy in this study has been to isolate political talk from its "natural" context in order to study it. I then use that information to make claims about how political talk is contextualized. That decision may seem strange, as if I have jettisoned context in order to save it. But this is actually a reasonable approach. The contexts in which political talk takes place naturally are too varied to treat systematically; by removing talk from its natural context and installing it in a carefully controlled, systematically varying set of "laboratory" contexts, I can gauge the importance of each context in influencing the content of the talk.

Like all methods used in social research, this one has some limitations. Selection bias is a potentially significant source of error. I tried to minimize this possibility by providing selective benefits to participation, reducing costs of participation, and avoiding specific discussion of the topics before the groups met.

Because I recruited participants for these discussions, I cannot assess their likelihood of participating in political deliberation in daily life. Furthermore, I am unable to study the actual behavior of these groups, since in these settings the "costs" of deciding to participate are lower—in certain cases much lower—than they would be in real life. Participants may therefore have advocated political activity that they would not normally have undertaken. Nevertheless, they often argued *against* participation, suggesting that they understood the hypothetical costs of involvement and incorporated them into their decisions.

Studies that observe real-world political discussions (e.g., Kleinman 1996; Lichterman 1996; Eliasoph 1998) solve the problem of decision versus action at the cost of allowing varying topics of discussion along with group contexts. Gamson (1992) assembled groups of friendly individuals to discuss a standardized set of topics, looking for "insight into the process of constructing meaning" (192). My research builds on that principle by ensuring that the focus groups are actually *groups* in a sociological sense—they are preexisting social collectivities, not collections of unrelated individuals. The participants are not randomly chosen, but satisfy the *interdependence* criterion that makes them truly groups in the sociological sense (Forsyth 1999, 5; Cartwright and Zander 1968, 46; Lewin 1948; Simmel 1950). Another classic study by political scientists Sidney Tarrow and Fred Greenstein used "semi-projective" interviewing (making interviewees complete stories) to evaluate children's attitudes toward political authority and laws in France, England, and the United States (Greenstein and Tarrow 1970). But these fascinating interviews sacrificed a group context, asking the children to complete the stories outside any conversational context. My approach enables us to gain comparative leverage on discussions *of the same topics* by presenting systematically differing, preexisting groups with the same standardized stimuli (Merton, Fiske, and Kendall 1956).

I analyze the discussions by breaking them down into "turns" (Sacks, Schegloff, and Jefferson 1974; Ford, Fox, and Thompson 1996). Each turn is a contiguous block of speech by a single participant, beginning when she starts talking and continuing until she stops or is interrupted. Breaking discourse down into discrete turns downplays the back-and-forth nature of discussion, since it understands each turn separately. However, by capturing the group context of each turn, the overall model does include the likelihood that turns' characteristics are influenced by those of the turns surrounding them.

While the motivation for this research is the possibility that differences in political thought and discourse might explain previously observed differences in political *mobilization*, the data allow only for locating differences in the structure of political *discussion*. There is an association between differences in political talk and those in political behavior, but the data for this study do not provide direct evidence of a link. However, some recent work on citizenship (e.g., Habermas 1989; Conover, Searing, and Crewe 2002; Eliasoph 1996) suggests that political discussion is, in itself, a citizenship practice; in that sense, these data provide a direct measure of the relationship between group participation and citizenship. By organizing the political microcultures discussed in chapter 2, civic life— along with other opportunities for discussion—structures citizens' capacities for politics as well as their cultural approaches to the public sphere. An individual's cognitive repertoire of politics is constituted by the intersection among the political microcultures she has experienced; at the same time, those political microcultures are made up of the interactions among members' cognitive repertoires of politics. Insofar as political discussion itself is a practice of citizenship, political microcultures constitute spaces for citizenship practices in themselves. In addition, since citizens' understanding of political life is likely to structure their modes of involvement, political microcultures may offer a partial mechanism for the often-observed link between participation in civil society and political activity.

In order to control for the political environment within which the groups existed, all twenty focus groups were conducted in the same section of Alameda County, California, within a four-month period. The aim is to make the different groups themselves the most significant variation in the study design, holding constant as many other characteristics as possible; however, this does introduce regional and historical particularity to the specific results. That is, the prevalence of particular themes—either across groups or within specific group types—may be the result of issues or repertoires specific to northern California during the spring of 2000.

A final limitation of my study is that unobserved differences in status among group members—stemming from prior interactions, ascribed characteristics, or group dynamics within the discussion—may have influenced what participants said (see, e.g., Berger et al. 1998; Berger, Ridgeway, and Zelditch 2002). Beyond taking into account individual members' demographic characteristics, there is no way to address this concern.[13] But no firm line separates political microcultures from status dynamics within groups. Constructing such dynamics is one way in which civic groups nurture political microcultures.

13. In a more technical article (Perrin 2005b), I use a statistical test to show that prior logics used by group members had little or no influence on each turn's logic.

In the next few chapters, I report on the dimensions of political talk in the focus group discussions. I use these analyses to fill in the gaps in the framework presented here. By the end of this process, we will have a good map of the contemporary American democratic imagination.

The Contours of the Discussions

To figure out where, when, and in what circumstances democratically imaginative talk happens, we can look for a few key pieces of political discourse. In the following chapters, I present an analysis of political discussions that pays attention to three elements of political talk: *logics* of action, *methods* of involvement, and argumentative *resources*. Logics compose the repertoire of ways of *interpreting* a situation and options for addressing it. Methods of participation, by contrast, are directly compa-rable to sociologist Charles Tilly's repertoires of contention (1992, 1995): actions people can imagine taking in the public sphere. Strategic compar-isons and sources of information are *resources* used by participants to bol-ster arguments and provide content to positions (see chapter 4 for more on how resources fit into political argument). Table 3.2 contains the list of codes.

Logics

The first major decision a group of citizens must make is what logical framework to use in evaluating a situation. Is this primarily a question of morality? Of personal interest? Of community concern? Does it involve our children? Our neighborhood? Or is it "distant" and therefore, per-haps, either less compelling or less threatening to address? Both overtly and covertly, participants set the stage for further discussion by categoriz-ing situations according to one logical framework or another.

I identified and coded for five types of logics in the data. These are ideal-typical logics; not all claims necessarily fit neatly into one or another of the categories, but these logics encompass the majority of approaches to the issues. Furthermore, when participants explicitly debate what logic to apply to a situation, the candidates are these five:

1. Interest-based and other pragmatic logics. These logics are based on (*a*) the speaker's or group's self-interest (an *interest* logic) or, more generally, (*b*)

TABLE 3.2 **Focus group coding categories**

Logics	
Interests	
Interest	Self-interest on part of speaker
Personal	Discussion of others' self-interest
Pragmatic	What works, what's necessary
Voluntarist	Not our (collective) problem, individuals' own fault
Ideological/moral	
Ideol	Ideological or moral argument
Legality	Does a situation contain a legal issue?
Populism	"The people's choice," and so forth
Standpoint	Based on one's identity
Environment_Absolute	Environment as moral good (Sandman 1986)
Capacity	
Efficacy	Ability to make a difference
Resources	What do we have available to address the issue?
Expanded self-interest	
Children	"For the children"
Local	Seen as affecting one's immediate community
Mediation	
Methods	
Governmental	
Bureaucratic	Ask the appropriate personnel to fix
Electoral	Vote, don't vote, and so forth
Legislative	Pass laws
Donate	Give money to have things done
Public	
Educate	Spread a message, particularly when seen as nonthreatening
Letter	Write letters to either media or government
Organize	Build/use group capacity to address an issue
Petition	Circulate a petition
Protest	Demonstrations, parades, pickets, and so forth
Revolution	Violent, radical solution
Private	
Exit	Just leave
Explore	Find out more about the situation
Narrative resources	
Anecdote	A story told to illustrate a point or concept
Comparison	Comparing the current situation to another situation
Entertainment	Ideas based on movies, TV, and so forth
History	Discussion of past situation similar to this one
Doubt	Mistrust authorities and/or information

expectations that others act principally out of self-interest (*pragmatic* logics). *Pragmatic* logics deal similarly with the politics of interest, but they are more broadly stated to include the interests of others along with those of the speaker.

2. Ideological or moral logics. This is the kind of logic most easily seen as "political." Speakers employing a logic of morality or ideology argue for a position because they see it as intrinsically right; they do not base their arguments on self-interest or the feasibility of action. Others have called this mode of

reasoning the logic of "abstract rules" (Bellah et al. 1986, 151–52). I do not dif-
ferentiate between arguments based on morality and those based on ideology
because they are structurally equivalent; each argues that a course of action is
simply *right*, rather than using externally debatable standards to judge it.

3. Capacity-based logics. Such logics focus on the question of whether successful
   involvement is *feasible* or not, regardless of its value or moral weight. They consider the ability of an individual or group to participate effectively in a public-
   sphere activity.

4. Logics of expanded self-interest. Others have noted strategies that people use
   to justify ideological positions without expressly stating them (Eliasoph 1997,
   1998; Lamont 2000b). Eliasoph argues that Americans say issues are worth acting on when they are "close to home." She notes that people use the phrase
   even when it is literally incorrect; they use it to justify getting involved (or not)
   in an issue when simply taking a politically charged position is taboo. She also
   notes that children are a sort of synecdoche for ideologies, "licensing" adults to
   take political stands that otherwise appear too controversial to be appropriate:
   "The phrases 'close to home' and 'for the children' worked hard; they were piv-
   otal in allowing volunteers to maintain that feeling that the world made sense"
   (Eliasoph 1998, 64–65).

   In certain cases, participants used a logic similar to interest-based logics, but
   focused on the interests of collectives to which they belonged. The two logics
   in this category matched Eliasoph's findings: I have called them logics of the
   local and of *children*. As Eliasoph suggests, participants used these as licenses
   to make moral or ideological statements that otherwise would have been taboo
   in these contexts.

   I count these logics separately both from interests and from ideol-
   ogy/morality because they show features of both. They adopt the language of
   self-interest, but because they refer to groups assumed to be good (children
   and communities) as the interested parties, they serve to frame moralistic arguments.

5. Mediation logics. In using mediation logics, participants look for systematic ways to offer solutions to the scenarios presented. The two subcodes
   included—*compromise* and *roles*—refer to their suggestions that the conflict
   being discussed could be solved through discussion, reason, and the normal
   channels.

Sometimes, participants explicitly debated which of several competing logics they would employ to address a particular problem. However,

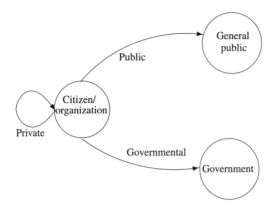

FIGURE 3.3. Active relationships in methods of involvement

logics are often the subtexts of anecdotes whose meanings must be interpreted.

Methods

Participants discussed three types of methods, each of which I treat more
thoroughly below: (1) *governmental* methods; (2) *public* methods; (3) *private* methods. Figure 3.3 shows the relationship each type of method expresses. Governmental methods typically involve either the *bureaucratic*
task of trying to find the appropriate official to solve a problem, or the
political task of electing someone to or removing someone from office.
They share the idea that politics—and, by extension, citizenship—is basically about governmental actors. Citizens can be effective by contacting
the correct official, whether she be a city council member, state representative, or president. If that person fails to fix the problem, she should be
voted out of office.

Thinking about citizenship in terms of governmental methods includes
many of the ways we think most often about politics. The government is
the representative of the people, and citizens who are concerned or dissatisfied appropriately bring those concerns to the government. It excludes,
though, a whole range of citizenship activities and decisions that involve
people's relationship to the *public* at large, as well as those that involve
primarily individual changes aimed at solving a citizen's immediate concern.

Public methods involve alerting the general public to a problem and seeking a resolution by having the public get involved. The audience here is not the government, but an assumed, even imagined, public (Warner 2002) that is attentive to concerns and available to put pressure on governmental actors as well as organizations, businesses, and other institutions. These methods include educational campaigns, writing letters to editors, organizing groups, circulating petitions, boycotts, protests, and in some cases starting a revolution.

Finally, it is important to understand that deciding strategically *not* to do anything about a situation is also a citizenship decision, as is deciding to do something without announcing that decision. For example, selecting a product or a store with local roots is a citizenship decision that has no public component. I call these decisions "private" because the citizen decides to address things for himself instead of engaging either with the public or the government. These methods include "learning more about the situation" (a common suggestion on how to participate) and *exit*: simply withdrawing from the situation, either by physically moving or by refusing to discuss an issue.

Resources

To make their cases more convincing, participants used ideas and knowledge available from elsewhere. These resources fell into two groups: *narrative* and *doubt*. Chapter 4 goes into much more detail about how these resources worked; I provide a short overview here. Resources differ from logics because they are rhetorical strategies used to bolster logics. Logics constitute the point a speaker is trying to make, whereas resources are the "evidence" the speaker draws on to support that point.

One of the most common strategies was to compare scenarios with other, real-world events. I call these narrative strategies because speakers use the comparisons with other stories, known by other group members, to avoid making explicit their own evaluations of the situation the group is considering. The use of narrative, that is, allows the speaker to take a position without incurring the risk that might be involved in taking ownership of that position. The onus is placed, instead, on a would-be disagreer, who is deprived of an explicit opinion statement with which she could disagree. These comparisons included *anecdotes* (stories known personally by the participant or a friend or family member); *entertainment* (comparisons with television, movies, or other fictional stories); *history* (comparisons with well-known prior events); and other comparisons.

The resources I call *doubt* bypass the intricate, comparative strategy employed by narratives. Participants who use doubt simply claim that the information provided in the scenarios, or by actors in the scenarios, is false. This mistrust is nearly always part of an argument *against* involvement, since action based on untrustworthy information is suspect.

Putting It Together: The Structure of the Democratic Imagination

We started this chapter in search of elements for evaluating political talk: benchmarks and signals to guide our investigation of the democratic imagination. Taking seriously the idea that the democratic subject—the citizen in a democratic society—is charged with "processing" information, ideas, arguments, and symbols, we need to understand how that processing works. I use the term *processing* to underscore the different kinds of activities a citizen is charged with: taking in cues from her environment and, *often at the same time*, generating, reconfiguring, and interpreting those cues for others in social interaction.

My claim in this book is that the democratic imagination is that processing system: the core that makes thinking, talking, and doing citizenship an active, creative set of activities. Furthermore, *the democratic imagination is rooted in citizenship talk*. Beyond simply being an accessible expression of the democratic imagination, citizenship talk is the form of the democratic imagination itself. We do not simply *express* imagination by talking; we *enact* it (Gumperz 1982; Austin 1962). The dimensions outlined above provide a framework to map specific democratic imaginations in specific social settings—the task of the next few chapters.

CHAPTER FOUR

Mistrust, Information, and Legitimation: Justifying Citizenship Decisions

"The Moody Land was only a story, Haroun," Rashid replied. "Here we're somewhere real."
When Haroun heard his father say *only a story*, he understood that the Shah of Blah was very
depressed indeed, because only deep despair could have made him say such a terrible thing.
— Salman Rushdie, *Haroun and the Sea of Stories*

Engaged political talk can be both the result and the cause of other
kinds of citizenship. Crucially, thinking, talking, and practicing citizenship can *reduce* the scope of the democratic imagination too. Indeed,
in many of the settings where we might otherwise expect Americans to
discuss politics, social norms discourage them from doing so (Eliasoph
1997, 1998, 1999). Rules of politeness, for example, prohibit talking about
politics and religion in many situations (Brown and Levinson 1987; Friedman 1995) and often increase existing inequality in society (Ridgeway and
Bourg 2004; Mills 2003).

But because elements of the democratic imagination are "sticky"—
citizens gain them in one setting, then consider deploying them in
another—we are forced to guess what kind of talk is likely to be convincing or welcome in a particular setting. Some kinds of talk are likely
to "mark" the speaker, encouraging other members of the group to discount what she says later. Eliasoph and Lichterman, for example, present
cases of activists who marginalized themselves (or worried about doing
so) by expressing views that fell outside the boundaries of the current
"group style" (Eliasoph and Lichterman 2002, 755, 763). Not only is that
talk ignored, but points the speaker wants to make in the future may be

considered suspect because of the transgression.[1] No matter how well a speaker knows the others in the group she is addressing, such a faux pas is always possible. A discussion partner may be offended by any number of seemingly innocuous points, or may understand an example differently. Several recent studies have shown that most people, in the United States and in other democracies, interact regularly with people who disagree with them (Huckfeldt, Johnson, and Sprague 2004; Huckfeldt, Ikeda, and Pappi 2005). Speakers therefore face real uncertainty in their ability to gauge their audience's reactions to political points. Understandably, this kind of uncertainty when facing a new conversational setting—or even a new meeting in an old setting—tends to make people cautious; speakers can be forgiven for "walking on eggshells" as they seek to maintain long-term relationships with conversational partners and also make a point.

In a classic article, psychologists Amos Tversky and Daniel Kahneman found that such caution permeates human interactions: when people are unsure how others will respond to their behaviors, they tend to fall back on being cautious. They also seek ways of fixing mistakes they do make in the course of estimating others' expectations (Tversky and Kahneman 1974). In the most general way, *uncertainty about others' views encourages caution and restraint.*

A speaker who wants to make a point must try to gauge the group style and creatively intervene. She may also need to have alternatives or repair strategies available: ways of justifying, retracting, or amending statements that fail to garner the expected response from others. To manage this complicated set of interactions, people use a set of what I call *strategic resources*. They provide authenticity and substance to arguments for political positions, and citizens mobilize them strategically in order to bolster those arguments and shield them from unwanted scrutiny. Although participants often appear to be simply "telling a story," they select and narrate their stories so as to support their own arguments and undermine those of opponents.

The strategic resources people mobilized in the focus groups fall into three general categories: (1) those based on personal experiences or the experiences of friends; (2) those based on reading or viewing the news

---

1. An extreme example of this is presidential candidate Howard Dean's infamous scream following the Iowa Democratic caucuses in 2004; as portrayed in the news media, it was such a violation of accepted group style that his later political persona was "polluted" by the memory of the scream.

media; and (3) those based on fictional "experiences" such as those in movies and television programs. These resources are similar in that they generally take *narrative* form: they are stories told in strategic context; as such, unpacking their meaning in the group becomes a significant interpretive task for other members.

Using Narratives

Telling stories is an important part of human experience, and stories play a similarly important part in communicating and evaluating political ideas. Narratives constitute a kind of storytelling with its own particular history, and its own strengths and limitations (White 1987; Belsey 1980). A narrative consists of an introductory phase, in which a cast of characters is convened; a plot, in which these characters interact with one another and with external events; and a conclusion, in which the characters and events come to a resolution.

Real life, of course, does not always work like that.[2] "Characters" enter and exit the stage at different times and in different ways. Countless "plots" intertwine as people deal with the relationships, groups, institutions, and environments that shape their lives. And, perhaps most important, clusters of characters and events rarely come to neat conclusions that make room for the next narrative to begin.

In her best-selling book, *The Spirit Catches You and You Fall Down*, writer Ann Fadiman investigated the case of a Hmong family's interaction with the American medical establishment. She noticed that the Hmong immigrant community understood social life in a way that differed dramatically from the neat, short narratives Americans expect. Preparing a class presentation to describe the preparation of traditional fish soup, a Hmong student began way back with his family's origins, since there is no "natural" boundary between the story of fish soup and the culture's origins: "[T]he world is full of things that may not seem to be connected but actually are; ... no event occurs in isolation; ... you can miss a lot by sticking to the point" (Fadiman 1997, 12–13).

Such an approach is, of course, wildly inefficient, and people generally find ways to convey ideas and information more efficiently. Narratives are

---

2. Indeed, narrative structure closely mirrors that of the anthropological theory of the *ritual*, whose role is also to set apart special or unusual events (Durkheim 1995; Turner 1980).

one way of handling that task; we use them to organize the confusing whirl of new information and ideas into coherent, well-bounded units. But efficiency comes with a cost: some potential interpretations, some relevant characters, some significant historical background must be jettisoned in order to convey the story efficiently.

The narrative form seems "natural" to many people, and offers a way of recounting events that conveys both the speaker's experience and the intended meaning of the speech. As Bearman and Stovel (2000, 70) write, "Narratives provide one mechanism for organizing and generating social meanings." Other sociologists, including Voss (1996, 252) and Bologh (2000), argue similarly that narratives structure the way people think politically. William Gamson, a political sociologist who pioneered the study of political talk, looked at the ways social movement activists use personal narratives. Taking these narratives seriously, he argued, offers everyday political actors the opportunity to frame and develop their own identities. They do so by choosing the characters, emplotment, time frame, and interpretation of the stories they tell. Narratives can therefore be empowering (Gamson 2002).

Empowering they may be, but they are far from "natural." As the literary theorist Catherine Belsey tells us, narratives have an insidious capacity to seem to interpret themselves:

> [T]he reader is invited to *construct* a "history" which is more comprehensive still. The gently ironic account of Mr. Tulliver's treatment of his horse [in George Eliot's 1885 novel *The Mill on the Floss*] is presented without overt authorial comment. The context, however, points more or less irresistibly to a single interpretation which appears as the product of an intersubjective communication between the author and the reader in which the role of language has become invisible.... Through the presentation of an intelligible history which effaces its own status as discourse, classic [narrative] realism ... does the work of ideology in suppressing the relationship between language and subjectivity. (Belsey 1980, 72)

Narratives, in other words, stand in for speakers' arguments. They don't contain arguments, though—they allow speakers to take positions without explicitly advocating them. Charles Tilly identifies much the same pattern in his essay, "The Trouble with Stories" (Tilly 1999). He points out that understanding the social world as a collection of stories stands in the way of identifying underlying and superimposed causal processes.

These two ideas—that narratives are empowering and that they strategically exclude and frame ideas and information—are not in competition. Both are true; indeed, narratives are empowering precisely *because* citizens can use them to maneuver in the uncertain and symbolically competitive world of political talk. Furthermore, even though narratives may not be truly natural, they *feel* natural to speakers using them. Using narratives is, itself, a principled decision: people use the personal anecdote form, for example, because they believe in personal experience as the primary source of wisdom and knowledge.[3] In suggesting here that narratives serve also to mask speakers' underlying political agenda, I am not accusing speakers of being disingenuous. I am claiming instead that this argumentative form, like all others, is not neutral: it allows speakers to avoid engaging with some of the issues others might want to bring up.

Participants in the focus groups understood that balance intuitively. Clementine Richards, a woman in a Catholic church group, cautioned about approaching a city council without appealing narrative stories: "You have to have something to back you up. Because if you know it's happening, you need to go to the city council and present it there as a group of concerned citizens. But you have to have some backup stories, you just can't go in with your feelings, you know, just one case" (C4). Her concern is that, presented with falling crime rates and concerns about racial profiling, the city council will disregard the issue of racial profiling without a collection of compelling anecdotes to illustrate the problem. Since the racial profiling scenario asserts that systematic data support the claim of racial profiling, we have to conclude that Clementine Richards expects individuals' stories to be *more* convincing than overall data. Throughout the focus group discussions, participants employed various kinds of narrative resources to bolster their positions.

Experiences and Anecdotes

During the focus groups, stories about experiences that were similar to those in the scenarios were a staple of discussion. Indeed, quite frequently the first rhetorical move after the introduction of a scenario was to refer to a similar situation elsewhere:

3. I am grateful to a reviewer for pointing this out.

THOMAS HAMBRON: This is a San Jose issue.

VALENTIN WOOD: What do you mean it's a San Jose issue?

PAULA THOMPSON: It's an L.A. issue.

VALENTIN WOOD: Name a city, this is an issue.

THOMAS HAMBRON: Name a state.

VALENTIN WOOD: Really. New York, L.A., go on. (S3)

The principal role of such narratives is to make a speaker's position more tenable by backing it up with examples: evidence based on "real life" (even when experienced through news or entertainment media) is far harder to contradict than are general points made without such backup. The very sense that narratives are "natural" and therefore beyond the taint of bias makes them convenient and convincing rhetorical tools. Consider this exchange from a sports group discussing the airport scenario, in which an airport near the group's homes has recently expanded, resulting in greatly increased noise:

KEVIN ELDER: I live under the flight patterns of the Hayward airport, I'm a mile and a half from the airport. And I knew that airport was there when I bought that house in 1950. You know, airplanes go, they don't bother me. In fact I look up, oh, there goes Jim. And we've had arguments, and I've been to the city council meetings and airport advisory committee meetings and what not on noise over there, and people from the village would come over there. And we had just one brilliant man who was over there and he was one of the loudest ones in the group complaining about that noise. And we brought up, say hey, you knew that airport was there when you bought your house, he says no I didn't. You didn't know the airport was there? No, I bought my house at night! Well, all right. All right. You want to go out and buy your house at night, don't find out much about the neighborhood, well.

URSULA OSSELIN: That's hard to believe.

KEVIN ELDER: We couldn't figure out whether he was that dumb or he thought we were that dumb.

ZEKE QUIMBY: We had the same problem when I was working, I worked for flood control especially out in Fremont. We had these little creeks running all over out there, you know? And no problem, and they built all these houses, and they built all the houses upstream, up in the hills up there. And people living down there, they planned to do something with the flood control channels 'cause the creeks wouldn't hold. It was coming out and going all over. People really hollered.

LANCE ZEEMAN: I'll bet they did.

ZEKE QUIMBY: They did. That creek was there when they bought.

LANCE ZEEMAN: But did it flood? It wasn't flooding when they bought it.

ZEKE QUIMBY: I'm not sure about that, sometimes it did. (S1)

Kevin Elder is arguing for a voluntarist logic: this issue, he wants to claim, is not one of public interest at all, but simply a matter of individuals' poor choices. But stating that position outright would risk drawing a direct rebuttal; if the logic is stated openly, it can be refuted *as a logic* by someone who disagrees. An anecdote cannot be refuted; it takes the form of objective fact, a list of experiences presented by their protagonist and presumably relevant to the topic at hand. A challenger can raise objections to the anecdote's *relevance*, or offer alternative anecdotes or alternative interpretations of the same anecdote. She cannot, however, easily challenge the logic underlying the anecdote's recital.

Elder exploits exactly this dynamic by telling his story. "I live under the flight patterns," he explains, so his position cannot be dismissed as callous; after all, he finds himself in the same situation. So what standard does he suggest for when it would be reasonable to get involved in the issue of local airport noise? When it is new or unexpected: "I knew that airport was there when I bought that house. . . ." Furthermore, a neighbor who tries to invoke the standard is ridiculed: "We couldn't figure out whether he was that dumb or he thought we were that dumb."

The combination sets up a nearly impossible standard for would-be challengers in the group. Kevin Elder begins by placing himself as the actor, deflecting any charge of hypocrisy. He then sets a standard that seems unassailable: willful versus nonwillful decision to be in the situation. Finally, he attacks an absent challenger as "dumb."

Unsurprisingly, no challenge is presented. Instead, an ally (Zeke Quimby) joins in with his own anecdote, somewhat further afield from the original topic. He reinforces the willful-decision standard: "That creek was there when they bought." This time, though, the anecdote is less successful; Lance Zeeman challenges the standard's applicability ("I bet it wasn't flooding when they bought it"). Quimby's response is weak, but the crucial task—establishing voluntarism as the operative logic—is accomplished without ever making the claim explicit.

Another characteristic of this exchange merits attention. According to the scenario text, "the number of airplanes flying over your home has more than doubled" since a recent airport expansion. Arguably, that makes Elder's anecdote inapplicable to the situation; indeed, his willful-decision standard might be countered by the actual scenario. But no other group member brings up the discrepancy; the anecdote's relevance to the situation is presumed. Only later, when I explicitly asked, was that issue addressed:

MODERATOR: Let me ask you all this, particularly the two of you who live near the Hayward air terminal. What if, say, UPS says, we need more capacity in the Bay Area and the big airports are, you know, they're at capacity, we can't use them? So what we're going to do is we're going to build a whole new cargo terminal at the Hayward air terminal, and so we'll be flying in, say, fifteen DC-8s a day, back and forth to Lexington.... You know, we'll pump in that much money to your economy, we'll employ that many people, but you know, it's going to mean there's a lot more noisy planes going in and out. You bought near the airport, no one's saying that you didn't buy near the airport, but you bought when the airport was a lot smaller.

LANCE ZEEMAN: That changes the whole argument, doesn't it? Because you didn't buy the house with those DC-8s flying over, you bought it with the Piper cubs flying over.

. . .

LANCE ZEEMAN: So that would change my total attitude.

KEVIN ELDER: Well, the San Jose Reid-Hillview airport is a small general aviation airport similar to Hayward down near the San Jose airport. And there's a lot of planes landing there, and they land in the north-south direction not the east-west direction that we do here.... And there were a line of houses, development built after the airport, out on the flight pattern. And they, that neighborhood, got all up in the air about all the traffic and what not because the traffic has increased.... And the people that were raising all the Cain, when the results came out, they shut up and disappeared. Because their recommendation, the independent consultants' decision on the best thing to do was to buy all those homes in the flight pattern, tear them down, and lengthen the runway. Was the most inexpensive and the best thing to do. And those people, no.

EMILY ISSERMAN: And that's what's going to happen here with the traffic too.

LANCE ZEEMAN: If they gave them fair market value, I'd say bye-bye.

EMILY ISSERMAN: I don't know, to me that wouldn't make a difference. Because I realize that any community is going to expand. Any community will expand. (S1)

Presented with the reminder about the scenario's provisions, Lance Zeeman starts out by noting its difference from the willful-decision standard. Kevin Elder, though, is unfazed; he responds with a new anecdote closer to the scenario, renewing his claim on the logic and outcome of the discussion. Emily Isserman clinches it, making Elder's argument explicit: "any community is going to expand," so the new standard is even stricter; presumably, a resident should not organize against airport noise in *any* situation, since community expansion is an individual, voluntary risk. The conversation ends at this point, with no interest from any group member in pursuing action of any sort.

In the following excerpt, a business group uses the same strategy to discuss the Chemco scenario:

BRENDA XAVIER: I wouldn't say close them down, but I would say they've got to abide by some of the guidelines and clean it up. I think that there are measures, I mean I worked in the semiconductor industry for many, many years. Of course we never polluted! Of course, I mean that's why you have BI and diffusers and everything else. But I mean so there are alternatives and sure I mean we could have been forced to close down, had we not done what we had to do.

LAURA OLIVER: And it's expensive, and they may have to affect their bottom line, and maybe their stockholders will have to give up a, you know, some of their quarterly income from their shares or something. But I worked at a printing, the only printing plant left in northern California, and they bought, they went around and bought the environmentally unused environmental rights to pollute, and I'm not saying that's good. I'm not saying it's the right way to go, but it is one way to keep the pollution at supposedly the acceptable level and keep a company open who employed 350 people. This is posturing. (B3)

In these two back-to-back anecdotes, the speakers were clearer about the position they advocated: taking a tough line with Chemco in order to comply with legally founded regulations. The strategy, though, is the same: recount personal experiences (in both these cases, work experiences) and imply the comparison to the situation at hand.

Narratives can be, as Gamson has argued, empowering to citizens trying to figure out whether they can make a difference (Gamson 2002). In a business group, participants were trying to determine whether they could change the airport noise situation:

MORGAN KRAMER: How many people did it take for the bar to turn the radio down? How many people did it take to make a voice for that when you . . . ?

it up, the one movie I want to see is the one that they just made about the one woman who got 634, Ellen something. She went out and got 634 [families], she went up against PG&E and she got big bucks because they were doing the same thing, polluting the environment, and on her own she got a community involved. So yeah, I'd go.

WENDY CHARLES: Is that Julia Roberts?

EILEEN HAMILTON: Yeah. They had the real person on TV yesterday. She's an amazing woman, a single mom on her own with three kids, no support, and she dresses the way she does in the movie. Begged for a job and then changed the world. (B1)

The film to which Eileen Hamilton is referring—*Erin Brockovich*—was based on a true story, but by all accounts it was significantly fictionalized. Furthermore, there were significant, relevant differences between the Chemco scenario and the story told in *Erin Brockovich*. Nevertheless, that film provided rhetorical ammunition in four of the focus groups' considerations of the Chemco scenario:

DEBORAH MAY: I'd still have to see really. Like politicians, they can say one thing and . . .

OLIVIA WALTERS: But I think definitely the community would have to get together with some sort of larger organization.

ELLEN CHESLEY: That's why I'm saying, this would be a way to hit the extra keys from [use the resources of] a bigger company that, a group that has done this before and fought other battles.

OLIVIA WALTERS: Right. *Erin Brockovich*, I'm telling you. Great movie. It was really good. (S3)

A similar film (*A Civil Action*, starring John Travolta, and presenting the case Eileen Hamilton discussed in the preceding dialogue) anchored two other groups' discussions of Chemco. Woody Allen's *The Sleeper* provided ammunition for another participant to argue that scientists had only a poor understanding of what posed a real threat to health and, by extension, the environment:

STEPHANIE GORMAN: That's exactly what I was going to say. You know the FDA this year, it's just fine and take it, you know, don't drink decaffeinated coffee or whatever the issue. And next year, oh yeah, just fine, drink it, no problem.

MARTIN ESTRELLA: Do you remember the movie *The Sleeper*, with Woody Allen?

NADINE THOMPSON: Well I don't know, my husband and I took them to court. And we first went to council. And they did.

MORGAN KRAMER: So it was just you two made a difference.

NADINE THOMPSON: Went to the city council. Yeah. And they had lawyers.

MORGAN KRAMER: So that was a big enough voice.

NADINE THOMPSON: Well yeah, and course what that does though is that if you start trouble, whatever it is, the person, the one that's in charge, though, of the airplanes won't like it. I mean he'll look into it. . . . The restrictions were great enough that the fellow sold it.

MORGAN KRAMER: Wow.

NADINE THOMPSON: So you can make a difference. I mean it all depends if you're right. I mean if it's a right/wrong thing. But when you're far enough away and when that sort of thing goes on, you don't have to put up with it. (B2)

Similarly, in a different business group, Tina Nickleby offers a story of successful environmental activism to suggest that participants could do something about the Chemco scenario:

TINA NICKLEBY: . . . I'm from Massachusetts. In my hometown we had a river that ran through town, and when I was growing up, it was very polluted. Extremely polluted. Everybody knew that the reason why it was polluted was from a paper company upstream. And I lived about maybe a quarter to a half mile away from the river. And on a hot summer day, let me tell you, it was raunchy. I moved away from Massachusetts a long time ago. And one year I went back for a visit, and they [had] cleaned up the river. It was gorgeous. There were fish in it and it was beautiful and clear and you know. People could swim in it. The plant was still there. There are things that a company can do short of shutting the stupid place down that you can do to fix your polluting problems. If this is such a successful company, it can do it too. And they better not think that they're better than the rules and laws of the state of California because it doesn't work that way. And there are ways to make it work both ways. (B3)

In both these cases, distant experiences were retold as allegories: stories with a specific interpretation and purpose. They sought to tell others in the group that a difference could be made and that citizen involvement could be successful.

This is not to suggest that stories and anecdotes are bad ways of arguing or that they constitute bad-faith discussion. I present these examples, rather, as evidence of the ideological role stories play in framing political discourse. Anecdotes, comparisons, information provision, and other resources offer citizens access to content with which to animate logics of evaluation. They constitute nodes of experience to which current situations are compared. But personal anecdotes were not the only kind of resource utilized; participants also referred to issues in the news media to bolster their arguments.

Media Narratives

Like direct anecdotes, reports in the news media can fuel discussion by providing knowledge of real-world events on which to pin logics and ideas. Although participants distrusted the news media, they also looked to the media to provide them with useful information about the issues. For example, the following exchange occurred in a business group discussing the Halfin scenario, in which "their" senator is involved in a campaign-finance scandal:

LANA SMITH: I think it's been around too long.

MODERATOR: And do you want to do anything about it?

NADINE THOMPSON: It's in the paper lately. I agree it's nothing new that hasn't been, that doesn't mean it shouldn't be an issue, but I mean it's been going on and on and on. (B2)

Nadine Thompson's memory of reading of a similar situation in the paper provides factual validation that it is a real issue. But in addition to such positive reinforcement, news media also provide fodder for an attitude of mistrust:

OSCAR CEVILLA: I think you need more information. You don't know, when you vote for a candidate you're not going to just go on what you see on television or read in the paper or see in the political mail you get in the mailbox, but you're supposed to go out there and look at their voting record if they have something in the past and talk to other groups who had some kind of contact with that person, see if they really did work for them. Go out there and do some digging yourself before you vote.

VELMA MARTIN: You do, and who even wrote this article? Maybe they were not for this candidate or against this candidate. I mean, where's the source of the information coming from?

. . .

OSCAR CEVILLA: Could be a newspaper that was for the other candidate, yeah. (C1)

Unlike personal anecdotes, media reports do not provide factually incontestable narratives. Rather, they provide a measure of an issue's centrality in current events as well as one pole in a presumed debate among interests. Mistrust of the news media is substantial; the idea that "a newspaper that was for the other candidate" would skew news coverage, for example, was so obvious as to be assumed in many cases. Indeed, the fact that the Halfin scenario was presented in the form of a newspaper article offered participants the opportunity to leverage mistrust of the media (Kiousis 2001; Tsfati 2003) in order to discount others' concerns. The other three scenarios, which were presented as generic descriptions, did not offer that opportunity.

Participants in a sports group expected the media to be part of the problem, but also suggested *using* the media to address it:

ELLEN CHESLEY: Don't you also think though that the newspapers who [are] also reporting this, you know, isn't this mayor great, he's pushing the crime rate down, you're also thinking that in your media as well.

UPTON WILSON: This came out of the media.

ELLEN CHESLEY: Right. But that's what's going on in town, right?

OLIVIA WALTERS: Yeah but again, I mean we have so little information, so it's hard to know. But it's hard to know what they're reporting. That's why I asked the question about what he attributes the reduction in crime rate to be. Is it specifically 'cause he's allowing the police department to do racial profiling? I don't know. So I don't know how aware the community is to begin with. But I would say if our community was unaware that using the typical albeit frustrating channels is a good way to bring it to light. (S3)

Fictional Narratives

In a similar vein, entertainment media—principally movies, but also television shows—provide another check on the salience and reality of an issue, as in this excerpt from a business organization discussing the Chemco scenario, in which a local factory is in violation of EPA emissions regulations:

EILEEN HAMILTON: Would I get involved? Damn right. Any company that thinks they're better than the environment is going to take on a lot more people than just Eileen. I think I'd get involved in this one because now we're talking about me breathing what you're putting into my air space. And the one, just to bring

STEPHANIE GORMAN: Oh yeah, yeah, yeah, yeah.

MARTIN STRELLA: First thing he said he found out that the new health food was chocolate sundaes?

STEPHANIE GORMAN: You mean your basic food group? (B4)

In many discussions, participants invoked movies to address the *feasibility* of involvement: if John Travolta or Julia Roberts can take on the big interests and win, so can we. Here, the deceptive character of the narrative form is most revealing. The stories made it to the big screen precisely because they were anomalies, yet they serve to convince viewers of the possibility of similar actions in their own lives.

This dynamic in American culture is not new; in 1945 social theorists Max Horkheimer and Theodor W. Adorno wrote about the glamorous draw of movies in the United States:

> [T]he starlet is meant to symbolize the typist in such a way that the splendid evening dress seems meant for the actress as distinct from the real girl. The girls in the audience not only feel that they could be on the screen, but realize the great gulf separating them from it. Only one girl can draw the lucky ticket, only one man can win the prize, and if, mathematically, all have the same chance, yet this is so infinitesimal for each one that he or she will do best to write it off and rejoice in the other's success, which might just as well have been his or hers, and somehow never is. (Horkheimer and Adorno 1972, 145)

To the extent that citizens "think with" movies, television shows, and other fictional narratives, their estimation of what is possible, normal, and even potentially moral is skewed: everyone "thinks with" narratives that virtually nobody experiences. This phenomenon is called *pluralistic ignorance* in social psychology. As an early discussion of the phenomenon puts it, pluralistic ignorance is a state in which "no one believes [in a particular ideal], but ... everyone believes that everyone else believes" (Krech, Crutchfield, and Ballachey, 1962, 248). In our case, virtually nobody has experienced these narratives, but everybody believes that others have done so.

Avoiding the Issue? Tangents and Policy

Participants in the focus groups were asked to decide whether to do anything about each scenario and, if so, what they would choose to do.

Although the groups clearly understood this charge, in practice they often veered well off course. Two of the most common distractions were *tangents* and discussions of group members' *policy* preferences. In both cases, taking the conversation off course is directly relevant to how the group evaluates the issue at hand. As the French sociologists Luc Boltanski and Laurent Thévenot have shown us, the task of evaluating new and changing situations is essentially about *comparing* them to situations we already understand (Boltanski and Thévenot 1991; Dodier 1993). Citizens use "off-topic" points such as tangents and policy to establish the grounds for comparisons: How should the group decide what a new situation means?

Tangents

We have already seen that the directions participants took with anecdotes and entertainment sometimes led them far afield from the scenario with which they were presented. So far, though, the examples have been of *comparisons* participants made between the scenarios and other stories, whether they were experienced firsthand or mediated. Equally impressive is the tendency to draw the topic itself far from the scenarios. Participants referred to ideas and concerns that were only peripherally related to the topic at hand.

When I was conducting the focus groups themselves, I was deeply concerned that the participants had failed to understand the directions. Why else would their conversations fail to address the questions put to them? Upon further analysis, though, I believe the answer is more interesting: much like the narratives they employed to make their arguments, the tangents and policy pronouncements served as resources the speakers used to frame the way they thought about the scenarios themselves.

For example, in four of the focus groups, the topic of the Electoral College came up while discussing the Halfin scenario. These conversations took place in the spring of 2000, well before the 2000 presidential election, so the Electoral College was not yet a topic of general debate at the time. The following excerpt is from a sports group discussing the Halfin controversy:

CAROL BONILLA: . . . we all go out to vote but it's never the guy we've all voted for. I mean you know, particularly, because of this electoral thing, see. The popular vote doesn't really count, I mean.

URI TESSELMAN: The electoral vote has outlived its usefulness. I mean I could see it years ago when there was no communications, but today . . .

CAROL BONILLA: Well look, some states have what, I mean, California has what, 200 or 400 or something electoral votes?

. . .

URI TESSELMAN: California's the largest state, has the most electoral votes.

CAROL BONILLA: Yeah. But there may be another state that doesn't have that much less population than we have, but they have a lot less electoral votes.

URI TESSELMAN: Maybe, I don't know.

DARREN DAVIDSON: I think if they could get more people out to vote, there's a high percentage of people that don't vote, even in this last elections. I don't know if it's 50 percent, or . . .

URI TESSELMAN: Last year it was 49 percent.

DARREN DAVIDSON: People get disgusted, they won't go anymore because of what's going on. And I think if we could stir up enough people, you know, so we could get 90 percent [of the] people to vote, maybe we could vote some of these people out of office. But that's the trouble.

CAROL BONILLA: But there again you need the popular vote to do that.

DARREN DAVIDSON: Well yeah, you need more people to vote is what I'm saying.

MODERATOR: Well here we're talking about the Senate, though, so there is popular vote for the senator.

CAROL BONILLA: Still doesn't seem to matter, they seem to get back in all the time you know.

BRAD GARFIELD: Look at Strom Thurmond. (S2)

Carol Bonilla begins by putting forward a sense of inefficacy: "We all go out to vote, but it's never the guy we've all voted for." She is disavowing participation in the Halfin situation because, quite simply, she feels entirely removed from the electoral process and unable to affect it.

Her reason, though, is unrelated to Halfin, who is a (fictional) senator and therefore not subject to selection by the Electoral College. She continues on the topic, showing in addition that she misunderstands other facets of the Electoral College. After I correct the original misunderstanding, she reiterates the general claim she is making: "[It] still doesn't seem to matter." Brad Garfield comes to her aid, offering a comparison: "look at Strom Thurmond." The comparison is not elaborated—Garfield simply assumes Thurmond (then an eighth-term U.S. senator from South Carolina) means to others in the group what he means to him.

Similarly, in a Catholic church group, a participant spontaneously brought up the Electoral College: "Well you know the other thing too is that electoral vote thing. That's ridiculous. I mean you could win by the popular vote but, or lose by that, and you win because of the electoral votes" (C1). The central message here, again, is one of efficacy; the group is addressing the question of whether they *can* make a difference in the electoral arena. The seemingly tangential discussion of the Electoral College is not, in fact, tangential; it offers a point of common agreement (if not knowledge) to cement the general conclusion of inefficacy. The tangential narrative, though, is clearly *not* offered as evidence in the traditional way, since the tangent's message was reiterated even after the story's relevance was denied. Tangents like this one operate, then, to stand in for explicit arguments. Citizens understand them as claims, not as real stories; their power lies in the fact that citizens agree with the underlying claim, not in their actual truth.

Policy

One particularly revealing form of tangential discussion in the focus groups was *policy*. Participants often chose to discuss what *should* happen in a situation—that is, what the government or other officials should do—rather than whether they would be interested in making it happen. Consider, for example, this excerpt from a Protestant church group:

MODERATOR: Sounds like there's pretty much unanimous agreement you want to do something about it. What do you want to do about it?

ALBERT LAVELLA: Profiling. Stop it. Period.

MODERATOR: How?

ALBERT LAVELLA: Well number one, the directive has to come from the top. The directive came from the top to start with, the directive comes from the top to stop it. And if the directive is coming from the top to stop it, and it isn't stopped, severe penalties should be paid. If the citizen complains, they shouldn't cover up the complaints. However, the police department has their ways of doing things. We all know that they can cover up what they want. And as long as they can continue to get away with it, they'll continue to do it. And I think harsh punishment should be dished out to those that do it. And if they continue to do it and it goes so far, well, you know, put them in the place where they have put the people that they've punished. Don't give them the country club car and say, okay you're going to do time, but you can play golf in there, you know? That's, to me that's not right.

MODERATOR: How would you go about, this is for any of you all, how would you go about getting to that point? You know at this point, the mayor's saying, well, crime's cut in half, I don't feel like doing anything about it. The police chief is saying, well, I cut crime in half, I don't feel like doing anything about it. You as a group of people who want to do something about it, what are you going to do?

ALBERT LAVELLA: Let me bring up my point. You say the police chief says he's cut crime in half. That's all fine, and that doesn't have anything to do with profiling. Okay? So crime can be cut in a lot of different areas, take into consideration. However, the issue here of the black and brown profiling wasn't on the table. Okay? So they put that issue in and then they add all crime. Well all crime hasn't gone down. (P4)

The group had already decided, unanimously, that profiling was wrong. They had been instructed to decide for each scenario what, if anything, they wanted to do about it. Yet the prospect of their own involvement was remote, at best.

Albert Lavella responds simply that profiling should be stopped. When prompted further, he suggests what officials *should* do—not, though, how they might be convinced to do so. When prompted yet again, he responds with an argument about the ineffectiveness of racial profiling—once more avoiding the question.

This phenomenon brings us back to the role of opinion in American political culture. Practicing what political scientist Ron Jepperson and sociologist Ann Swidler call "efficacious citizenship" involves reaching a decision as to the appropriate *outcome* (Jepperson and Swidler 1994). Decisions on the active process involved in practicing citizenship are often difficult even to discuss.

Similarly, groups' approaches to the Chemco scenario (in which a local factory was releasing too much ozone-depleting pollution) often focused on policy: "[Paula Oldham:] I think the root of it is the regulations stand, they're already ... well, that's what needs to happen, they need to stand by the regulation and shut the place down" (B1). This statement reveals how citizens use tangents to avoid committing to a decision to get involved. Oldham's sentence is in the third person: "[T]hey need to ... shut the place down," implying that the work is to be done by someone else.

Considering the role of these tangents in the citizenship triangle (fig. 2.1) is instructive. These citizens are clearly deliberating—that is, *talking citizenship*—in the classic way. They have taken up an issue, discussed its merits, and reached a conclusion on its outcome. But their democratic imagination is constrained in terms of *practicing citizenship*; they are unable, or unwilling, to make the connection between successfully evaluating a new situation and engaging in activities to deal with it.

Mistrust and Doubt

The other important kind of argumentative resource is doubt, or mistrust in institutions, individuals, and information. In a sense, expressing doubt about the basis of another's argument is a desperate intervention, since it presents no alternative. For the same reason, doubt-based reasoning nearly always favors the decision *not* to get involved, since uncertainty about the situation is disempowering. Doubt also has special theoretical significance because of claims that social capital builds trust, and that this trust-building function is central to a healthy polity (e.g., Putnam 2000, 134–39; Fukuyama 1995, 61).

Perhaps the most striking difference among group types was in their use of *doubt*. Sports leagues used far more doubting language than did any of the other kinds of groups. The following extended excerpt, from a bowling league discussing the Chemco scenario, displays the radical mistrust that typified sports leagues' discussions, particularly of the Chemco situation.

EMILY ISSERMAN: I don't think you can let all these chemicals fly in the air without some kind of problems. And we already know that there's a lot of problems up in the atmosphere.

KYLE YARBOROUGH: We do?

EMILY ISSERMAN: Yes.

KYLE YARBOROUGH: How do you know?

LANCE ZEEMAN: We've been told.

KYLE YARBOROUGH: Somebody's told you that. And do you believe them?

EMILY ISSERMAN: Do you stay outside for any length of time?

KYLE YARBOROUGH: Oh yes, I spend 90 percent of my time outside.

EMILY ISSERMAN: Have you ever got skin cancer?

KYLE YARBOROUGH: Huh?

EMILY ISSERMAN: Have you ever got skin cancer?

KYLE YARBOROUGH: From the sun, yeah. But that's not from the chemicals, that's from the sun.

EMILY ISSERMAN: No, because it's breaking down. The layers are breaking down. The sun is getting stronger. Now that's a fact. The sun is getting stronger. It is stronger now than it was twenty years ago.

KYLE YARBOROUGH: I don't believe that.

EMILY ISSERMAN: You don't?

KYLE YARBOROUGH: I do not! I mean it's the same thing. Clinton said yesterday that every day there are fifteen children killed by guns. You believe that?

EMILY ISSERMAN: I have no idea.

EYLE YARBOROUGH: You realize how many children that is a year? And you know they come out with these, they throw these figures out. There are so many people dying of AIDS, there are so many people dying of smoke-related things. And when you start adding up these figures, everybody's dead.

LANCE ZEEMAN: Seems like.

KYLE YARBOROUGH: If I walk across the street and I stop in the middle of the street to light my cigar and a truck hits me, it's because I'm a smoker.

LANCE ZEEMAN: That's right.

KYLE YARBOROUGH: Because if I wasn't a smoker, I wouldn't have stopped and the truck wouldn't have hit me.

LANCE ZEEMAN: Tobacco got you.

KYLE YARBOROUGH: Right! No, I'm sorry. I have a hard time believing all the rhetoric we're getting from these people about global warming and all this. And they're saying well the hole in the ozone is so much larger today than it was years ago. Wait a minute, how do you know? Did they measure ozone then? No. Fact you go back far enough they didn't even know there was ozone. (S1)

There is also doubt about the intentions or identities of actors in an issue, as in this softball team's discussion:

ELLEN CHESLEY: I'm somewhat cynical too about what Airwatch is interested in. What exactly are they, you know, what are they going to do in this community? Are they going to start picketing? Are they going to just say, you know, fine them all you can? What are they going to do with this group? (S3)

The contrast with the following discussion in a business group is impressive. The business group principally uses comparisons (as opposed to

doubt) as its resource, and comes up with a significantly different outcome:

PAULA OLDHAM: Well that $400,000 fine probably would have taken a nice little
chunk out of what they had to do. And you know if they can get away without
doing it, it's just like our kids. You know, they're going to do it until you just
grab hold of them and say excuse me, this is getting done.

EILEEN HAMILTON: Yeah. Well, and the fact that the EPA says, you know, that's
one action. They can continue, and again coming from Pacific Bell, recently
retired, they got hit a lot of times with fines. And your first fine is a wake-up
call. But if you start getting hit again and again and again with that same fine
and or greater because you choose not to acknowledge it, then as a society
everybody starts getting involved. But then again then they start picking on
the nit-picky things, it's like okay. But this one's a big one, this is hurting the
community and the area. And I'd side with EPA on this one, and I'd probably
be out with my little protest sign out in front, we want to shut it down now.
(B1)

The principal effect of doubt is futility and powerlessness. Citizens
who think in terms of mistrusting information and authority use those
thoughts to dissuade themselves from involvement. For example, a union
member discusses the case of Senator Halfin, the seemingly corrupt
senator:

CLAUDIA WILSON: I wouldn't get involved in this because I have a very, very, what
do I want to call it? View of politics. Everything about it disgusts me. I don't
think it would matter who you put up there, the same thing would happen
sooner or later. It's been so long since anybody had any spine or backbone and
really had any conviction. (U2)

The Halfin scenario inspired such responses from a variety of groups, such
as this one in a Protestant church group:

BRIAN FORZER: If I were to pick up the paper and read this, I might as well say
to myself, Was this yesterday's paper or the day before's? Because big-shot
politician influenced by money, right? And so it depends on how jaded you are
about the system, and I would be kind of on the jaded end of things, and it
wouldn't be a shock to me, it wouldn't incite me to take immediate actions for
that issue. (P1)

The next is from a different Protestant church group:

ASHLEY KING: I think everybody's in collusion with everybody else and it's all about
     money, it's all about gain, it's all about getting what you can as creatively or
     uncreatively as you can. And I agree that I think that the real ethics of the
     person, the morality of the person, comes with their history and their pattern
     and performance when it comes to the real issues that they have to deal with. I
     think that this is everyday politics, it happens. Somebody's in somebody's back
     pocket. You know.
ALBERT LAVELLA: It's a game they all play. (P4)

This attitude—a familiar element of American political culture—is particularly interesting both because it is widespread and it is at once *critical*
and *disempowering*. Citizens develop an idea of what's wrong with the
political system, but that very idea also teaches them that they cannot effectively combat it.

Imagining with Narratives and Doubt

The stories we share with others—fictional, news-based, and personal—
constitute the stuff of which collective democratic imaginations are made.
While I want to resist the idea that narratives are the *natural* or absolute form that thought takes,[4] they are nevertheless enormously powerful
ways for citizens to argue, convince, and direct conversations.

The democratic imagination is like a web. Each memory, each story,
each possibility, is attached to the others by means of comparison. When
we need to evaluate a new situation, the most urgent task is therefore
to determine what previous situations we will compare it to, and how we
will understand those comparisons. Narratives help build that web by providing comparative cases: preevaluated, or at least self-evaluating, events
that lend moral and intellectual meaning to new situations.

These narratives, though, are not politically neutral. Again turning
to sociologist Michael Schudson, we should notice that the messy social reality that journalists—and, by extension, citizens—encounter has
to be "cooked" to make it comprehensible: "News in a newspaper or on

---

4. See, for example, Smith (2003, 63–94), for an argument about narratives as fundamental
human ways of thinking.

television has a relationship to the 'real world' ... in the way the world is incorporated into unquestioned and unnoticed conventions of narration, and then transfigured, no longer a subject for discussion but a premise of any conversation at all.... News is not fictional, but it is conventional. [These] conventions help make messages readable" (Schudson 1995, 54–55). Just as Schudson warns us about accepting journalistic narratives uncritically, we should be both concerned and impressed with conversational narratives' power to frame a topic, illuminating some directions while obscuring others.

As powerful as they are, though, narratives do not trump all other forms of discussion. Doubt is one resource citizens can use to temper the power of narratives' preevaluation. In all the focus groups—especially in the sports groups—speakers sought to undermine others' narrative positions by introducing doubt about the truth of the narratives and the trustworthiness of the people involved.

Narratives and doubt, then, are two of the building blocks for the democratic imagination. They play out in conversations—whether in civic groups like my focus groups, or in workplaces, schools, and families—as citizens seek ways to understand political scenarios. We turn text to another dimension of the democratic imagination: the logical standards citizens use to evaluate situations.

CHAPTER FIVE

Morality, Ideology, and Interest

We've got to realize we're on spaceship Earth, there's only so much here. We've got to take care of it. We can't have this blatant attitude that we used to have that it doesn't matter as to the environment. — Business group participant

Well I don't know. I'd rather have my son and husband go out and find another job than die of something that's in the air that shouldn't be. — Business group participant

I think we have too many boundaries that I think that sometimes as so-called Christians, we're supposed to be open-hearted and try to accept people, and sometimes I think best to try to be in their community and then you see how they feel, because they feel the same way as what you're saying right now. You know they feel fear about white people or Hispanic people, because they're thinking everybody's out to get them, or they try to do good but it doesn't come out that way. . . . But you have to try to think good. You know, Christian, that he's going to do the right thing. — Catholic church group participant

While I like Robert's idea of trying to mediate it, you know the bottom line is the fact that it affects my pocketbook, and if it's going to increase my taxes or my ability to have federal funding for certain things, then I would probably be more cut to the chase, let's just try to get [the plant] closed down and be out of here with this. — Protestant church group participant

A group discussing a new issue must do a lot of work to determine what standards it will use to decide on whether and how to become involved. This process is largely hidden; participants make claims that *imply* a logical standpoint more often than they explicitly consider multiple logics and select one. The two most common ways of framing an issue are in terms of *morality* and in terms of *interest*. That initial choice—implicit as it may be—sets a course for a decision about getting involved. Once a group has begun discussing an issue in terms of interests, it becomes difficult for a member to shift the ground of the discussion to the morality involved. Similarly, discussions that begin with morality inhibit participants' ability to raise concerns about their own interests. In the context of morality, interest appears selfish and even tainted. In the context of interest, morality seems naive and preachy.

Consider a fairly straightforward example of interest and pragmatic logics applied to the racial profiling scenario. Presented with this scenario, a fifty-six-year-old Latino in a business group approached it this way: "[Martin Estrella:] I don't really object to the idea of profiling, having owned property in a high-crime area, drug area. Driving while black, or driving while brown. It does work in a high-crime area. Can't fault them for it, there is an area of danger" (B4). Estrella begins by expressing a policy preference (racial profiling as a potentially appropriate way of reducing crime). He then defends that position (even though it has not yet been challenged), and in the process he sets up the standard of judgment on the issue of racial profiling to be one of pragmatics and interests. Does profiling succeed in reducing crimes? Then it should raise no objections. The standard is pragmatic, as evidenced by his justification: "[I]t is an area of danger." Police decisions, he implies, need not be justified by moral principles but only in terms of the actual presence of things worth fearing.

Later in the same discussion, another participant tries to shift to a moral argument, but with important caveats to justify his argument:

FRANK ARNOLD: I'm taking probably a little wider view that if we're successful in profiling drivers and we reduce the crime rate, where do we stop? Is it other groups? Other types of cars? Other characteristics? Other kinds of situations, because if it's that, I can be stopped in my automobile because of my race, my age, my gender, the kind of car I drive, the time of day or night that I'm driving, then what about my home? What about my business? Is there a line in the sand that gets drawn? And I think it can be a runaway situation. The second point I have is would we be trading fear of criminals for fear of the police? In totalitarian countries, the crime rate is low because the police terrorize the citizens. Yeah, it's safe to walk the street at one o'clock in the morning because you're not going to be mugged by a criminal but you could be picked up by the police for spitting on the sidewalk, so to speak. And I'm concerned about freedom, and what are we free from? Free of crime, or free of our liberties? (B4)

Frank Arnold is concerned about more broadly moral or ideological issues than Martin Estrella was. He introduces his rejoinder by excusing

himself for "taking probably a little wider view." He is quite clearly worried about the ideological problem of increased police power—not because of its pragmatics but because of its moral meaning. But because
Estrella has already couched this discussion in terms of interests, Arnold
reframes his own argument to match Estrella's. Arnold has effectively
decided that interests will determine the logical terrain on which this conversation will take place.

Contrast Estrella's approach with another introductory comment—
this one from a fifty-two-year-old white man in a Catholic church group—
that applies a moral logic to the same scenario:

WENDELL QUARLES: When you look at profile stops, it's like you're beginning to
    infringe upon civil rights of people because of their racial or ethnic background,
    and I don't think that's right. And I think there could be other avenues, other
    ways of reducing crime but not because you're black or Hispanic or whatever,
    you get pulled over, and trying to find out to see if you've done anything wrong
    is not an appropriate way of reducing crime, because not everybody's on the
    same page. (C5)

Wendell Quarles begins by offering an evaluation based on moral criteria:
"I don't think that's right." He continues, though, to offer an argument
as to why his position is *better* than the competing logic of pragmatism:
"[T]here could be . . . other ways of reducing crime." Other members of
the group, then, have a choice. They can choose to follow Quarles's moral
line of thought, or they can accept the interest-based logic, in which case
Quarles heads them off at the pass by claiming that the immoral policy is
also ineffective. The presence of a moral position, combined with a rebuttal to the (presumed) pragmatic argument, is a formidable foe.

Nevertheless, later in the discussion Laureana Magpuri and Quinto
Juarez seek to raise concerns about effectiveness and self-interest that, to
begin with, seem at odds with the absolute character of logics of morality:

LAUREANA MAGPURI: I think somebody higher than the mayor should get in this
    thing because maybe it will stop crime or lower it, but in the long run I think it
    would increase crime. Because people, you know, people are like kids. The
    more you tell them not to do something, the more they do it. And if they
    are pressured to this kind of thing, I mean, they're going to do something be-
    hind somebody's back, they're going to do it when nobody is looking or they
    think nobody is looking, they're going to do it more. Sometimes to tease them,

see, we can, see if they catch us. Let's see if they catch us. You know, the more
I think, it's going to increase it. I don't think it's going to, maybe it lowered it
in half, but that's maybe three years. But in the long run, four, five years, it's
going to increase crime. So I'm not for it. I think somebody should monitor
Mayor Jones.

. . .

QUINTO JUAREZ: I think there's a danger in [protesting against] this issue. And the
danger is that if crime rates have dropped dramatically in that time frame, you
know, there's this kind of an acceptance that, you know, what do we want? Do
we want crime? And so long as you're not in the category of the racial profile
that is being stopped, you're probably going to be more likely to go along with
the program in saying, well, you know what, they're making our streets safer. So
I think that there's a whole educational process that needs to take place here.
And so, you know, to get involved in this issue, I don't know if it's primarily to
stop that or is it to educate the others about the people that are being stopped?
(C5)

In both statements the speakers try to protect themselves by returning
to moral arguments (Laureana Magpuri) or by attaching the concern to
"others" instead of the speaker (Quinto Juarez).

Moral and ideological logics have a unique place in the scheme of
political discussion. As Jepperson and Swidler (1994) point out, Americans tend to consider opinions elements of their individuality, and their
expression a means to "enact a canonical identity of efficacious citizenship" (367). In other words, Americans consider it crucial to hold opinions
on a variety of topics, even when information is irrelevant to evaluation.
We often use the phrase "that's just my opinion" to *end* a conversation,
placing opinion outside the boundaries of discussion. Similarly, Benjamin
Page and Robert Shapiro report that "survey respondents can be per-
suaded to offer opinions about nonexistent, fictitious congressional policies" (Page and Shapiro 1992, 437). Having an opinion is, in a sense, sacred: it is afforded respect simply for its existence, not usually because it
is better or more convincing than the opinions of others.

In the focus groups, the contest between logics of morality and
ideology and those of self-interest and pragmatism was complicated.
Once morality had been introduced, it became essential for participants
who originally based their arguments on interest to respond within a
moral framework, at least temporarily. This is not to say that *competing*
moral positions could not be discussed, but logics based on self-interest,

pragmatics, or convenience had to be explicitly justified after the introduction of a moral logic. Similarly, when pragmatic logics were introduced
first, morality-based ones had to struggle to be adopted.

This observation is somewhat at odds with Nina Eliasoph's (1998,
1997) observation that citizens must give themselves permission to speak
in large, ideological, or moral terms, often through the use of subjects of
presumed value such as children and one's local community. She argues
that, in a sense, moral and ideological arguments are taboo in American political culture. Subjects must contort their claims to fit in a logic
of self-interest in order to make it palatable. Political scientist Katherine
Cramer Walsh illustrates how this kind of politics-avoidance works. She
observed the informal political conversations held at a coffee shop by a
group of "old timers" who gathered to pass the time. Talking to "John,"
she writes,

> I explained that I was interested in political conversation. This was more of an
> admission than I had yet made during my observations, and John ran with it:
> "Yeah, well, I don't think any of us in here are that intense. I mean, we're up
> there in years, you know, and most of us have been through a lot of crap in our
> lives. And I tell you, you're uptight twenty-four hours a day [when you're work-
> ing]. Take him—Bill—I could never have done the job he did—I would have
> killed somebody, dealing with human relations, listening to gripes all day long.
> It would have driven me nuts. Now, I don't want that aggravation anymore."
> To the Old Timers, politics is about impasse and petty griping. John's interpre-
> tation is that they do not talk about politics very much because they are done
> with bothering themselves with such aggravation. However, his definition of
> political talk does not include the many conversations that are relevant to pub-
> lic affairs but do not appear as "opinionated" or "gripes" because the members
> have similar views. In addition, defining political talk as contested *issues* over-
> looks their many conversations that do the work of defining whose interests are
> at stake, whose opinions are worth considering, and where they place people
> like themselves on various issues. (Walsh 2004, 39)

The phenomena Walsh and Eliasoph highlight occurred in my focus
groups as well. It was certainly necessary for participants to couch some
ideological talk in the rhetoric of expanded self-interest (that is, in an
expanded realm of interest that included family and community). They
frequently resorted to the two phrases Eliasoph notes ("for the children"
and "close to home"), using them to justify the ideas they held. Indeed,

85 participants (59 percent) used one of the two concepts at some point during the focus groups, and they were used in nineteen of the twenty discussions. Using these rhetorical devices gives speakers a "middle ground" between the starry-eyed idealism of morality-based arguments and the *realpolitik* of interests and capacity. Speakers could shore up their moral positions with support from the presumed-important actors of children and community. Still, far from being taboo, morality-based logic was the most commonly used (479 statements, or 45 percent) of the five major logics.

Also, as Walsh's example shows us, these people are not actually avoiding politics. Rather, they are avoiding talking about what they think politics means: griping, impasse, Washington. In taking these rhetorical detours, they are also reinforcing ideas about the permissibility and interest involved in politics. One example of this use of interest-based logic to bolster moral arguments occurred in the following exchange from a business organization's discussion:

RAMONA WANG: Since I'm a minority and I come from Asia, I totally don't agree about the profile stops because ... it's like prejudice because it's not a racial problem, it's a crime problem. We have to look at the crime.

LAURA OLIVER: The thing that bothers me, or one thing that really bothers me, is that it's totally against everything that we stand for. If the police force can take it, or the mayor, and through the mayor's office the police force can do these kinds of things, they can do anything.... If they don't like the height of your fence or the kind of dog you own.... They just can't get outside their powers this way. And if we citizens let it happen, it'll happen one way or the other to all of us at some time or the other.

BRENDA XAVIER: Well the question before us though is should we get involved. Is this something you want to get involved [in]?

LAURA OLIVER: Well, yes I, this is why I'm saying I think we definitely should. 'Cause we're all at risk here. (B3)

Ramona Wang begins the passage by arguing essentially pragmatically: "[I]t's not a racial problem, it's a crime problem." She implies that we can expect the policy to fail, since it addresses the wrong problem. Her colleague, Laura Oliver, switches logics, making an ideological argument: "[I]t's totally against everything that we stand for." The discussion is now in the realm of right and wrong; however, Oliver doesn't let it stay there for long. She quickly returns (somewhat awkwardly) to assure her fellow participants that it's also about self interest: "[I]f we citizens let it happen, it'll happen one way or the other to all of us."

Once participants switched the discussion onto the ground of moral issues, it became necessary for those who disagreed with them to justify a move onto other logical turf. If a position is wrong (immoral, unjust, etc.), participants must work to be allowed to make arguments based on interests, pragmatism, or other grounds.

In the following passage from a union group discussing the airport scenario, an ideological position is challenged from the point of view of self-interest:

PURVI MEE: I'm looking at this in a little different light, too, that it's like you have people who live in, you know, the ghettos or whatever, and they have to deal with roaches and water and, you know, all these kinds of problems, but you don't see associations over there. I mean, I rarely hear about associations over there, you know? Hooting and hollering about that. You know, we're lucky we can afford a house, you know what I mean? So I don't know, to me as an individual I just don't think it's, I wouldn't waste my time with this.

MARY NELSON: I don't know, Purvi, because when you have a lot of, not that we have a lot of money invested in our home, but we have most of our assets invested in our home, and we're looking at our home as being something that we can use as an asset until it's time to retire, and as you see that the things that you've worked for are being degraded because your home is going to lose value when you live under an airport ánd you have those bad things, I think that you may feel like you need to do something because it's affecting your ability to retire, where you can be, how you're going to live, because your home is worth less. I mean if you've worked really hard to establish yourself, you might feel like you need to do something. Or, like Zubin Lopez said, maybe you would need to feel like you get out before it gets worse. (U2)

Purvi Mee begins the dialogue by arguing morally: she's lucky to own a home and to have a place to live, and she's concerned about the implications of complaining about the airport noise. After all, "they have to deal with roaches and water . . . but you don't see associations over there." The moral point is that principles of fairness and equality should trump those of narrow self-interest.

Mary Nelson responds defensively, arguing that the individual harms are significant enough to override Mee's moral concerns: "[W]e have most of our assets invested in our home; . . . it's affecting your ability to retire, where you can be, how you're going to live." Nelson succeeds here in overcoming the power of a previous moral argument by stressing the degree to which her interests would be harmed.

Sometimes, then, the selection of a logic for discussion resembles the children's game "rock, paper, scissors," in which each choice wins against one of the alternatives and loses against the other. Participants select logics strategically, hoping that their choice will prevail against the strengths and weaknesses of others' selections. Once these initial selections are made, the process of negotiating over logics begins.

Although different logics may be strongly associated with specific positions for which people are arguing, they are not entirely matched. Using a moral logic does not imply adopting a position perceived as altruistic, and arguing based on interests or capacity does not necessarily imply the perceived "selfish" conclusion. For example, one Protestant church member put it this way:

FELICIA BILLINGTON: I feel that once profiling is going on, then we're all on the defense, whether we did anything or not. Every time we see an officer, we think that we could be harassed or something like that. Like you said, escalating, even if you weren't doing anything, you know that, okay, this is the enemy and now I have to be on defense. (P4)

The logic here is based on interests: "[W]e're all on the defense," which is not a desirable way to live. The conclusion, though, is in line with bigger-picture ideas about how society ought to work. The speaker does not allow interest-based logic to lead her to think in terms of the immediate, anticrime benefits that the city's leaders ascribe to the racial profiling program. Instead, she uses interest-based logic to bolster an argument against the program. Conversely, in a different Protestant church, Bob Thomas uses an ideological argument to defend the racial profiling program:

BOB THOMAS: We depend on the policemen for their judgment, and I don't think you can ham-string them. I do think that it's probably abused on occasion, but to me I think that the police need, they need the authority to be able to do this, and they do need to be careful to do it even-handedly. But I don't believe we should be screening the police officers from doing what it takes to cut the crime down. These people are probably victimized at times by the policemen, but crime also has its victims. (P3)

Emotion

Emotional appeals were notably absent from the focus group discussions. We know from a variety of research that emotions often set people up to think and act in particular ways. And in the press we often hear politicians criticized for appealing to citizens' emotions instead of their rational faculties. Indeed, no less an observer of American democracy than Alexis de Tocqueville noted the emotional content of our periodic elections:

> One may consider the time of the Presidential election as a moment of national crisis.... Intrigues grow more active and agitation is more lively and wider spread.... The whole nation gets into a feverish state, the election is the daily theme of comment in the newspapers and private conversation, the object of every action and the subject of every thought, and the sole interest for the moment.
>
> It is true that as soon as fortune has pronounced, the ardor is dissipated, everything calms down, and the river which momentarily overflowed its banks falls back to its bed. But was it not astonishing that such a storm could have arisen? (Tocqueville 1969, 135)

Frank discussions of morality are anxiety-producing. They are parts of "unsettled times" (Swidler 1986; Perrin et al. 2006) in which cultural production is more active. Psychologists and linguists, too, have noticed that visions of morality are often paired with emotional language.[1]

There were a few isolated references to emotion, as in this Protestant church group:

WANDA GAMBERI: When I hear a company say that they cannot afford to upgrade their equipment, it makes me very angry. ... I think the very least that even as a group we could do would be to, you know, send a letter of support for the EPA and a letter to Chemco stating, you know, hey, continued violations of the regulations, you should be shut down.

LINDA ROBINSON: I may lose my job if you send that letter. And so as part of this community group, I'm really opposed to your sending that letter [or] trying to get the rest of us to send that letter.

RENA WRANGEL: I think there needs to be some compromise; ... my recommen-

---

1. Linguist Zoltán Kövecses presents a fascinating discussion of this in *Metaphor and Emotion* (Kövecses 2000).

dation would be to support the EPA in negotiating some kind of timetable for these folks to reduce their ozone-depleting chemical emissions over time. (P2)

Wanda Gamberi begins with an emotional appeal, noting her anger at the Chemco violations. The emotion is quickly tamed, though. Linda Robinson protests that Gamberi's angry response threatens her self-interest, and Rena Wrangel seeks to compromise between the two. Compromise, though, doesn't acknowledge Gamberi's anger; it simply looks for a meeting point on what outcome to choose.

On the whole, though, emotional language was largely absent from the discussions. Why? My suspicion is that emotional appeals are less likely when citizens expect to be talking about specific issues—particularly hypothetical issues that are not actually affecting them at the time of the discussion. Instead, they assume that discussion is supposed to be reasoned and conciliatory. The anxiety and nervousness that Tocqueville discusses—and that political scientist George Marcus has argued is crucial to a "deliberative mood" (Marcus 2002)—is absent when citizens actually sit down to deliberate.

That pattern, though, should give us pause. Citizens are more likely to evoke moral positions—that is, frankly to consider issues of right and wrong—when they feel free to express emotional commitments (Sandman 1986). If the forums we set up for deliberation discourage citizens from expressing emotions, we may end up inadvertently discouraging moral discourse.

Negotiating over Logics

When participants disagree about what logic to apply to a situation, they negotiate over which one (or what combination) they will use. Discussing the Halfin scenario, three members of a business group argued about the Clinton impeachment controversy:

ROBIN JACKSON: The grassroots did not want him tossed out of office for this scandal. And yet we're saying his whole character has been like this from the time he's ever been in public office; we couldn't trust him, and he's done this many times over and over. And the American public did not get up in arms about this and say, toss the crook out. They're all saying ignore this situation, let it go, don't vote him guilty.

PAULA OLDHAM: What does that say about our entire society? We abort one-and-a-half million children a year, we have no problem with divorce because, you know, you didn't get meatloaf for dinner. There is no, we're so concerned about an individual's rights that the overall good of anybody has absolutely no value.

EILEEN HAMILTON: I have to say, for what Paula said, I was one of those people that said, why impeach a man for having an affair with an over-aged-twenty-one-year-old who knew what she was doing, excuse me. And the man politically, when we saw what he was doing politically, he was running the government the way we wanted it at the time. He wasn't doing anything politically wrong to be impeached. You don't impeach him for having an affair, okay?

ROBIN JACKSON: Do you impeach the president 'cause he lies? If he lies to you about something like this, he's going to lie to you about other things.

EILEEN HAMILTON: Well that's what my parents said. But I mean when you looked at what he did government-wise, I mean, we impeached a president. We impeached Nixon because he bold-faced lied about what he was doing government-wise to this country. And that's when the people all got together and said, you're gone. Because this is not what our country represents, okay? But now what, then again we're getting away from scenario number two [the Halfin scenario], but what Clinton did he did maybe on government property but he didn't take a nation to disaster. And Nixon was taking the nation into a disaster. (B1)

Robin Jackson sets the stage for a moral discussion, expressing disgust at the moral character of the country for tolerating Clinton's misdeeds. Paula Oldham seizes the opportunity, expanding the argument into a general indictment of contemporary American morality and the danger of privileging individuals' rights over the common good. So far, the discussion is entirely on moral and ideological terrain.

Then, Eileen Hamilton challenges this position, implicitly claiming that the logic for evaluating the impeachment controversy should be narrower, based on the pragmatic needs and expectations for which elected officials are chosen: "[H]e was running the government the way we wanted it at the time." That creates a disconnect: Jackson is *morally* offended, while Hamilton is *practically* satisfied.

The resolution to this conflict comes when Jackson offers a *pragmatic* defense of her previously *moral* position: "If he lies to you about something like this, he's going to lie to you about other things." Jackson provides an *alternative* defense for her position of outrage: Hamilton is sacrificing not only her moral integrity but *also* her own pragmatic interests by allowing Clinton's lies to go unpunished.

In terms of which logic prevails, Hamilton has "won." Jackson has been forced to argue based on Hamilton's chosen logic (pragmatism), abandoning her prior moral logic. That does not mean, of course, that Jackson's *position* has changed, although that is a possibility. What is important here is that the structure of the discussion—the rules about how the political discussion will be conducted—have been set. Jackson is forced to rejustify her opinion on the issue.

This process of negotiation is crucial to understanding the structure of political discourse. The selection of a logical approach to a political problem has significant implications for the direction the discussion takes and, quite possibly, its outcome. The options for logics going into the discussion and the negotiations over which of these options wins out are keys to political decision making.

The Chemco scenario inspired logics both of mediation and of expanded self-interest. For example, in a union group, a vocal participant took this position:

XAVIER CLEMENT: Let's work with this company, maybe get them a grant, maybe the government can give them a loan or something to help them do the improvements that they need to do. If you listen to what he gave us [as] information, it wasn't cost-effective for them to do the repair. They'd rather close up because it's going to cost too much money. So instead of letting them close up because it's going to cost too much money, let's give them a grant or something. I mean it's nothing different from any terrible neighborhood in this Bay Area down here, they have loans, 1 percent loans to fix up your homes and stuff like that. (U1)

Xavier Clement's position is clearly one of mediation: find a way in which neither side of the dispute wins entirely. In terms of expanded self-interest, both the community and children were big players in the Chemco scenario. Reluctant to get involved, a participant in a Catholic church group eventually comes down on the side of the EPA for reasons of children and community: "[Oscar Cevilla:] I guess *if I lived in that exact town*, and it wasn't my job, I wasn't going to lose my job, but *I didn't want my kids to grow up in an area that was, you know, in a future that would be unsafe for them*, I probably would say follow the rules *if I lived in that town*" (C1; emphasis added). Cevilla is unhappy about feeling that he must get involved in the situation; fundamentally, it does not interest him. But his sense that children and community were at stake forces him to back up his implicit principle of expanded self-interest by agreeing to get involved in the Chemco dispute.

Similarly, the following excerpt from a discussion of the profiling scenario shows the intermixing of all three active logics (interests, morality, and expanded self-interest):

RANDALL PHELPS: It seems to me that crime is down, our police department is either determining that crime is committed by people who drive or people who drive that are also minorities. Seems that's the way the statistics are presented in this case. Now since putting crime down is a goal, since crime hurts all society, then the question that I have is, is this not a good policy because after all, people who have nothing to do, that are mobile, probably are looking for problems more than looking for entertainment. And if the police make a mistake under those circumstances, that certainly is easy to determine. It would be a lot more difficult to stop an individual walking for any particular reason, investigate what their purposes are, anything like that today, than it would be for someone who's driving. A minor excuse to pull them over to question them may be a better tactic regardless of the ethnicity of the person or the group.

HENRY EATON: I would probably say that a car or a person that is, that had children in it, driving to a specific spot, or a … parent, grandparent, something like that, driving to a specific spot [who] really has one agenda in mind probably aren't going to be the target of the police to do that. So probably the people that these police departments are looking at are probably people that they know either have been in trouble or are maybe related to people that have been in trouble. So I would agree with Randall, I agree with Bob that this, you know, what they're doing is bringing the statistics down, bringing the crime down. Being a parent of children, that to me is very attractive. That to me would be, even if it does, you know, step on some people a little bit, maybe there's a lesson to learn there. Maybe they should be evaluating their, reevaluating their goals and their attention on what needs to be done.

PEGGY AXTON: I think [that] depends on the type of things for which they're being stopped. If it's speeding, if it's pulling in and out of traffic in an unsafe way, whether it's a single individual, more people in a car, whether they're young or older, I think that's a very legitimate reason and a very dangerous thing to do. And then there is certainly reason for them to be stopped. And I think that doesn't have anything to do with the color, the race consideration.

. . .

VIRGINIA KENNEDY: The thing that I was thinking about is, if I'm driving down the street and I have a taillight out, am I going to get kind of a nod and not even be pulled over, where a young black man of eighteen to twenty-five is driving with a taillight out, he's going to get pulled over even though he's obeying laws. Those kind of things would concern me. (P3)

Randall Phelps begins the excerpt with a pragmatic logic, arguing that the policy is good because it is effective. He then expands this into expanded self-interest ("putting crime down is a goal, *since crime hurts all society*"). Henry Eaton and Peggy Axton largely agree, but then Virginia Kennedy brings up the moral concern: that the police practices violate norms of fairness.

It is hard to argue, therefore, that (as Boltanski and Thévenot [1991] imply) modes of evaluation are primarily functions of the sphere of life under discussion.[2] They are, rather, the product of constraint, selection, and negotiation by participants. Speakers must creatively, actively select and combine these logics to construct a coherent intervention in the discussion.

Sports groups were the heaviest users of logics of interest, while unions were the lightest; sports groups were nearly 10 percent more likely to use such logics than were unions. Returning to the racial profiling scenario, consider this exchange from a bowling league:

KEVIN ELDER: I think they should be left alone, let the police do their job.

URSULA OSSELIN: There's too much high-speed chases, criminals that get away with things that, perhaps if they can stop the small infraction it might not have happened. I think they have a right to, I agree with you.

KEVIN ELDER: I've seen a lot of people going through red lights, I mean totally red lights, without stopping. Instead of slowing down, they go, they put on the gas and step on the accelerator. That's one of the infractions I'm talking about; there's several others, I can go on and on. In fact I do a little bit of it myself, but I don't do it intentionally, it happens, but I'm not thinking sometimes, you know?

EMILY ISSERMAN: And would you like them to pull you over every single time that you're just not thinking?

2. To be sure, Boltanski and Thévenot do not exclude other influences, but they seem to claim that modes of evaluation mostly follow the topic of discussion.

KEVIN ELDER: Yes. I wouldn't, yeah, if I made a mistake, yeah.

EMILY ISSERMAN: Every single time?

KEVIN ELDER: Well, I don't make that many mistakes, so I don't think it'd be that often. (S1)

Kevin Elder begins the discussion by expressing a general lack of sympathy with those concerned with profiling. His colleague, Ursula Osselin, agrees, tangentially citing the abundance of petty traffic crimes, and thereby initiates a logic of interests. Emily Isserman continues the logic, arguing that Elder should reject profiling on the grounds that it might be problematic for his own life. The mode of evaluation here is entirely based on interests.

By contrast, a union group approaching the same scenario discusses it as follows:

LAWRENCE CABOT: I think that the police department's categorizing people [is] taking the wrong approach, however it sees fit, I just totally disagree.

XAVIER CLEMENT: Of course this is happening in many communities, especially in the Bay Area. I think that there's very little that can be done because the majority of the people in the area are going to look at crime going down as a good thing. Sometimes people don't look at the way you get to solve the problem as long as the problem's been solved. All they're interested in, people that get pulled over and harassed, it's just a lot of people say it's worth it to keep the crime down. So, I mean, I wouldn't, I wouldn't get out and protest about it, I would just keep myself clean, since I am a minority.

. . .

LEON PATANGA: I think a lot of them are misusing their powers, you know. So I think we, there's not a whole lot that we can do about it, but I think we can let people know in authority that those kind of practices are going on within the police department.

. . .

ZOHAR LI: I think that things, giving the police the power that as a community we're not giving them, they're not showing us, we're not giving them respect, all power but they're not producing respect out of it.

LEONARD ROBINSON: I believe the same thing too, that the police are going to abuse their power if they can, but if it is cut and dry that this guy's giving them the power to do that, maybe next election time don't vote for him. Get somebody else in there that's not going to give the police that power to do that, and maybe, you know, go back to the way they should be neighbors. 'Cause he's giving them the power to do it, so, you know, take it against him and get him out of office; get someone else in who's not going to give them the same power. (U1)

From the beginning, this union group approaches the problem as a moral one: abuse of power, discrimination against minority citizens. Xavier Clement's decision to "keep myself clean" because he is a minority is closest to interest-based reasoning.

Unions are strong users of logics of capacity (discussions of whether, and how, they could be effective in a situation). In the following excerpt, a union group approaches the same profiling scenario in terms of the group's ability to affect the situation:

HADLEY KAUFFMAN: I agree but I just don't know how you do it. Like you say though, and I understand, and it is wrong. But how do you get the majority of the people that just don't give a damn? They don't care. They're so stupid.

WILHEMINA VINCENT: Well you know our media controls a lot of this. I mean when you turn on the television you see, you know, black male does this, Hispanic male does that. And it's prevalent that they pick out specific things, so we'd have to probably get media attention to draw, take away from that. In the newspaper when you read issues about crime, I mean, unfortunately if it's a white person, you know, that's not the caption that's read or the face that's looking at you. There was predominantly put in that the minority person, so everyone said, oh it's them, it's them, it's them, it's them. (U3)

It is tempting to conclude that, in the union setting, capacity is really just a stand-in for morality; that is, that union group members believe that the morally right option is necessarily one that is also doable. On one level that is, of course, correct: we can assume that a speaker thinks whatever she advocates is right. But that does not mean that the *mode of argument* is moralistic; speakers defend their positions using capacity when they believe their positions are most easily defensible in terms of feasibility.

The other strong point for union groups is expanded self-interest: use of community and children's interests as licenses to make moral arguments. These logics, along with logics of capacity, form the basis for the following discussion of the Halfin scenario in a union group:

ZUBIN LOPEZ: That's actually probably why as a new teacher I got involved in the union in the first place, because it feels like you can actually, on the local level, you can actually do stuff that works. I mean you can go to the community, you can do stuff. Once you get to Washington, as far as I'm concerned, it's so far away that I don't know what you can do other than, you know, kind of vote for the lesser of two evils, basically.

MARY NELSON: I mean I vote and I do all that stuff, but sometimes these big, big issues, senators and presidents and stuff, are so far out there that it doesn't feel like you really have that much control. You know, you're voting for somebody who's agreed to vote for them, it's like, well, you know, the whole two-party system is all skewed to the person that can run to the edge of the pack with their big bag of money. So it's kind [of] a cynical way of looking at it, but I really don't think that you can honestly run unless you have an awful lot of power and money behind you. And if you're not in one of those two parties and have a lot of people behind you, you can't possibly make it.

ZUBIN LOPEZ: Unless you're Jesse "The Body" Ventura.

CLAUDIA WILSON: He had a lot of people behind him.

MARY NELSON: And he was well known.

CLAUDIA WILSON: I would like to work toward some reform laws of voting so that . . . if people vote, you know that your vote's going to go right to that person and not to somebody else who could decide to vote differently or whatever else. I would rather put my energy to something that might actually happen.

JANE QUONSET: Yeah, and something, either that or more local. For me. (U2)

The two sets of logics—capacity and the virtues of the local—intertwine here as group members fall over themselves to validate not getting involved in the Halfin scenario. It's too far from home (even though it involves the group's "own" senator); it's therefore both less important *and* less amenable to citizens' actions.

Which Comes First?

All this brings up the following question: Do participants, in fact, reason by beginning with a standard for judgment and then determining whether the facts support that standard? In other words, do logics structure people's political positions, or do people first determine what position they hold, then justify it by mobilizing the ideas and resources at their disposal? There is significant support for both possibilities: that people use logics to justify prior decisions, rather than using logics to determine those decisions, and that people make decisions about action after following through a selected logic. In support of the latter possibility, commonly, numerous logics are mobilized to support a single position. As an example, consider the following excerpt, spoken by a union member:

ZUBIN LOPEZ: If probably, ... once an event hit close to home, for instance, if I had a student whose elder brother ... was harassed in my neighborhood because, by virtue of being black, or brown whatever it is, that might concern me enough to want to start doing stuff about that. At least investigating it more closely. I mean certainly I see both sides of the issue. I would like to feel safe in my own neighborhood, but at the same time, when do you allow the laws to start abridging the individual's rights? When do you start having laws that say, well, by virtue of statistics, you fall under this category because of your skin color, therefore we're going to take away some of your rights, which is really what's happening, I mean, and so that would be the issue. Until there was some kind of major problem that presented itself, you know, it's true that three times, 300 percent of the people that get pulled over were African American, yet a large percentage resulted in arrests of people who had prior convictions or something like that, I would probably, I probably wouldn't get involved, and also I'm really busy most of the time and wouldn't get involved. But once it got to the point where it struck home, I can certainly see, I mean, the first thing that goes up in my mind would be ACLU or getting some civil liberties, you know, finding out if you could get some pro bono case. But I think you have to have a case to start with. So that would be my issue. (U2)

During the course of this statement, Zubin Lopez uses five different logics: *local* ("once an event hit close to home"); *interests* ("I would like to feel safe in my own neighborhood"); *ideology* ("when do you allow the laws to start abridging the individual's rights?"); *capacity* ("I'm really busy most of the time"); and *legal* ("I think you have to have a case to start with"). In addition, he suggests modes of participation and what actors might be interested (the ACLU, in particular).

Another union member (from a different group) similarly uses several different logics to argue for getting involved:

IRA TENLEY: I'm not a minority, but I do know that this does exist, and they have a big problem with this, but as anything, one person really can't do too much about anything. But if you really unite and you tell, you know, as a group, and you say if you went to the mayor and you protested in a way with petitions, and you said that I want something done about this, this is ridiculous, you know, as all black people, all minorities got together and said you know, enough is enough, we can't take this, I mean, because they do, they'll single out just that one person for that reason. But you have to go on a higher scale I think to do something about it, to stop it. Just saying, well it exists and I'm going to accept it, I can't understand, I wouldn't accept that. If I was, if it happened to me, I wouldn't accept it, I would take it higher up. Say, this isn't going to happen to me again. Because it's not right. But you can't do it, like I said, as one person. You have to be united, and you have to do it in the right way so that you can get people to understand. Yeah, I think you should take it to the mayor. And if that doesn't work, take it up higher. Keep going as high as you can go. Until, if you have to go as high as possible until you get some action. Because this isn't just in one city, this happens throughout the whole country. It's a big problem. (U1)

In this statement, Ira Tenley also uses four distinct logics: *standpoint* ("I'm not a minority, but . . ."); *interests* ("[I]f it happened to me, I wouldn't accept it"); *ideology* ("[I]t's not right"); and *efficacy* ("[Y]ou can't do it . . . as one person"). She also mentions three public methods of involvement (petitions, organizing, and protest) and one private method (taking the matter to governmental officials). In both of these situations, it is difficult to consider the speakers' positions as the *result* of applying their preexisting logical frameworks; there are simply too many of them. Rather, the speakers felt that their course of action was correct and generated a list of useful logics and ideas to back up their feelings.

At other points, however, participants explicitly choose a standard by which to judge their participation. This is particularly true in church groups, perhaps because the church context grants a license to put on a "morality hat." Consider this participant in a Catholic church group:

LORETO NESILLA: I think we have too many boundaries that I think that sometimes as so-called Christians that, you know, we're supposed to be open-hearted and, you know, try to accept people, and sometimes I think best to try to be in their community and try to work in that community, and then you see how they feel because they feel the same way as what you're saying right now. You know they feel fear about white people or Hispanic people, because they're thinking everybody's out to get them, or they try to do good, but it doesn't come out that way. People I see that are incarcerated say the same thing, you know, that white man, he won't let me have a piece of paper, won't let me have a pencil to write a note to somebody. But you don't know, your mind is thinking, well, that's what he's going to do, but maybe he'll turn around, sharpen it, and, you know, stab somebody. But you have to try to think good. You know, Christian, that he's going to do the right thing. I mean I work late at night and I come home at three, four in the morning, and I get near a guy, but there's a certain power inside I guess as a woman, or maybe just what I've been working on, see so many different things. (C1)

Her overriding concern is that the outcome of her decision be "Christian." Christians, she says, are "open-hearted" and "accept people," and these are the standards to be applied when judging a potential decision or activity. Indeed, in this passage she never even approaches the topic itself; her entire discussion concerns the standards she intends to apply. Only later does she return to the subject of racial profiling, arguing that it is un-Christian to allow the police to judge individuals based on race.

I call this form of logical selection *standard-setting and evaluation* because it involves first choosing a standard of evaluation, then considering evidence as to whether the option under consideration meets the standard. This process is not unique to logics of morality. People also begin statements by arguing that issues are most important when they affect their own interests or those of their communities:

VICTOR TRUJILLO: I think more than anything it's going to come down to how much it affects me directly, to be realistic. I think it's going to be like Paulo was saying. Much as I disagree with this, unless it truly affects me, that this causes me to lose my job, you know, I probably won't be motivated to get her out of office as if I was, if I still had my job and got raises and promoted and so forth in the next four years. So I think most of the people that are going to take action against her are probably ones who were directly affected by what she did. 'Cause they'll certainly remember it in four years. (U4)

The standard here, for evaluating action on the Senator Halfin situation, is self-interest. It is stated at the outset and subsequently applied to the question of whether or not to get involved.

The standard need not apply only to the specific situation being evaluated. In one case, a participant gave a general argument for getting involved in community life; the situation was of secondary importance:

YELENA NAVARRO: I guess in the past, many of us do not get involved in these situations. We read about it, and I think in order for all of us to—this is my first time ever discussing something like this in an opening case. I think many of us should get more involved to see what our mayor is actually doing for the good of our city and what kind of tactics is he really actually doing. And as we do hear a lot of the crime is rising or crime is going down low or comparing it from years past or from different cities, I think we should have more of this sort of [discussion] to the public. (C5)

Clearly, the question of whether logics precede decisions or vice versa has no simple answer. In some situations, participants clearly stated logics they felt were appropriate for addressing situations and then used them to evaluate the situations. In others, they apparently began with a decision, then "worked backwards," adding reasons for their decision later.

Conclusion

Perhaps the most important elements defining how a group discusses politics are the logics they use to frame them. How emotional the discussion is, and whether the discussion is grounded in interests or morality are crucial for the group's initial consideration of its charge. Different kinds of groups do this in different ways. It is important, and not surprising, that church groups were particularly strong users of morality, while business, labor union, and sports groups considered politics to be mostly about competing interests.

The next chapter builds on this information. We turn there to the methods groups imagine for participating in politics. Having decided whether, how, and why to get involved, what can a group actually *do*?

CHAPTER SIX

Capacity and Expression: The Tactical Repertoire of Citizenship

I would rather put my energy to something that might actually happen. — Union focus group participant

Every single issue here is important. There's not one on here that's not, well maybe one, but for the most part they're important, but you only have so much time in your life and you have to pick your shots, and this is not one of my shots. — Protestant church focus group participant

Spurred into action by concern with an issue, groups need to decide what to do about it. In this chapter, I examine how they make that decision. What kinds of citizenship actions can citizens imagine? What are citizens looking for when they think about how to get involved? What makes one kind of citizenship more attractive than another?

What Can Citizens Do?

At particular historical times and places, citizens show surprisingly little variation in the actions they choose. Sociologist Charles Tilly has shown, for example, that the British food riots of the eighteenth century were rarely "about" food. Rather, they were the way the English working class best understood political protest—whether it was about food, working conditions, taxation, or any other grievance. They used food riots to voice their discontent because food riots were one of only a few elements in their "contentious repertoires." Like most citizens, they lacked the extraordinary imagination to create new tactics out of whole cloth (Tilly 2004, 1995, 1978; Taylor 1996).

The repertoire of possible citizenship actions is one of the most important contributions of a civic context to a citizen. People in one or more
civic contexts—and with experiences in them—build a mental list of possible activities from which they can draw when it becomes necessary.

EILEEN HAMILTON: I'd side with EPA on this one and I'd probably be out with my
   little protest sign out in front, we want to shut it down now.
   . . .
EILEEN HAMILTON: If I didn't work at the company I'd be there.
ROBIN JACKSON: I would stand out with a placard for something like EPA, you
   know, before I'd do it for some other things. I mean this is a really important
   cause. And it seems to me too many people think it's not important, and they
   say, well, you know, so it's a little more stuff in the air or this or that. We've
   got to realize we're on spaceship Earth, there's only so much here. We've got
   to take care of it. We can't have this blatant attitude that we used to have that
   it doesn't matter as to the environment. (B1)

Note that, in this excerpt, Eileen Hamilton skips the process of evaluating competing ways of getting involved. She assumes that the appropriate
tactic is going "out with my little protest sign." Her implicit concern is
simply whether or not to get involved; the method is never called into
question.
   The Chemco and profiling scenarios elicited very similar discussions of
method. They are associated with boycotts (unsurprising for the Chemco
scenario in particular) as well as further exploration and education, as in
this excerpt:

REGINALD QUIMBY: Well first of all we would have to find out if this is going on in
   Fremont, which is almost impossible. You know, these police chiefs, they know
   about stuff. They have their own codes and everything and have their men and
   women at attention before they send them on the street. And you could be
   standing here listening to them. And they can drop one or two words that's
   going to mean everything to these people. And to you they mean nothing. So
   you got to know what they're saying. Same way with the press, you know? So
   often these guys think they're so smart, you know? And they have no idea what
   the police do. And that's just the way it is. You know, so we could find out, . . . I
   think it would be harder working in a place like Fremont or Union City because
   it's so small. And just looking around, it looks like both police departments are
   represented fairly well with minorities. (B3)

The airport-noise scenario, on the other hand, brought up a hodge-podge of community and governmental methods: education, legal responses, bureaucratic responses, protests, organizing, and petitions. It is also the scenario most closely related to the *exit* method: deciding simply to leave a situation (in this case, to move out of the area) instead of engaging in a public debate. All of these methods can be seen as essentially administrative; they respond to the sense that something was *done incorrectly*, as opposed to a sense of political or community disadvantage. Political scientist Danielle S. Allen points out that this tendency—to view politics as a matter of effective administration instead of conflict—is one of the fallacies Americans adopt that make the rational deliberative ideal so appealing (Allen 2004, 54–55).

The collection of methods associated with the airport scenario is substantively distinct from the methods associated with the Senator Halfin scenario: letter-writing, legislation, electoral involvement, donations, and revolution. Whereas participants proposed dealing with the airport scenario by using methods that were linked to an *administrative* violation, they understood the Halfin scenario as linked with the political process and proposed responses accordingly.

In general, the methods associated most closely with logics of capacity are relatively non-confrontational; these include bureaucratic solutions, electoral involvement, organizational involvement, donations, letter writing, legislation, and petitions. Participants came up with these solutions when they were looking for *effective* ways of addressing a problem:

URI TESSELMAN: There is one way I think you could get around this. The people have the right to vote. And if they would exercise that right, you could get rid of these congresspersons.

CAROL BONILLA: I don't think so.

URI TESSELMAN: I think you can.

CAROL BONILLA: I don't think so.

URI TESSELMAN: But the problem is that when the news media gets through with you they're going to change the way you think and you're going to vote for, you'd have to have the populace say no, we're not going to do it that way, regardless. (S2)

The two most confrontational methods—boycotts and revolution—were discussed quite differently from one another. Boycotts came up very frequently, mostly in connection with the Chemco scenario, and their effectiveness was often touted as an important feature. For example:

JEFFREY JOHNSTON: I say boycott.

BRENDA XAVIER: You betcha.

LAURA OLIVER: Yeah, just don't buy any more Chemcos.

TINA NICKLEBY: That's right, I didn't need them anyway.

JEFFREY JOHNSTON: What do they produce?

MODERATOR: They produce a variety of household chemicals. Cleaning supplies.

LAURA OLIVER: So we could order a shopping, supermarket boycott.

TINA NICKLEBY: Oh, we could boycott.

LAURA OLIVER: Just like we did the grapes.

. . .

LAURA OLIVER: But there's a possibility here. I mean if they produced something we didn't use, we wouldn't have that possibility.

TINA NICKLEBY: If it was something like you only needed when you built a house or something. But this is something we use every day. Well some of us do.

JEFFREY JOHNSTON: Some of us do. (B3)

Revolution, by contrast, was discussed only once, and in a dismissive tone that spoke principally of its ineffectiveness:

WALTER FURMAN: Well I think we're all kind of slaves to the system so to speak, and we're the probably the bottom of the elephant pile or something.

VALERIE WHITE: What are we talking here, revolution?

ARNOLD WALTERS: No. *Throwing bombs won't do it.* (S4; emphasis added)

Numerous reasons could be provided for not favoring revolution. Indeed, one can imagine moral arguments (the degree of violence), interest-based arguments (the danger involved), expanded self-interested arguments (the danger to one's children and community), and mediation arguments (the sides should come to a compromise). Arnold Walters's response reveals the appeal of the efficacy argument over the others: there can be no argument about the importance of efficacy in deciding how to participate. Impugning the efficacy of a suggestion offers two advantages. First, it helps to overcome the power even of a moral argument, since *failing* at doing the right thing is not considered a goal. Second, it avoids disagreement over the appropriate mode of judgment, since any method must be both effective *and* appropriate.[1]

1. Other research (e.g., Lichterman 1996) has noted that activists in social movements actually have a *low* sense of efficacy; they do not expect their activism to have results. My findings do not directly address this issue, since (1) participants in my focus groups were not

Method selection is less polarized than logic selection, but there are still some significant differences. Catholic church groups were very likely to consider government-based responses—more than 16 percent more likely than Protestant and union groups:

WENDELL QUARLES: For me, this is a quality of life issue. If I lived in this neighborhood and I wouldn't be able to talk when planes were flying overhead or the house was moving and shaking, I would do something about it—why wait? Because to live like that day in and day out and every minute of the day, it's not something that, you know, you look forward to when you come home from work or whatever. You want to see what maybe elected officials or what strong mayor or someone in the area or your neighbors are thinking to say, we got to do something about this because it's not right that this type of a business is impacting the way that we live, the way that we want to live. And we would need to do something to meet with the officials to say that this has got to stop, and it's got to stop because, you know, it impacts the way that I live.

. . .

QUINTO JUAREZ: This is a real issue. This is a real issue for Union City. Recently the San Francisco airport tried to reroute their flights coming from the north to fly directly over Union City, which is where we are and which is our home. The problem is that the arriving flights from the south approaching the Oakland airport already go over Union City. So what they were going to do is they were going to have aircraft that were going in opposite directions directly over Union City. So what's happening is San Francisco airport is forever expanding, and they're trying to change these flight patterns now. The problem is they would continuously increase the number of flights going in opposite directions directly above Union City. One of the issues that came to my mind immediately was not only the possibility of a crash above Union City, but you know with that increased air traffic I started thinking about loss of sleep, some of the emotional issues that would be attached to it. I know that it would create irritability, that there would be probably higher levels of divorce, of stress-related illnesses. And so I started thinking about some of the medical research. When the city council addressed this issue, this is exactly some of the issues that they were talking about. Luckily for us they had done their homework on this, and so the FAA, they needed to, they asked Union City about this, and they needed a response. So luckily for us our public officials had already been informed about

---

activists; and (2) efficacy was addressed here only in the context of deciding on particular actions, not as a general question.

this before it became a problem for the local neighborhood. If this was the local neighborhood and the public officials had not been informed prior to, then I think that's the entity that I would like to attach myself to and gain support from so that we could address this issue with the FAA, the local airport, to see if we could possibly reroute flights, like right here in Union City if we can get flights to go over the bay on their approaches to the airports as opposed to flying over residential neighborhoods. So I think that I would look at routing unpopulated areas as opposed to routing flights over the populated areas. But I myself would probably approach local city government and try and gain their support to move the issue. (C5)

Contrast these suggestions to the ones that predominated in Protestant groups, which tended to focus on public actions rather than governmental ones:

BOB THOMAS: Well if I was very upset and I lived in the neighborhood, I would probably get my neighbors together and petition the airport for noise abatement or to move the darn runway so it goes over your house instead of mine. (P3)

HELEN CRANDALL: I grew up like this. I would get on really friendly terms, really friendly terms with my neighbors and start talking about it and finding, you know, standing out in the neighborhood and really finding out how much of an effect it had on them as well and trying to organize. I mean it's a very disruptive thing to have happen to your home. It's like having an earthquake hit at your house over and over and over all day long, and into the night.

ROBERT DENNIS: I agree with Helen. I would work to form a neighborhood organization. They're very effective on issues like this. There's nothing like having a hundred people, families, banded together on an issue. Get a lot of attention. A lot more than an individual. (P1)

Similarly, union groups were the most likely to consider private methods, such as in this discussion of the airport noise scenario:

CLAUDIA WILSON: My question is, does it do any, I haven't ever seen a home association stop any kind of an airport anything.

MARY NELSON: That's exactly what I was thinking is I don't think I'd want to waste my time with the association 'cause I don't think I'd be able to stop it, and if it was really going to affect my quality of life and I couldn't take it, then I'd want to move. Or, you know, take, I mean, I feel like, got to take care of my self and get out of here. 'Cause we spend a lot of time and a lot of energy and fighting a huge, you know, SFO or something like that, it's not going to happen. (U2)

Mary Nelson's proposal here is what I have termed *exit* (referring to the concept proposed by Hirschman [1970]): simply leave the neighborhood, since organizing will prove fruitless, and the noise is unbearable. This provides a striking contrast to the previous three excerpts, also about airport noise, in which participants suggested public and governmental responses—methods that understood the problem as fundamentally *social* and *political* rather than private.

The Operative Repertoire

As I discussed in chapter 3, we can group methods of involvement into three main categories: public, private, and governmental.

Public

Public methods involve sending a message to the public as a whole. They seek to "speak into the air," as communication scholar John Durham Peters has described modern, technical communication (Peters 1999, 6–7). Often, the media is the first way citizens can think of to get that message out. In one business group, Laura Oliver explicitly seeks to use the media to speak to an unseen, yet assumed, public:

LAURA OLIVER: As a group, if we were going to try to address this, I think we should get publicity. I think we should write, people should volunteer to talk to the radio stations, talk to the television stations, who knows who has contact in the organized community of people with experience fighting this. . . . I mean in Fremont we ought to be able to make a difference, six people should, noisy, loud people should be able to make a difference. If we were talking about Washington, D.C., or Los Angeles, you know, I don't know. And I don't really know about Oakland either. (B3)

Laura Oliver calls for going to the media in order to get the message out. She never addresses the question of who in power could fix the problem (essentially a governmental question), nor does she suggest individual remedies (a private solution). Rather, using the media offers her a way to speak directly to the public, at least in a city where the public is relatively small.

Similarly, in a different business group, Lana Smith mixes public and governmental approaches to the racial profiling scenario:

LANA SMITH: I mean I would hate to have that, I even feel sometimes we're a minority sometimes in the Bay Area, being white, for myself, sometimes. So I mean you can feel very uncomfortable in some situations where you go. So I think definitely you'd have to stand up for it and write letters. Especially if you met other people when you did say something that agreed with you, then you could band together and do something as a bigger group and as a whole to make something. And you know when you stand together, you have a bigger voice, and so you're heard more.

MODERATOR: Who else might you join with?

JANET QUINN: I think one way to approach it would be to bring it to different organizations' attention and see if there were other people that were feeling the same way about it, and so therefore you could make suggestions of things to do, you know, routes to bring this to the attention of the right people. (B2)

Lana Smith starts out with a media approach (writing letters), then adds community organizing to the mix: "[Y]ou could band together and do something as a bigger group and as a whole to make something." Janet Quinn's ultimate outcome, though, is governmental: "bring this to the attention of the right people." In this case, then, talking to the anonymous public is a step toward talking to government officials.

Boycotts are a form of public action because they organize citizens without the intervention of a government body. In a sports group, this typical discussion called for boycotting Chemco because of its regulatory noncompliance:

JIM FARMER: The only thing they understand is the cash register. Don't buy their product. That's right. You call them up and say, hey, you know, you're stinking up the neighborhood down here, I'm not going to buy your products, I'm going to encourage all of my friends and family and so forth not to buy your products.

BENJAMIN HALVORSEN: I agree. Boycott.

JIM FARMER: Yeah, basically a boycott of the product. (S4)

Private

Boycotts should be understood as separate, though, from purely individual decisions about what to buy. The latter are essentially private decisions; they allow individual expression without the involvement of either public speech or effectiveness. Contrast this Protestant church group
discussing Chemco with the sports example above: "[Brian Forzer:] I
wouldn't feel compelled to do much about it myself because they've already got them, as long as they keep after them, then I would be okay
with that. If they started letting up, then that would be a different thing.
If you really thought they were doing something bad, you just don't buy
Chemco's stuff, you know?" (P1). Brian Forzer provides no way for his
action (not "buy[ing] Chemco's stuff") to interface with the public or to
make much of an impact on Chemco's bottom line. Rather, his approach
is personal: keep *my* consumer dollars from flowing to a company whose
actions I don't like.

Private methods involve only the citizen making the decision. They
specifically exclude the general public or the government as partners, as
in this business group discussing the airport scenario:

MODERATOR: Anybody want to do anything about this?

JEFFREY JOHNSTON: Tell the people to move.

RAMONA WANG: The person if they get used to it, it's okay; if they don't like it, they
  should move. (B3)

Similarly, in a union group, an African-American man offers a private
method for dealing with the profiling scenario: "[Xavier Clement:] I mean
I wouldn't, I wouldn't get out and protest about it, I would just keep myself clean, since I am a minority" (U1). As I argued above, we should understand these private methods as still being citizenship decisions. They
are based on the same ideas about effectiveness, expression, and morality.
Citizens may adopt them after exhausting, in their minds, all public and
governmental solutions. They may also select them first, as they seek to
reassure themselves that individual activity can solve social problems (see
Swidler 1992).

Governmental/Institutional

Finally, governmental methods seek to involve the responsible governmental or institutional officials in solving the problem.

URI TESSELMAN: Well I think the only thing that's available to us is to write to the elected officials. In my experience with local and state and federal people, . . . some will answer you and some won't. And if it's not politically sound for them to give you an answer, they'll only answer part of your letter. As to whether it makes a difference or not, I don't know. Certainly I like to exercise that right. Whether it has an impact or not, I don't know. (S2)

In this sports group, Uri Tesselman moves immediately to writing to elected officials as the right way to deal with the Halfin scenario. He is concerned about the effectiveness of it—indeed, he states outright that "some will answer you and some won't." The decision here is almost fatalistic: little will help, but contacting the right officials is the most likely solution to work.

As with public methods that connect with governmental ones, governmental methods often end up with public backup, as in this Protestant group discussing racial profiling:

ROSALYN PINCKNER: I think we should address this issue with the mayor. And get some type of media attention, petition. Something in writing, something documented showing that we have presented it as a problem, so that when it comes up again we can have something documented showing that we have concerns about that particular issue and we want something done about it.
RODNEY ANDERSON: And start protesting.
ROSALYN PINCKNER: And doggone it, I'm not going to take it anymore. (P4)

Rosalyn Pinckner understands that the basic decision about racial profiling lies with the mayor, and it is there that her energies lie. But she proposes using public methods (media attention and protests) to augment her case with the mayor.

How Do Citizens Decide?

The most important distinction made in the focus groups was between kinds of citizenship that speakers felt would *make a difference* and those they felt gave them *voice*. Sometimes citizens are concerned with whether an action will be effective, and sometimes they are more interested in expressing themselves. The first concern I call *capacity*, since it demonstrates citizens' understanding of their political capacities. The second I label *expression*.[2] These are closely related to the long-standing sociological distinction, pioneered by Talcott Parsons, between *instrumental* and *expressive* actions (Parsons and Platt 1982; Parsons 1974). Instrumental action is intended to change something; people engage in instrumental action in order to get something done. Expressive action is designed to say something; people engaging in it value it intrinsically.

In a bowling league focus group, Amy Hamer and Uri Tesselman provide a clear vision of what I call expression:

AMY HAMER: You've got to open up your mouth. You have to voice what your problem is. What your thoughts are, what your ambitions are, what you must do to rectify the situation and whether it's to city officials, it's government officials, or to your neighbor next door. You must let your thoughts be known.

URI TESSELMAN: You have to communicate.

AMY HAMER: Yes, communication, exactly. (S2)

To highlight the contrast, another sports group (this time, a bicycling association) evaluated the Halfin scenario as follows:

ARNOLD WALTERS: We're not happy but we can't do anything about it.

JIM FARMER: We feel helpless.

BENJAMIN HALVORSEN: It'll always be there.

WALTER FURMAN: We feel helpless, yeah. There may be something to do about it, but we don't know.

JIM FARMER: If we had several billion dollars at our beck and call we could be like the soft money and put in politicians, and then we'd be just as guilty as they are. (S4)

These two ways of deciding whether, and how, to get involved reveal important differences in *what the two groups were looking for* in citizenship activities.

One element that goes into deciding whether expression or voice is more important is how *local* citizens understand the issue. Research shows that people think they can have a greater impact on issues that are "local," and that, in addition, they care more about these issues.[3] Those

---

2. Expression is a mode of what Hirschman (1970) calls *voice*: the ability of an actor to engage in communication, regardless of its ultimate effect.

3. See, among many others, Burns, Schlozman, and Verba (2001, 101–3).

dynamics make the relationship between how local an issue is and what kind of consideration it receives far from simple. On one hand, Oscar Cevilla considers voice particularly important, given the local character of the airport noise issue:

OSCAR CEVILLA: This is your house, you know, this is your sleeping and I think this is important. If you can't do something to protect yourself or to improve your way of living, then why are you here? So therefore, yes, you should start a committee, and, yes, you should have people come over to your house and discuss this, and what's the next step we should do? (C1)

Oscar Cevilla's standard for selection is based on the extent to which the problem interferes with his home and life.

The airport scenario highlights this concern because many participants thought they could have no influence over the airport's decision, either because big corporate interests would control the outcome, or because the flights had already begun:

BOB THOMAS: Well if I was very upset and I lived in the neighborhood, I would probably get my neighbors together and petition the airport for noise abatement or to move the darn runway so it goes over your house instead of mine. *I mean, you know, there probably is no solution to this.* (P3)

Thus, citizens who began encouraging action because of expression often ended up defending the feasibility of involvement:

PEGGY AXTON: I think the public does have influence, and I think the more we educate the public about these issues and what the problems are that are causing them, the better off we're going to be, and that's something that we can do about it as individuals. (P3)

Sometimes, though, the *first* matter of concern is whether citizens can influence the situation. After all, the reasoning goes, if we can't do anything about it, why waste valuable energy trying?

In drawing from the rather narrow menu of methods they considered, participants sought to balance the issue's importance, its impact on their lives, and their (perceived) ability to make a difference. For example, several participants in a Catholic church group approached the Senator Halfin scenario as follows:

JANE BALZER: I'd sign a petition for campaign reform, but I don't see myself going out with a clipboard and getting signatures.

WENDY KILLIAN: That's a good way of putting it.

AMBER FLYNN: I'd do something minor.

WENDY KILLIAN: As far as social policies go, or social issues, I would spend my time and do spend my time on other issues. I think this is important, it just isn't one that I would work on. (C3)

When this exchange opens, no participant has mentioned petitions or gathering signatures. Jane Balzer *assumes* that a petition is the appropriate method of involvement—even though she indicated on her questionnaire that she had engaged in several other kinds of citizenship as well.[4] She draws a distinction between *signing* a petition and gathering signatures for one—the former, of course, requires less cognitive, emotional, and literal investment than the latter.

Following Balzer's lead, Wendy Killian and Amber Flynn offer support for the position: the Halfin situation is bad enough to support signing a petition to reform the law the senator may have skirted. But because her behavior is perceived as distant and common, the group is unwilling to commit to more difficult involvement. Killian summarizes that position, while also complicating the picture of the issue's importance. She starts by arguing that other issues are more important and then qualifies that: "I think this is important, it just isn't one that I would work on." Such a global statement makes further discussion difficult.

Other scenarios aroused similar discussions. Presented with the Chemco scenario, a business association member reacted as follows: "[Martin Estrella:] I don't see where there's anything I can do except march in front of the gate or something like that" (B4). Offering this as the only option leads the speaker to discount all options. Both symbolically and literally, "marching in front of the gate" offers little in the way of success.

In this example from a business group, Blanche Evans complements her concerns about efficacy with her interest in local issues:

BLANCHE EVANS: I think it makes a difference whether it's on a local level or a national level as far as the election goes. Because I think you have more influence

---

4. Petitions are relatively common in California as an initial step in many of the "direct democracy" policies for which the state is famous, from ballot referenda to gubernatorial recalls (DeBow and Syer 1997).

over what happens locally than at the national level. But as Lana Smith was saying, you have the option then of not voting for someone in the next election because they haven't followed through with their platform, what they said they would do. (B2)

She is discussing the Halfin scenario, which intentionally combined local and national characteristics. Halfin represents the respondents' state, so she is their "local" senator, but the action takes place in Washington, D.C. Nevertheless, Evans's approach makes it clear that she feels ineffective because of the apparent distance of the situation: "[Y]ou have more influence over what happens locally." She does, though, propose an electoral method for dealing with the problem ("not voting for someone . . .") but only as a last resort, suggesting that that is the only option available for a dissatisfied constituent.

A similar dynamic is at work in Laura Oliver's discussion of the profiling scenario, which we examined above:

LAURA OLIVER: If we agreed that we should do something, then we ought to, every one of us individually, take on a section of it and do something about it. And it would depend on if we were dealing with a Los Angeles or a Fremont. I mean in a Fremont we ought to be able to make a difference, six people should, noisy, loud, people should be able to make a difference. If we were talking about Washington, DC, or Los Angeles, you know, I don't know. And I don't really know about Oakland either. (B3)

Again, the speaker uses the degree of locality to illustrate the importance of political efficacy in deciding whether and how to get involved.

By contrast (and, interestingly, in much the same spirit), this participant in a Catholic church group considers the Halfin scenario with the *competing* concerns of efficacy and locality:

WENDELL QUARLES: This is one area that maybe I should be paying more attention to, but I don't because I get frustrated with the political system and feel that this is such a global picture that what good would one voice do in trying to deal with campaign financing or reform or whatnot, and that this is something that took place in another state, but why do I need to pay attention to it. But I guess at the same time I do take my voting privileges very seriously, and I vote in each and every election, and I've done that ever since I was able to vote. So I'm probably speaking from both sides of the mouth, and I don't pay close attention to something like this, but at the same time as the election pertains to the local community and to my state, you know, I do my voting. (C5)

An alternative move, then, is to shift the terrain of efficacy—here, Blanche Evans agrees with a prior speaker that little can be done to combat racial profiling as it is already being practiced in town. But, she argues, perhaps the problem could be minimized by addressing it soon: "[Blanche Evans:] What my objective would be in talking to other people is to say, do something now even though it's not a big issue yet, so that we can at least maybe catch it right before it becomes something bigger" (B2). In a different group, a skeptic (also the sole African American in the room) lectures his colleagues about the dangers of getting involved in the profiling scenario:

REGINALD QUIMBY: You ever been to jail? . . . That's something you have to think about.

LAURA OLIVER: To go to jail?

REGINALD QUIMBY: Yes. Absolutely. In a hot minute. You're taking on the police force here. . . . This is our gestapo. And you know, I would be willing to work with any group to look into racial profiling or whatever is going on here. You know, but there's just some things that, you know, you would really have to be aware of.

. . .

JEFFREY JOHNSTON: So if we did get involved, you know, it would have to be an all-out battle. I mean I don't know if we six people have that much energy and time. (B3)

Ironically, even with the language of "gestapo" and admonitions about jail time, Jeffrey Johnston frames the decision in the cost-benefit terms of a rational actor. The question is whether "we six people have that much energy and time," not (for instance) whether actions that might provoke a jail term are too dangerous, or whether the possibility itself arouses moral indignation.

By contrast, in a Catholic group, participants sought to limit the amount of energy they would spend on the profiling issue, even as they understood it as a fundamentally moral concern:

OSCAR CEVILLA: I think if someone came, if one of the churches came over and said, we have a petition here, would you sign for it and, you know, and we're having a meeting, I guess it's basically, [the] reality of the thing is, I don't have that much time, but I would sign a petition, and if the time was convenient I'd go to the meeting 'cause I feel like it isn't fair, you know, their presentation of the case as stated here certainly isn't Christian. You know, and they have some good arguments, and I would probably sign their petition, and I would go to one of their meetings and see what can be done. (C1)

Here, the moral quality of Oscar Cevilla's analysis of the situation requires that he get involved. But there are potentially too many stresses on Cevilla's time, and so he tries to limit the impact of that moral valuation on his eventual schedule. Once again, the profiling scenario aroused competing concerns about morality and the cost-benefit calculation.

The Halfin Scenario

JEFFREY JOHNSTON: Silly me, how could I forget? Money talks, nobody walks. I'm not sure, what are the positions available for us to take?
TINA NICKLEBY: I think I will vote against her in the next election, period, end of statement. (B3)

The Halfin scenario aroused the most indignation about betrayal and unethical behavior, but also the most cynicism about involvement. Tina Nickleby's approach to the problem summarizes that position: Halfin deserves to be removed from office, but the limit of her involvement in that process is to "vote against her in the next election."

Later in the same business group discussion, Tina Nickleby again brings up the question of involvement:

TINA NICKLEBY: So, do we want to get involved or not? I vote no.
JEFFREY JOHNSTON: How active is an involvement; we're either going to vote her out or not vote her out the next time she's around.
BRENDA XAVIER: If I read this in the paper, I'd say yeah, yeah, and go to the sports section.
TINA NICKLEBY: Yawn.
JEFFREY JOHNSTON: What can we do about it anyway? Just vote her out or not vote her out. (B3)

The assumption in this and the other business associations was that actions must be effective to be appropriate. Furthermore, they must be *immediately* effective; there was no room left for considering activity that might make a difference in the long run.

Similarly, in a Protestant group, witholding one's vote is the method chosen for its effectiveness:

ROSALYN PINCKNER: I wouldn't even get involved in this. You know, it's a political arena that I don't think that we would have a lot of control over. Although I do agree with Ashley, I would look for a candidate's moral values and their character, but as far as the money side, I don't think we would have any control. Money is power, and whoever gets the most money buys the position. But I would look at the candidate that I would vote for on a moral issue more so than on money. (P4)

Contrast that standard to the one applied to the same scenario in a Catholic church group—composed, incidentally, of participants political scientists expect to be less involved. They were of lower class, in general, than the participants in business group 3 who debated involvement above, and more of them were nonwhite.

OSCAR CEVILLA: I think it's kind of sad we can't [do anything about Halfin] because it's one little person bucking an organization that's been going on for years, you know?

ANNE MORGENTHAL: Sure, you can't, as one person, or even as this group here, we couldn't do anything about it. I mean we're nine people here, we couldn't do anything about it.

OSCAR CEVILLA: I think the idea that you can do something, dedicate your time to something, you might succeed in something. You could never succeed at this, no.

JAVIER GUEVARA: Well, I belong to Greenpeace, or I subscribe to them. And that's one of the things a little man can do. You can contribute, and if you can't contribute you can still be a participant somehow. I forget how that works, but . . . (C1)

Effectiveness mattered in this group, too. But the evaluation of effectiveness was different in subtle, yet important, ways. Even after Anne Morgenthal confirms Oscar Cevilla's original claim that there is no effective response to the situation, Cevilla returns, looking for more: "[Y]ou might succeed in something." Javier Guevara enters by arguing that, in some situations, political activity might be effective, but by the time he does so, the distance between his experiential evidence and the Halfin case is great.

A similar logic was at work in a different Catholic church group, now discussing the Chemco scenario:

AMBER FLYNN: I think, from a distance, if this wasn't in my city, that's what I would do. I would boycott the products, and I would tell people. You know, I wouldn't, I probably wouldn't picket it or anything, but I would tell my friends, or ... I mean, I do that now, I mean, there's a lot of things I won't buy.

. . .

AMBER FLYNN: And I think it's hard 'cause sometimes you feel like you're not making a difference. But I think you do.

JOHN BALZER: You're making a difference, though, to yourself, aren't you?

AMBER FLYNN: Yeah, I just think it's important to talk about it, not just to do it.

JOHN BALZER: You were saying about an individual being able to do something, or not being able to do something about anything, okay, because you're just one person? We have a wonderful tool in our homes. The telephone. And if this chemical company was here in Newark, I would make a phone call. And just say, well, I live in the community and if you're hurting the community like the EPA says you are, then I would like to see you close your doors. (C3)

Capacity, here, is treated as one reason for selecting an approach to action, but emphatically not the only reason. Amber Flynn endorses "talk[ing] about it, not just ... do[ing] it." And John Balzer suggests individual telephone calls specifically because of the degree of *voice* they offer.

Indeed, exercising voice is sometimes seen as an element of good citizenship in itself, as when Peggy Axton exhorts her Protestant-church colleagues to contact their representative:

PEGGY AXTON: I think people have to write to their senators and their congressmen. They have to let their views be known, such as when we have the local meetings like we had yesterday with our congressman. We have to make our visions of what we want them to do known. And, sure, you're not going to have everybody have the same opinion. But if there are enough people who can tell their representatives how they feel, I feel that that's got to have an influence on the congressman or the senator. (P3)

Again, Peggy Axton is acutely aware of the possibility that capacity will be raised to counter her argument for expression; she acts to forestall that objection: "I feel that that's got to have an influence."

Another common solution to the problem of diagnosing efficacy is to involve greater numbers of people:

HERMINA LUMAPAS: Different people, more people involved, that makes a difference.

MABASA MARCOS: Yeah, because if you go by yourself, nothing.

STEPHEN CLARK: Nothing.

KATHRYN ENGSTROM: But, you know, you can't say that. Because it took one woman that started Mothers Against Drunk Driving, MADD. I mean sometimes it only takes one to get it started. You need help, but you need somebody to start it. People have done it. I'm with it. (C4)

This strategy spans all five types of groups; in each case, the perceived lack of capacity of a method in a particular situation can be fixed by appealing to a large enough group of citizens. It was used not only in Catholic church groups like the one above, but also in Protestant groups:

HELEN CRANDALL: I think that in our society in order for action to be taken, it needs to be, action needs to be taken by a person in power. And white people are in power in our society, so if you want something like this to be taken care of, it's not enough for a bunch of black people to be out there protesting about it. (P1)

It came up also in sports groups:

BRAD GARFIELD: Yeah, one dog barking doesn't get any notice. You get a group starting to bark then.

MELINDA ENGLISH: Step in the right direction.

BRAD GARFIELD: Maybe a petition.

. . .

URI TESSELMAN: Can we get a petition in the paper, have them put an editorial in there for us? Would they do that? I don't know.

AMY HAMER: It'd be worth a try.

DARREN DAVIDSON: It's freedom of speech, should be able to put whatever you want in the newspaper.

CAROL BONILLA: Yeah, but wouldn't that depend on the political view of whoever you went to ask to do that? I mean, you know, everything is so [political]. (S2)

Conclusion: Capacity and Expression

In evaluating what kinds of things they might do—and, by extension, what kinds of things they will decide *not* to do—citizens try to balance the *reasons* for action and the *criteria* for successful action. This chapter shows us that citizens are concerned both with effective action (capacity) and with the opportunity to make their voices heard (expression). They balance these two concerns in much the same way classical sociologists suggested they would: by understanding some actions as instrumental and others as expressive. Citizens also use creativity, imagination, and narratives about past political activity to construct ideas about what they can do and how different actions might affect the balance between instrumental and expressive actions.

Political Microcultures:
The Structure of Political Talk

The book began with an argument that we should think about citizenship as a creative task that integrates thinking, talking, and doing. Good citizenship, I claimed, can be identified through the civic contexts and discussions that give citizens the tools to define, pursue, and consider public concerns. The past three chapters have located a wide variety of types, contours, and shapes of the democratic imagination. Given the requirement to engage with a new issue of public concern, citizens deploy an array of rhetorical, informational, and interactional strategies to enact citizenship.

It is time now to take inventory. How do group settings shape democratic imaginations? What constrains and expands citizens' creativity and imagination? In this chapter, I pull together the theoretical and empirical threads that I have developed so far and use them to propose that we think about group settings as *political microcultures*. These are localized social settings that serve—just as political cultures do in general—to constrain and enable citizens' democratic imaginations. A key element of this idea is that *the same citizens, placed in different political microcultures, may think, talk, and practice citizenship differently*. Elsewhere (Perrin 2005b), I have developed a more detailed, technical version of this argument. Here, I describe the kinds of discourse that characterized the five types of civic groups I studied. This sets the stage for the final chapter, which examines how public policies might encourage a broader democratic imagination.

In order to describe the different types of discourse, I broke down all the focus group transcripts into *turns*. A turn is, simply, everything one person says until she either finishes or is interrupted by another person. Thus, turns can vary widely in length. Some consist of only one word, and others are much longer. The longest turn in the focus groups was 684 words—about two and a half typed, double-spaced pages. Most, of course, were shorter; 90 percent of them contained 106 words or fewer, and the average was only 40 words.

Thinking about conversations in terms of turns has a rich history in sociology and psychology, where conversation analysts use them to identify the power, inequality, and persuasion patterns among participants in a conversation.[1] Turns are important because they constitute one person's attempt to intervene in the conversation. That attempt may be completed or not (since someone else may interrupt), and it may be successful or unsuccessful. Just as I argued in the first chapter that citizenship is *creative*, a conversational turn is a creative act. The form and content of a turn are, of course, influenced by the context in which the turn is taken, but that form and content cannot be determined by the context.

If citizenship is a creative act, then this chapter traces many small creative acts of citizenship: interventions in conversations about citizenship issues. The two most important factors influencing how people in the groups talked were the *scenario* they were talking about and the *kind of group* in which they were talking. I present that information in figures 7.1–7.6. The raw data appear in tables B.2 and B.3 in appendix B.

How Topic Influences Discussion Style

By far the strongest influence on how citizens talked in the focus groups was *what they were talking about*—the scenario they were discussing. I start the discussion, therefore, by describing how the groups discussed each scenario.

Figure 7.1 displays the percentage of logic-based turns that considered each of the three major logics (morality, interests, and capacity). In other words, given that the speaker was using *some* logic in a turn, the graph presents the likelihood that she used each of the three logics I am discussing here. Since any turn may consider zero, one, or more than one logic, many turns are counted in more than one of the graph's bars.

---

1. See, for example, Ford and Thompson (1996); Ford, Fox, and Thompson (1996); Sacks, Schegloff, and Jefferson (1974); Gibson (2000).

CHAPTER SEVEN

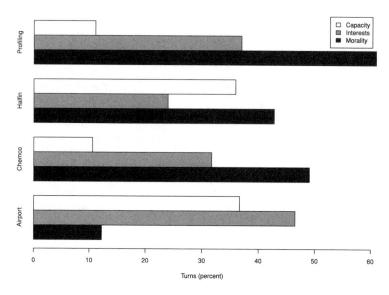

FIGURE 7.1. Logics by scenario

Consider, first, the use of the logic of morality. The racial profiling scenario elicited the greatest use of that logic; more than 60 percent of logical turns considering that scenario involved morality. By contrast, the second-place scenario (Chemco) was about 17 percent less likely to use logics of morality. The least likely to elicit the use of morality was the airport-noise scenario, which was 80 percent less likely to do so than the profiling scenario.

The logic of interests trumped the others when discussing the airport scenario: participants understood this principally as a problem of one group's interests in contest with those of another. In that context, they were quite ready to assert their own interests as legitimate: "[Vicky Randler:] I would be involved in this, and I would probably organize the group. 'Cause this one would really have an impact" (B4). In all the other scenarios, morality was more of a factor than interests were, although the use of the logic of interests varied substantially. The profiling and Chemco scenarios displayed relatively high levels of interest-based discussion, while the Halfin scenario showed the lowest.

The difference between scenarios in the use of logics of capacity is particularly impressive. About 35 percent of logic-based turns discussing the Halfin and airport scenarios were concerned with capacity: How effective can we be in addressing this scenario? For example, consider this Catholic church group reacting to the Halfin scenario:

OSCAR CEVILLA: I think it's kind of sad we can't because it's one little person bucking an organization that's been going on for years, you know?

ANNE MORGENTHAL: Sure, you can't, as one person, or even as this group here, we couldn't do anything about it. I mean we're nine people here, we couldn't do anything about it.

OSCAR CEVILLA: I think the idea that you can do something, dedicate your time to something, you might succeed in something. You could never succeed at this, no.

LORETO NESILLA: I tend to disagree in the sense that ever since I was a little child I was always a rebel, and I was taught, you know, the power is in the numbers. And if you join forces you will be powerful. One person cannot win, but the more people that stick together, the more strength that they're going to have. (C1)

Similarly, a sports group discussed Halfin as follows:

GERALD BRAMSON: Well, you're kind of at a dead end. Congress is the one that makes the law. And they're not going to change it. They can talk all they want, these politicians talk all they want. They're not going to change the program. 'Cause it benefits them all. It's just that simple. You can talk all week long, it's not going to make a difference. (S2)

By contrast, only about 10 percent of logic-based turns in the Chemco and racial profiling scenarios were concerned with capacity.

The two scenarios with the lowest scores for capacity had the highest scores for morality. This suggests an interesting way of thinking about new issues. When citizens understand an issue as being basically about morality—that is, about basic issues of right and wrong—they respond by preferring expressive to instrumental speech. Expressive speech is not susceptible to concerns about how effective it can be; citizens speak expressively simply to speak, not because they expect that speech to make a difference. Like many of the strategies we have considered here, this separation between instrumental and expressive speech is neither uniformly good nor bad. Purely expressive speech may be intrinsically important, as when groups seek recognition: their political goal is speech itself. Citizens are also not necessarily good at estimating capacity, so speech they

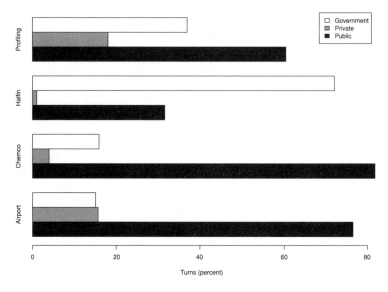

FIGURE 7.2. Methods by scenario

consider purely expressive could end up actually being effective as well. At the same time, though, separating instrumental from expressive speech encourages us to marginalize expressive speech. If it is not intended to have any effect, why should we pay attention to it?

Even more than logics, the methods that participants considered varied with the scenario they were discussing (see fig. 7.2). Public methods—such as demonstrations, picket lines, and letters to the editor—were mentioned often in three of the four scenarios, but played relatively little part in discussions of the Senator Halfin scenario. Respondents to the original screener survey labeled the Halfin scenario "distant," and it was the only scenario in which the protagonist was in a different city (the scenario was datelined Washington). By far the most commonly discussed response to the Halfin scenario was voting for an opposing candidate the next time around:

JIM FARMER: The only way that anything like this could be settled . . . [is] at the ballot box. And if the people don't like the particular people they put in there, vote them out.

CHIN-SHE LI: I actually don't agree that the only way to do it is at the ballot box. Because nowadays they don't even listen to what the people have to say. It's so what if you put it on the ballot, it's just going to be.

JIM FARMER: Well then you've got to vote them out.

CHIN-SHE LI: So what if you try to vote them out? They're just going to be voted right back in by the ignorant people. You know not everybody is smart about politics. (S4)

Furthermore, voting for an opponent was a method considered *and rejected* by some groups:

ZEKE QUIMBY: This alone would not change my vote in any way.

MODERATOR: How come?

ZEKE QUIMBY: Because I think it's normal rhetoric.

ELIZABETH PARMEN: We expect this from politicians, you see?

ZEKE QUIMBY: You know they're lying to you anyway.

LANCE ZEEMAN: Till they pass a law that says it's illegal for a politician to lie, you know they're going to lie. (S1)

Voting for an opponent—considered a governmental approach—explains why the Halfin scenario inspired so much more discussion of governmental methods than did the other three. Other governmental approaches were common too, and frequently consisted of working on ways to prevent Halfin's reelection:

BLANCHE EVANS: I think that it should be exposed when it's discovered so that everybody has an opportunity to make a decision based on that information, and so, you know, if an elected official, and you have an issue with how they've conducted their campaign, then your choice is not to vote for them. And I just fundamentally think that an elected official should reflect their constituency. You know I was elected on this platform and these principles and ideals, and I'm upholding that. You know, I like to think that if people voted that person in because of what she stood for and then she shifted her position mid-term, that money or not money next election campaign would be secondary. Would be on the basis of her beliefs. It's still smarmy. Because I don't think it's across the board fair. It's manipulative in the way that I think the people who give the money are trying to direct the country's agenda. I mean I know that when they filter money into certain places there's a higher likelihood that certain bills will or won't be placed. What is that? (B2)

Private methods were relatively uncommon in any of the scenarios but were much more common in discussions of the airport and racial profiling scenarios. In each of these scenarios, though, they took a somewhat different form. Private methods in discussions of racial profiling typically consisted of black participants suggesting that they would act more carefully to avoid arrest, as in this comment:

DAVID YOUNG: Me being a minority, I would not feel compelled to try to go by and try to get this person out of office.... What has been done that I know of is that people, minorities tend to start saying that they cannot change policies, they have to change how they live.... Because what happens is that they feel hopeless as far as trying to go up on the government route.... So what they do is they end up boarding themselves in their communities and so called watching their backs. (S3)

By contrast, private methods discussed in the airport scenario nearly always involved exit. Since participants rarely felt that they would be able to change the airport's expansion, the most attractive option for discussion was moving out of the neighborhood: "[Reginald Quimby:] Move! I can tell, you know, they're not going to move that airport!" (B3).

Differences in governmental methods are not surprising. The Halfin scenario—a situation in which a governmental figure is accused of wrongdoing—inspired the most governmental discussion. The other scenario in which a government agency (the police department) was the main actor was racial profiling, and that scenario garnered significantly more discussion of governmental methods than did the two scenarios (airport and Chemco) whose main actors were nongovernmental institutions. This pattern suggests a relatively constrained view of the capacity of the public sphere. Consideration of governmental responses is much more likely when the government is already involved, but relatively unlikely when a situation does not yet involve the government.[2]

The resources used for arguing varied by the topic of discussion as well. Narratives were used in discussions of all the scenarios, although they were most prominent in the airport scenario (see fig. 7.3). Not a single turn in discussions of that scenario expressed doubt about the scenario itself or others' intentions. Doubt was most common when discussing the Chemco scenario, which brought up issues of the trustworthiness of science and the regulatory practices of the EPA:

2. This is particularly striking in the Chemco case, in which the EPA, a government agency, *is* involved, but is not the main actor.

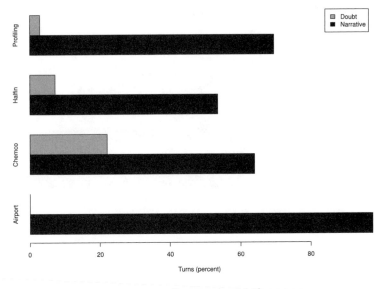

FIGURE 7.3. Resources by scenario

JEROME HASLER: Oh, okay, I thought maybe they are coming up with things and not showing conclusive proof that these are affecting the layer or what not. So therefore they're coming up with these stricter regulations anyhow or something. Maybe they're taking it as a personal attack, I don't know. It doesn't make sense, you know, I mean, if they're coming up with these regulations and they're saying that they can't meet them, then what does that tell you? (U4)

By contrast, the doubts expressed with regard to the racial profiling and Halfin scenarios were mostly about the truth of the scenario itself. Participants wondered, for example, whether racial profiling was really occurring and who provided the information about Halfin's alleged corruption:

OSCAR CEVILLA: I think you need more information. When you vote for a candidate, you're not going to just go on what you see on television, or read in the paper, or see in the political mail you get in the mailbox, but you're supposed to go out there and look at their voting record if they have something in the past and talk to other groups who had some kind of contact with that person, see if they really did work for them. Go out there and do some digging yourself before you vote.

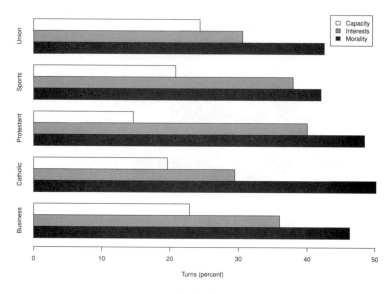

FIGURE 7.4. Logics by group type

VELMA MARTIN: You do, and who even wrote this article? Maybe they were not
    for this candidate or against this candidate. I mean, where's the source of the
    information coming from?

ANNE MORGENTHAL: Yes.

OSCAR CEVILLA: Could be a newspaper that was for the other candidate, yeah.

VELMA MARTIN: Yeah, so as I said, the checks and balances, they have to just work
    it out themselves. (CI)

Group Style and Political Discussion

An important part of the argument of this book is that the group context
in which citizens deliberate influences how they deliberate. A union is
not a church, which is not a bowling league; each of these constitutes its
own political microculture, including its own group style (Eliasoph and
Lichterman 2002). The second set of graphs displays the effect of the type
of group on the style of conversation.

Figure 7.4 shows the use of each of the three important logics in the
five group types. A glance at the graph shows that there is less variation
among group types than among scenarios (see fig. 7.1). But since each
group addressed all four scenarios, the presence of statistically significant

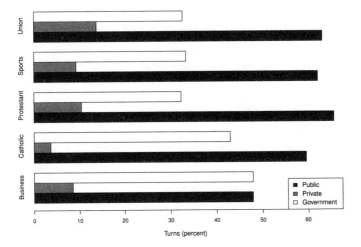

FIGURE 7.5. Methods by group type

variation here implies that the group type is an important element in the selection of logics, even when the groups are discussing the same topics. Protestant and Catholic church groups used morality the most often, while sports and union groups used it less.

The logic of morality competes with the logics of interests and capacity for reasons similar to those discussed above about morality and capacity. In Protestant and Catholic churches, for example, where the logic of morality was most prevalent, logics of capacity were least prevalent. But Protestants were much more likely than Catholics to use logics of capacity. Unions and business groups were the most concerned with logics of capacity. In both of these groups, the ability to get things done is an important element of their mission and, consequently, of their group discussion style.

Figure 7.5 shows that union contexts are more conducive to discussion of private methods than are the others. Nearly 13 percent of union discussions of methods of involvement was spent discussing private methods, compared to only 3.5 percent in Catholic groups. Business groups were the strongest users of governmental methods, with Catholic churches not far behind:

ROBIN JACKSON: Right, I would see this as something a person should do as an individual, maybe go to a council meeting or something like that and say, this seems to me to be a need, and how do we go about getting consensus that

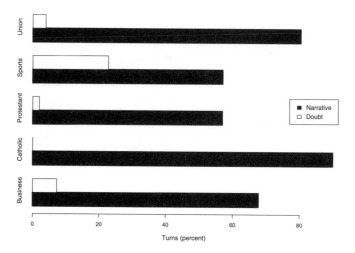

FIGURE 7.6. Resources by group type

we need a committee, and then get a representative committee to look into something like this. Think that might be the way to go, to approach a council person, and then I don't know if it can be handled in a public council meeting, but at least the council would have it under discussion and agenda. (B1)

This similarity, though, masks an important difference. Business groups talked of governmental methods with a sense of confidence: finding the administratively appropriate official would effectively get the job done. Catholic church groups approached them with a sense of deference; governmental methods were often the only ideas they could imagine.

MARIA RAMOS: Talk to the chief of police. Maybe like talk to the mayor or the city or something?

STEPHEN CLARK: We would have to go to a meeting.

MABASA MARCOS: . . . we can get the presentation if this is really happening. And then from there we have the facts and all the papers to present to them.

STEPHEN CLARK: To present to them.

MABASA MARCOS: From there to the city hall and go to the police department. Make an appointment with the chief of police or whoever. And then we can present, you know, that this is happening, or we think this is happening, and we have surveyed the community, these are the facts, and could you tell us how many of these are really, you know.

. . .

CLEMENTINE RICHARDS: Invite the chief of police to be there at that council meeting so that he can also hear about it. But we tried that, and they stood us up. (C4)

All the groups were heavy users of narratives, which underscores the importance of that form of discussion. The most striking connection between group type and the use of a resource (fig. 7.6) is the strong relationship between sports groups and the doubt resource. Sports-league participants spent more than three times as many of their turns as the next highest scorer (business groups) expressing doubts. This may be a function of sports leagues' relative insulation from public-sphere problems (what the great sociologist Georg Simmel [1910, 129] called "the essence of sociability" in play-related groups). Since (in most circumstances) sports leagues need not come up with explicit decisions on public actions, they are free to engage in the luxury of doubt. Civic contexts that are tuned to making decisions based on interests, ideas, and information likely provide a repertoire that allows for evaluating the quality of such information.[3]

At least since the 1950s, observers of American society have worried about Americans' "spinning apart." The best-selling sociology book of all time, *The Lonely Crowd* by David Riesman and his colleagues, examined Americans' cynical attitude toward politics and the common good. Then-current Americans, they said, were attracted to an "inside-dopester" view of political life that avoided important moral questions in favor of cynical predictions (Riesman, Glazer, and Denney 1950). More recently, observers like Alan Ehrenhalt have argued that the breakdown of communities makes citizens cynical and disconnected (Ehrenhalt 1995). Others have blamed the press corps's cynical attitude (Cappella and Jamieson 1997) or the culture in general (Stivers 1994). Given this background, another way of understanding the differential use of doubts in the focus groups is that civic organizations provide a defense against cynicism in the culture in general. Groups with shared moral or interest-based missions (such as unions and churches) are particularly good at buffering that cynicism, while those whose missions are primarily social (business groups and particularly sports leagues) are less good at that task.

3. I am not suggesting that the distinction is as clear-cut as the "instrumental" vs. "expressive" typology of associations (Gordon and Babchuk 1959); sports leagues, for example, become involved in political issues, and "instrumental" organizations frequently hold "expressive" activities, including sports events (see also Burns, Schlozman, and Verba 2001, 74–82).

Taken together, the information in this chapter goes a long way toward explaining how and when Americans can creatively discuss important issues of citizenship. First, citizens are able to zero in on important elements of a new situation, analyzing it relatively quickly and with relatively little need for additional information. The similar ways in which different groups talked about the same scenarios suggests that Americans in general use similar tools to interpret and evaluate new political information.

Those similarities, though, give way to important differences among the civic contexts in which citizens address these questions. Some kinds of groups encourage moral conversation, while others emphasize interests or capacity. Some privilege cynical, doubt-based discussion, while others do not. Some imagine citizenship activities as engagement in the public spotlight, while others concentrate on governmental and bureaucratic responses.

These differences in group style can explain why different kinds of organizations seem to mobilize their members in different ways (chapter 2). Furthermore, they can guide efforts to reinvigorate American democracy by showing us what kinds of civic contexts encourage their participants to think, talk, and ultimately act in ways that are expansive and creative. The next chapter takes these findings and builds an argument for supporting such political microcultures in the service of a rejuvenated democracy.

CHAPTER EIGHT

How to Use Civic Life to Build Citizenship

If democratic citizenship is in crisis, it is not—or, at least, not entirely—because citizens are renouncing the practices of citizenship but because the pool of styles, skills, habits, and ideas from which they can fashion creative responses to political events is thinning and dividing. The fact that democratic citizenship is more a characteristic of groups and communities than it is of individual citizens is a source of democratic strength, since it takes communities longer to disengage than it would take isolated individuals. Sadly, though, it raises the concern that, once communities begin the process of democratic decline, stopping or reversing that decline will be more difficult than simply changing individuals' attitudes and practices. This chapter offers conclusions about the character and state of democratic citizenship, along with some principles for policy measures to address it.

Creativity as a Democratic Skill

The evidence presented so far shows clearly that citizenship depends greatly on the contexts in which it is situated. These contexts have many more levels than the ones I have discussed here. Citizenship practices are, for example, situated within legal frameworks, which have received only a passing glance here. We can expect laws that reduce the difficulty of participating or increase the rewards of doing so to inspire citizens to behave differently.[1] Similarly, cultural norms and styles that emphasize harmony over conflict or that encourage citizens to understand politics as distant from their everyday practice make active engagement in politics less likely.

At its root, democracy is about citizens' ability to affect the decisions made on their behalf: what sociologists call *agency*. The most interesting recent foray into understanding agency in sociology is by Mustafa Emirbayer and Ann Mische. They understand agency as individuals' capacity to cause or prevent changes in social structure "through the interplay of habit, imagination, and judgment" (Emirbayer and Mische 1998, 970). Agency is, in that sense, a kind of creativity (Joas 1996): a patterned, structured process of creating new practices out of old ones.

As I suggested in the introduction, citizenship, too, is best understood as a form of creativity, nurtured and constrained by its environment but not reducible to the influence of that environment. Some other principles about citizenship follow from ideas about creativity:

1. Creativity involves *inventing, imagining, and recombining ideas, skills, and habits to accomplish new "projects."* These ideas, skills, and habits are not simply invented anew, though. They come from past experiences: those that citizens have been involved in and those whose histories have been preserved through various narrative retellings.

2. Crucially, therefore, *creativity relies on the residue of creative acts past.* The creative genius we attribute to isolated individuals—Mozart or Elvis in music, for example, or Monet in art—contains the creative and technical expertise of the social milieus in which they moved. That fact does not diminish the genius or the creativity of their work, but their contributions are the unpredictable products of their creative history.

3. Equally important, *creativity flourishes in the context of other creative minds.* Like a painter, chef, or musician who depends on a community of like-minded others who value and (sometimes) practice her craft—what sociologist Howard Becker calls an "art world" (Becker 1982)[2]—a good citizen is aided by a community of others who value and (sometimes) practice citizenship. Such

---

1. An example of this finding appears in the work of political scientist G. Bingham Powell, who compared voter turnout in the United States with that in eleven other countries. He found that the party system and registration laws were responsible for the bulk of Americans' tendency to vote less often than citizens of the other countries (Powell 1986).

2. In a less well-known, but very convincing, work, Barbara R. Walters has traced the development of French Impressionism to the blossoming of a social milieu that fostered it (Walters 2003).

community dependence is recursive—that is, a person whose citizenship is not inspired by her environment is also unlikely to provide an inspiring environment for others. In this sense, community dependence makes citizenship practices "sticky" over time.

4. Finally, *creativity is sensitive to the infrastructure and rules that evaluate it.* Psychologist Mihaly Csikszentmihalyi (1996) points out that creativity requires a "symbolic community" that can recognize and promote innovative ideas. In the language of evolutionary theory, this is a "selection effect": a characteristic of the environment in which an innovation occurs that determines whether the innovation will take hold or not (Aldrich 1999). That is, a great citizenship idea, fostered by a receptive community, will nevertheless tend to fail when the rules of the game are unfriendly, or when the institutions we rely upon to convey ideas ignore or denigrate it. The principal kind of institution that sets the rules of the game is government, which regulates much of how popular concerns reach public policy. Institutions that convey ideas include the news and entertainment media (whose selection of stories, ideas, and perspectives strongly determines what citizens perceive) as well as schools, universities, book clubs, and more.

Creativity is not limited to any one of the three corners of the citizenship triangle. Individual citizens, groups, and social movements practice what sociologist Doug McAdam calls "tactical innovation" in the context of *practicing* citizenship—they develop new methods and reinterpret old ones in the service of political goals (McAdam 1983; Voss and Sherman 2000). They demonstrate creativity in developing new approaches to citizenship. Similarly, confronted with new emotional, informational, and interest-based messages, groups and individuals can create innovative ways of thinking about citizenship. In practice these forms of creativity are not easily distinguished from one another; for example, social movement theorists such as Nancy Whittier and David Meyer (Meyer and Whittier 1994; Meyer 2000) have shown that an important outcome of social movements—that is, of *practicing* citizenship—is that they change the way other citizens *think*. Linking these two is the kind of creativity we have observed in this book: innovative interventions in ongoing political discussions, or creativity in citizen speak.

Creativity and the Generative Public Sphere

Citizen speak deserves special treatment, since it is through talking that thinking becomes doing and doing becomes thinking. Furthermore, we can observe innovations in citizenship talk far more easily than in citizenship thought, and somewhat more easily than in the practice of citizenship.

Most recent discussion of citizen speak has focused on the concept of *deliberative democracy*: an ideal form of democratic governance in which all actors consider information and interests from the point of view of all others. In the words of deliberation's most vocal proponent, German philosopher Jürgen Habermas, "[F]rom this interlocking of perspectives there emerges an ideally extended 'we-perspective' from which all can test in common whether they wish to make a controversial norm the basis of their shared practice" (Habermas 1998b, 58). Deliberation, in this view, takes place in a public sphere: a space in which all citizens come together to exchange rational concerns and ideas on issues of the day. In practice, some observers have suggested that the New England town meeting is such a public sphere. Political scientist Frank M. Bryan and his research team visited thousands of town meetings throughout Vermont, reporting on what he argues is "real democracy" in practice (Bryan 2004). Others have claimed that various communicative media—television, newspapers, the Internet—provide a virtual, "mediated" (Clayman 2004) kind of public sphere.

George Marcus (2002) has shown that citizens are more able to think deliberatively when they are in specific emotional states, suggesting that the deliberative ideal is relatively specific to particular kinds of contexts. Michael Schudson points out that the ideal public sphere has never been realized in American history (Schudson 1992a). Beyond these questions about the extent or possibility of the deliberative public sphere, though, one striking thing about this vision of democracy is that it is *not* creative. Citizens have interests and concerns that are objective and, essentially, privately formed. They carry these interests to the public sphere, where they are presented with the task of discussing and refining them. Emotions, conflicts, tensions, divisions—these are absent from the ideal public sphere.

Political theorist Seyla Benhabib has taken Habermas's ideas about the public sphere and suggested that we view the arenas of everyday life as ground for deliberation:

> A [public] space emerges whenever and wherever, in [Hannah] Arendt's [1972] words, "men act together in concert." . . . [A] town hall or a city square where people do not act in concert is not a public space. . . . But a private dining room

in which people gather to hear a *samizdat* or in which dissidents meet with for-
eigners become public spaces; just as a field or a forest can also become public
space if it is the object and location of an action in concert, of a demonstration
to stop the construction of a highway or a military air base, for example. These
diverse topographical locations become public spaces in that they become the
sites of power, of common action coordinated through speech and persuasion.
(Benhabib 1992, 78)

In Benhabib's vision, citizens create public space by engaging in public
talk. She thereby inserts the importance of creativity—that is, of citizens
making, not just consuming, the public space.

Because citizenship is deeply creative, and because creativity is deeply
social, citizenship is (to return to the great French sociologist Émile
Durkheim) an eminently social thing (Durkheim 1995; Fields 1995). The
traditional image of the public sphere therefore contains an important
flaw. We cannot assume that citizens' ideas and views are formed in isolation and then brought to a common space for public discussion. Rather,
patterns of thinking, talking, and practicing citizenship are forged in the
context of social interaction (Adorno 2005).

The Citizenship Triangle Revisited

I claimed in chapter 2 that each of the three elements of citizenship behavior—thinking, talking, and practicing citizenship—causes and is caused
by the other two. Most important, encouraging one of the three elements
without supporting the other two is unlikely to produce the democratic
revitalization many observers have been calling for. Voter-registration
drives and voter education, for example, are important in encouraging
citizens to vote. But citizens whose democratic imaginations are impover-
ished cannot lend vitality to the tasks of citizenship simply by voting.

To illustrate that point, consider the many citizens who do not vote—
in recent presidential elections, that has been roughly 50 percent of the
eligible population, and substantially more in local and state elections.
Most public opinion polls suggest that these citizens do not hold opinions that are significantly different from those of the voting public. If they
had voted, analysts reason, the outcomes of the elections would have
been similar (Teixeira 1989, 1988). Indeed, political scientists Raymond
E. Wolfinger and Steven J. Rosenstone, in their classic study of voting,

report that the opinions of nonvoters are "virtually a carbon copy of the citizen population" (Wolfinger and Rosenstone 1980, 109). Some analysts take that to mean that increasing voter turnout is an unimportant goal, since nonvoters are adequately represented by those who do vote. Wolfinger and Rosenstone continue with a revealing point: "Those most likely to be underrepresented are people who lack opinions" (109).

That position misses the point. As several sociological theorists have pointed out, public opinion is more than the collected opinions of isolated individuals (Adorno 2005; Bourdieu 1979; Warner 1992). It is the collective, deliberative, and interactive product of our collective democratic imagination. Thus, *we cannot know* what nonvoters would choose if they were actively engaged in thinking and talking citizenship.

I have shown in this book that different civic contexts are associated with different ways of thinking about and imagining action with regard to similar political issues. Beyond simply connecting individuals with social networks that foster greater political participation (Putnam 2000; Lin 2001), these civic contexts constitute environments for encouraging, directing, and, yes, stifling political thought. Citizens' civic experiences (alongside, presumably, noncivic experiences such as work, family, and friendship networks) provide them with a store of resources for political thought. Encouraging and engaging in rich dialogue on public-sphere issues is, in itself, a way of practicing politics. Political activity cannot be separated from citizen speak.[3]

Nina Eliasoph's (1998, 231) concern to discover the contexts that encourage citizens to wear their "democratic citizenship hats" is well-placed: the organizational, civic contexts of citizenship do structure citizens' political imaginations. If political culture is a schematic web of interconnected ideas, styles, habits, and evaluations that structures and enables citizens' political views (Boltanski and Thévenot 1991; Swidler 2001), then associational life is a crucial territory for building citizenship, as others (e.g., Putnam 2000) have suggested.

But this research, and the concept of political microcultures that emerges from it, suggests a more specific response. The principal contribution of civic life to citizenship is *not* the formation of individual friendships and connections among organization members but the provision of nodes and ties to citizens' schematic maps. It is in this way that civic life undergirds a culture's political imagination.

3. See M. E. Warren (2001, 70–82) for an excellent theoretical discussion of this.

Revitalizing democratic citizenship, then, requires attention to all three corners of the citizenship triangle. An imaginative citizenry is, at root, a social goal: it is the product of richly patterned and connected relationships among people and groups. Public and private policies to support civil society can help develop those connections.

What Can We Do to Build the Democratic Imagination?

The eminent political scientist Theda Skocpol ended her 2003 book, *Diminished Democracy*, with a corrective to the increasingly popular communitarian and social capital theories of democratic renewal. Noting the importance of national-scale problems and policies, she argued that revitalizing American democracy required forms of civic association that go beyond the local and take part in frankly conflictual politics (Skocpol 2003, 292). While Skocpol is certainly right that current democratic dilemmas require more than a retreat to local connections, she gives short schrift to the cultural, social elements of civil society. For associations do not simply connect citizens to one another, nor do they serve only to communicate citizens' needs, preferences, and desires to the powers that be. They provide a fertile context in which people can learn to think, talk, and practice citizenship.

Whether or not American democracy and the public sphere have actually realized the romantic ideals to which nostalgic treatments look back (Putnam 2000; Ehrenhalt 1995; Schudson 1992a, 1998), we can imagine a kind of democracy in which creativity, imagination, discussion, and deliberation are the cornerstones of a vigorous public discussion about vital decisions. Whereas recent discussions about social capital and democracy have been concerned with enlarging civic life *in general*, the differences among political microcultures embedded in different civic contexts suggest that citizenship would be best served by stimulating the growth of associations that engender vigorous citizen speak (see Hart 2001; Beem 1999).

I conclude with some principles for fostering creativity and the democratic imagination:

1. *The key is access to ideas, not specific practices.* Citizens who are convinced of the importance and excitement of active citizenship will be motivated to register, vote, follow the news, and find other ways of doing citizenship. But

citizens who are goaded into practicing citizenship without access to the ideas that come from thinking and talking citizenship are less likely to form a thick democratic imagination.

2. *Simple solutions probably won't work.* Access to ideas and discussion must be accompanied by cultural changes that reduce or eliminate the desire to "avoid" politics. Citizens need to be encouraged to link everyday talk to public-sphere problems; if they think politics is boring, unapproachable, or impolite, they will not do so.

3. *Policies should target the ideas and institutions that underlie citizenship, not citizenship itself.* Policies aimed directly at underwriting citizenship will probably fail. The American public's understanding of citizenship is caught up in a toxic cycle. Government and public policy seem foreign, unapproachable, and inscrutable. Citizens and the media "read" and reinforce this image of the citizen as powerless and unable even to understand the actions of government. Citizens learn that they are uninterested in active citizenship. They will therefore not attend forums, discussions, and other events that they perceive as "political."

4. Evaluating the success of measures designed to generate creativity is very difficult. Therefore, *measures designed to generate creativity need enough time, space, and flexibility to develop their own directions.* Creativity is, almost by definition, unpredictable. A creative solution to a problem is generally one that seemed far from obvious when the problem arose. Policies and projects that aim to underwrite creative citizenship, therefore, must accept the possibility that their outcome cannot be determined in advance. Furthermore, the time frame for such outcomes is long—measured, probably, in years.

5. *A strong program for building the democratic imagination should engage citizens' interests and emotions along with their information-processing capacities.* We have seen that citizens use all the resources at their disposal to form responses to political situations: narratives, both fictional and true, personal stories, radical doubt and cynicism, morality, interests, and more. They process these messages in many different ways. A policy to bolster the democratic imagination should take seriously the power of fiction (including television), news, and other mass media as forms of public interaction, along with the political microcultures I have considered here.

The main message of this book, though, is not a recipe for public policy. It is a plea for conceptualizing democratic citizenship in all its nuance and self-contradiction, and for recognizing the democratic potential of creativity. Public policy—as promulgated both by government and by public institutions like schools, workplaces, and media—matters, and these institutions can be a part of democratic revival. Citizenship is a lively, creative, imaginative process, deeply ingrained in social life, and improving democracy depends on nurturing citizen speak.

Methodology: How Associations Mobilize

In this appendix, I detail the formal statistical models that demonstrate the points in chapter 2. The principal data source for chapter 2 is the 1990 American Citizen Participation Study (Verba et al. 1995). In addition, I use the combined 1972–98 General Social Survey (Davis and Smith 1998) to supplement the analysis. The ACPS is based on 2,517 lengthy in-person interviews done in the spring of 1990. It contains detailed information on respondents' civic and political participation, including questions about participation in twenty different kinds of civic groups. The information on political participation is especially rich, including a range of activities from voting and contacting officials to membership on community boards and involvement in protest activities. These detailed data allow us to look for complicated relationships among demographic, organizational, attitudinal, and environmental factors predicting different kinds of political participation. It has two drawbacks: first, the relatively small sample size makes analysis of important subsamples problematic; second, there may have been changes in the structure of political participation since 1990. Nevertheless, at least five other books are based in part on ACPS data (Verba, Schlozman, and Brady 1995; Nie, Junn, and Stehlik-Barry 1996; Oliver 2001; Burns, Schlozman, and Verba 2001; Walsh 2004), and we have no reason to assume that the links between civic and political participation changed dramatically between 1990 and 2000, when the research for this book took place.

The 1972–1998 cumulative General Social Survey (GSS), when pooled, provides a much larger sample size: 20,881 respondents. A substantial number of these interviews (4,984) were conducted in the years since 1990, when the ACPS interviews were completed.[1] Unfortunately, however, the 1987 sociopolitical participation module provides the only detailed data on political participation in the GSS. In addition, the categories into which the GSS divides civic participation are even less discriminating than those used in the ACPS.

In the research reported in chapter 2, I used the ACPS and GSS to determine whether some types of civic activity predict political participation better, and in different ways, than do others. To test assumptions made in the literature about civil society and political participation, I work with two hypotheses drawn from assumptions or claims made in that literature.

Hypothesis A.1 Other things being equal, citizens who participate in group-oriented activities will be more actively involved democratic citizens than their less civically involved peers.

As suggested in chapter 1, those lamenting the decline of civil society imply that participating in civic life makes people better citizens by increasing the stock of social capital available. The very act of being involved in an independent, voluntary organization should therefore increase political participation.

According to these theorists, it is involvement in civil society *in itself* that underlies democratic engagement. Therefore, we should see little difference among types of organizations in terms of their members' mobilization.

Hypothesis A.2 There will be little difference among types of civic organizations in their capacity for predicting democratic citizenship.

The purpose of the analysis in this appendix is to determine the general patterns of the relationship between civic and political participation and, thereby, to form the basis for targeting citizens to participate in focus groups.

I consider civic participation to be involvement in organized groups whose purpose is not *explicitly* to push for goals in the public sphere. Thus, while Nie, Junn, and Stehlik-Barry (1996) categorize groups as

---

1. Both of these numbers are for the GSS ballots that included the organizational membership questions. See Davis and Smith (1998) for more information.

nonpolitical only when they *never* take political stands, I exclude only those organizational types that are explicitly political. I therefore include all organization types except political issue groups, liberal or conservative organizations, and organizations involved in elections. This more open approach allows for the possibility that an organization may not be strictly political or apolitical; an organization may choose to take part in public-sphere debates on a contingent or strategic basis. Therefore, simply *ever* taking political stands should not disqualify an organization from being treated primarily as a civic group. Since I do not combine these organizational memberships into a single variable as in Nie, Junn, and Stehlik-Barry (1996), this relatively broad inclusion of organizational memberships should not introduce error into the results.

Table A.1 contains the lists of organization types, as they were presented to survey respondents, for each of the surveys. Respondents in each survey can be (and often are) members of more than one type of organization; for example, a single respondent may be a member of a civic organization, a labor union, and a religious organization. Respondents can also belong to several organizations of the same type, which would be impossible to discern from the data.

In addition to the organization types in the ACPS, I added a dummy variable for membership in a church or synagogue by recoding separate questions about membership and attendance at church or synagogue. Respondents who were members of a church or synagogue and usually attended that church or synagogue when they went to services were coded as being church or synagogue members. This allows for direct comparison with the other organizational membership variables in the survey.

In both the ACPS and the GSS, income is coded in tiers, and the tiers differ between the surveys and among years in the GSS. I constructed a measure of household income by simply taking the center of each of the reported income tiers. Income for respondents in the lowest tier was set at 75 percent of the range, and for those in the highest tier, at the tier's lower limit. For example, an income category of $0–$1,000 would be set at $750, and the category $50,000 or more at $50,000.

Race and sex are coded as dummy variables. Race is interpreted as being nonwhite (0 for white race, 1 otherwise). Sex is coded as being female, that is, 1 for female and 0 for male.

I calculated two measures of political participation in the ACPS. The measure of *routine political activity* is a five-point score designed to measure relatively routine, electorally oriented political activity. Respondents

ACPS	GSS
Service clubs or fraternal organizations, such as Lions, Kiwanis, or a local women's club, or a fraternal organization at school	Fraternal groups
	Service clubs
	School fraternities or sororities
Veterans' organizations, such as the American Legion or the Veterans of Foreign Wars	Veterans' groups
Groups affiliated with [the respondent's] religion, such as the Knights of Columbus or B'nai B'rith	Church-affiliated organizations
Organizations representing [the respondent's] own particular nationality or ethnic group, such as the Polish-American Congress, the Mexican-American Legal Defense and Education Fund, or the National Association for the Advancement of Colored People	Nationality groups
Organizations for the elderly or senior citizens	
Organizations mainly interested in issues promoting the rights or welfare of women, such as the National Organization for Women, the Eagle Forum, or the American Association of University Women	Political clubs
Organizations active on one particular political issue, such as the environment, abortion (on either side), gun control (again on either side), consumers' rights, the rights of taxpayers, or any other issue	
Nonpartisan or civic organizations interested in the political life of the community or the nation, such as the League of Women Voters or a better-government organization	
Organizations that support general liberal or conservative causes, such as the Americans for Democratic Action or the Conservative Caucus	
Labor unions	Labor unions
Other organizations associated with [the respondent's] work, such as a business or professional association, or a farm organization	Farm organizations
	Professional or academic associations
Youth groups, such as the Girl Scouts or the 4-H	Youth groups
Literary, art, discussion, or study groups	Literary, art, discussion, or study groups
Hobby clubs, sports or country clubs, or other groups or clubs for leisure time activities	Sports groups
	Hobby or garden clubs
Associations related to where [the respondent] lives—neighborhood or community associations, homeowners' or condominium associations, or block clubs	
Organizations that provide social services in such fields as health or service to the needy, such as a hospital, a cancer or heart drive, or a group like the Salvation Army that works for the poor	
Educational institutions: local schools, [the respondent's] own school or college, or organizations associated with education, such as school alumni associations or school service organizations like the PTA	School service groups
Organizations that are active in providing cultural services to the public, such as museums, symphonies, or public radio or television	
Other organizations	Other organizations

Source: ACPS (Verba et al. 1995); GSS (Davis and Smith 1998).

received one point for working on a campaign in 1988; one for being registered to vote; one for voting in "most" or "all" presidential elections since having been old enough; one for voting in most or all local elections since having been old enough; and one for attending a meeting of a local government board or council in the previous 12 months. I also reproduced the measure used by Nie, Junn, and Stehlik-Barry (1996, 208) for participation in "difficult political activities." This four-point additive measure consists of one point for each of the following: contacting public officials; working for political campaigns; being a member of or attending meetings of a local board; and engaging in other informal political activity. I did this in order to capture the kind of "democratic citizenship" I want to consider. This is superior to simply capturing voting behavior for the following reasons:

- Voting is the least "public" of all forms of political activity except simple exit.
- Voting is the least costly of virtually all forms of political activity; thus, the incentive structure for voting is likely to differ from those for other forms of citizenship.
- Social desirability bias is likely to be higher for the generally normative act of voting (Abelson, Loftus, and Greenwald 1992; Silver, Anderson, and Abramson 1986; Presser 1990) than for less-common forms of citizenship. That makes it more likely that we will capture real citizenship activity than inflated estimates.

The two crucial intervening variables in this model are *civic skills* (see Verba, Schlozman, and Brady 1995, chap. 11) and *political efficacy*. Civic skills is an eight-point scale consisting of one point for each of four skills (writing a letter, attending a meeting, planning a meeting, and giving a speech) plus one additional point for each of these skills used in more than one setting (church, work, or organization).[2] *Efficacy* is also an eight-point scale. For each of four elements, one point was awarded for answering that the respondent felt "some" efficacy, and two points were awarded for answering that the respondent felt "a lot." The elements of efficacy are whether the respondent felt she could have influence on local government

2. Verba, Schlozman, and Brady (1995, 559–61) use a somewhat different scale, adding the four skills in each of the contexts to come up with a twelve-point scale. I have elected to flatten the curve slightly by awarding only one point for each skill used in two or more contexts, since this more directly represents the concept that these skills are generic and transferable (Verba, Schlozman, and Brady 1995, 312–13).

decisions; whether she felt local government officials would pay attention to her concerns; whether she could have influence on national government decisions, and whether national government officials would pay attention to her concerns.

I use a combination of ordinary least-squares (OLS) regression analysis and path analysis to address these issues. First, to test the contribution of membership in each civic organization type to both the routine and difficult political activity measures described above, I use the dummy variables for involvement in each organization type as the independent variables and the measures of political activity as the dependent variables. I include civic skills and efficacy in the equations to allow for separating the direct effects of organizational membership from those mediated by civic skills and efficacy. Finally, I use the organizational membership variables as predictors of civic skills and efficacy to complete the path model. I do a similar analysis with GSS data, using only voting in the immediately previous election as the dependent variable,[3] since there is no more political participation information available in multiple years of the GSS.

I then proceed to use path analysis to illustrate the causal models. These models estimate the relationships among civic participation, efficacy, civic skills, and political engagement. Path models allow for testing and presenting each pathway clearly and separating these connections from each other (Fischer 1975; Duncan 1966; Blalock 1964). These models underscore the direct influence of involvement in nonpolitical civic activities on political participation as well as the same relationship mediated through two other variables: efficacy and civic skills.

All the results for the ACPS data use the weight variable designed to represent the population of the original fifteen thousand telephone interviews that formed the basis of the study (Verba, Schlozman, and Brady 1995, 535–36). Since the GSS data are a representative sample to begin with, no weight is used. For each model, independent variables are flagged as significant if they meet the two-tailed test with $p < .01$. Adjusted β-scores are reported to indicate the magnitude of the variable's predictive power, and two-tailed significance scores are reported as well.

Relevant control variables are included in all the models. These are family income, age, sex, race, and years of education. As previous studies

---

3. For ease of comparison, I use OLS regression instead of logistic regression for the GSS data, even though the independent variable is dichotomous. See table A.6 for the results of a logistic regression on the GSS data. The results are substantially the same for both techniques, and the OLS method allows more direct comparison to the ACPS models.

of political participation have shown, some of these variables are highly significant by themselves; others are not. For each model, findings regarding the control variables are reported alongside the organizational predictors.[4]

The Kinds of Mobilizing Organizations

I begin by evaluating three separate connections: those between organizational membership and political participation via the routes of (a) efficacy and (b) civic skills; and directly between organizational membership and political participation. Then I combine the relationships into a single path model to estimate the total effects of organizational involvement on political participation.

Who Has Efficacy?

The strongest predictor of efficacy is education. Most group memberships are not significant predictors of efficacy. Among the types of civic organizations that independently predict their members' efficacy, churches and synagogues are the highest, followed by educational institutions, organizations interested in women's issues, and youth organizations (table A.2). Family income also significantly predicts efficacy.

Who Has Civic Skills?

By contrast, independent of the control measures, some organization types show large and significant relationships with civic skills, and some show small, but still significant, relationships. Age and sex are both significant predictors: older respondents and women had, on average, fewer civic skills than younger, male respondents. Again, education is the strongest predictor here, and family income also has a substantial, significant influence on civic skills.

Organizations whose members have slightly, but significantly, more civic skills than their peers are "other" organizations; groups concerned

---

4. Analyses in this section were performed using SPSS for Windows, version 7.0, under Microsoft Windows NT 4.0. Some basic demographic data come from the initial telephone screening interviews instead of from the in-person surveys. I am indebted to Henry Brady for his assistance in making the data available in a useful form.

160

APPENDIX A

TABLE A.2 **Predicting efficacy (OLS standardized regression coefficients)**

	Std. β	$p(H_0)$
(Constant)		0.887
Age in 1990	0.040	0.089
Education	0.142	0.000*
Family income	0.063	0.004*
Nonwhite race	−0.026	0.204
Female	−0.041	0.040
Member of service club/fraternity	−0.013	0.512
Member of veterans' organization	0.045	0.025
Member of religious group	0.042	0.032
Member of nationality/ethnic group	0.030	0.128
Member of senior citizens group	−0.021	0.359
Member of group interested in women's issues	0.054	0.006*
Member of a labor union	0.020	0.309
Member of a business, professional, or farm group	0.016	0.453
Member of a nonpartisan or civic organization	0.032	0.099
Member of a youth group	0.054	0.006*
Member of a literary/art discussion group	0.012	0.547
Member of a hobby/sports club	0.030	0.129
Member of a neighborhood or homeowners' association	−0.002	0.937
Member of a health or service organization	0.008	0.710
Member of an educational institution	0.072	0.001*
Member of a cultural organization	0.049	0.015
Member of another organization	0.031	0.106
Member of church/synagogue	0.094	0.000*

Source: ACPS (Verba et al. 1995).
*Significant at $p < .01$.

with women's issues; service groups and fraternities; literary, art, and discussion groups; educational institutions; churches and synagogues; health service groups, and youth groups. Those with large and significant relationships with political civic skills were religious organizations and business, professional, and farm groups (table A.3).

Who Participates?

THE AMERICAN CIVIC PARTICIPATION SURVEY. In the ACPS data, only two group memberships were statistically significant, direct predictors of *routine* political participation such as registering to vote and voting: (1) church or synagogue membership, which has a relatively strong and significant predictive value; and (2) neighborhood/homeowner organization membership, which has a relatively weak but nevertheless significant relationship. The bulk of routine participation is explained by demographic characteristics of individuals and by the civic skills and efficacy they bring to the political arena, developed either through organizational

TABLE A.3 **Predicting civic skills (OLS standardized regression coefficients)**

	Std. β	$p(H_0)$
(Constant)		0.000*
Age in 1990	−0.052	0.006*
Education	0.209	0.000*
Family income	0.142	0.000*
Nonwhite race	0.008	0.642
Female	−0.093	0.000*
Member of service club/fraternity	0.059	0.000*
Member of veterans' organization	0.004	0.819
Member of religious group	0.122	0.000*
Member of nationality/ethnic group	0.023	0.151
Member of senior citizens group	−0.047	0.010
Member of group interested in women's issues	0.053	0.001*
Member of a labor union	0.030	0.059
Member of a business, professional, or farm group	0.201	0.000*
Member of a nonpartisan or civic organization	0.026	0.107
Member of a youth group	0.098	0.000*
Member of a literary/art discussion group	0.061	0.000*
Member of a hobby/sports club	0.020	0.217
Member of a neighborhood or homeowners' association	0.034	0.039
Member of a health or service organization	0.091	0.000*
Member of an educational institution	0.079	0.000*
Member of a cultural organization	0.027	0.105
Member of another organization	0.050	0.002*
Member of church/synagogue	0.082	0.000*

Source: ACPS (Verba et al. 1995).
*Significant at $p < .01$.

involvements or through other channels such as the workplace or schools. Age is the most powerful predictor of routine participation, with efficacy, civic skills, and education also playing large and significant roles.

By contrast, *difficult* political activity, such as writing letters, demonstrating, and participating in collective action—the kind of participation that best represents active citizenship—has little to do with individual or demographic characteristics. Civic skills and efficacy are, again, the strongest predictors, but membership in a variety of organizations has an independent effect on the likelihood that people will take part in difficult political activities. The type of organization associated with the strongest effect is the neighborhood/homeowner organization. Seven other organizational memberships are associated with smaller but still significant effects (table A.4).

GENERAL SOCIAL SURVEY.   The GSS data do not allow for measurement of civic skills or efficacy, and the only indication of political participation they provide is whether a respondent voted in the previous presidential

TABLE A.4 **Predicting political activity (OLS standardized regression coefficients)**

	Routine participation		Difficult participation	
	Std. β	$p(H_0)$	Std. β	$p(H_0)$
(Constant)		0.000*		0.345
Age in 1990	0.283	0.000*	0.006	0.781
Education	0.117	0.000*	0.029	0.177
Family income	0.082	0.000*	0.025	0.202
Nonwhite race	−0.062	0.001*	−0.009	0.606
Female	−0.013	0.471	−0.044	0.015
Efficacy	0.141	0.000*	0.169	0.000*
Civic skills	0.124	0.000*	0.173	0.000*
Member of service club/fraternity	0.018	0.317	0.044	0.016
Member of veterans' organization	0.040	0.024	0.064	0.000*
Member of religious group	−0.007	0.669	0.029	0.104
Member of nationality/ethnic group	0.011	0.538	0.012	0.505
Member of senior citizens group	0.011	0.569	0.028	0.159
Member of group interested in women's issues	0.034	0.052	0.039	0.027
Member of a labor union	0.040	0.021	0.030	0.089
Member of a business, professional, or farm group	0.019	0.324	0.028	0.156
Member of a nonpartisan or civic organization	0.043	0.012	0.094	0.000*
Member of a youth group	0.020	0.258	0.089	0.000*
Member of a literary/art discussion group	0.004	0.810	0.026	0.137
Member of a hobby/sports club	0.038	0.032	0.072	0.000*
Member of a neighborhood or homeowners' association	0.056	0.002*	0.105	0.000*
Member of a health or service organization	0.036	0.045	0.074	0.000*
Member of an educational institution	0.034	0.067	0.073	0.000*
Member of a cultural organization	−0.031	0.081	0.006	0.738
Member of another organization	−0.022	0.199	−0.001	0.942
Member of church/synagogue	0.174	0.000*	0.054	0.002*

Source: ACPS (Verba et al. 1995).
*Significant at $p < .01$.

election (table A.5). Nevertheless, the large sample size and availability of data for multiple years make these data a useful source for information on civic and political participation.

As in the ACPS data, age, education, and income are the three strongest predictors of routine forms of political participation (table A.6). However, unlike the ACPS data, GSS data demonstrate that membership in several organization types also significantly predicts voting behavior. This finding suggests that civic skills and efficacy lie behind the mobilizing power of the organizations listed in the GSS data as well. The ACPS data show that these intervening variables explain most of the relationship between organizational membership and routine political participation; it is

TABLE A.5 **Predicting voting in previous election (OLS standardized regression coefficients)**

	Std. β	$p(H_0)$
(Constant)		0.000*
Years since survey taken	0.000	0.955
Income (indexed to yearly mean)	0.154	0.000*
Nonwhite race	−0.026	0.000*
Female	0.000	0.972
Age	0.249	0.000*
Education	0.125	0.000*
Member of fraternity	0.024	0.002*
Member of church group	0.105	0.000*
Member of farm organization	0.005	0.493
Member of greek organization	0.000	0.973
Member of hobby group	0.015	0.044
Member of literary group	−0.001	0.931
Member of nationality group	0.003	0.722
Member of other group	0.040	0.000*
Member of professional group	0.058	0.000*
Member of school group	0.041	0.000*
Member of service group	0.031	0.000*
Member of sports group	0.038	0.000*
Member of labor union	0.029	0.000*
Member of veterans' group	0.013	0.079
Member of youth group	0.002	0.780

Source: 1972–1998 Cumulative GSS (Davis and Smith 1998).
*Significant at $p < .01$.

therefore reasonable to expect that, if it were possible to measure these variables in the GSS, the analysis would follow a similar path. Indeed, most of the group types that predict voting behavior in the GSS predict civic skills in the ACPS data. The GSS data validate the ACPS findings, suggesting that similar types of organizations promote political participation; the ACPS's indicators of efficacy and civic skills provide insight into *how* these organizations mobilize their members.

Paths from Organizational Membership to Citizenship

Combining these results, we can generate an overall predictive model to estimate (1) the general likelihood that membership in certain organizations predicts political participation; and (2) whether such predictions are associated with organizations that promote greater civic skills or efficacy ("indirect mobilizers") or those that do not do so ("direct mobilizers").

The path model presented in figure A.1 estimates the predictive strength of five pathways that predict political participation:

TABLE A.6 **Logistic regression and OLS standardized β predictors of voting**

	R	$p(H_0)$	Std. β	$p(H_0)$
(Constant)		0.000*		0.000*
Years since survey taken	0.008	0.071	0.000	0.955
Income (indexed to yearly mean)	0.110	0.000*	0.154	0.000*
Nonwhite race	−0.008	0.070	−0.026	0.000*
Female	0.000	0.531	0.000	0.972
Age	0.220	0.000*	0.249	0.000*
Education	0.134	0.000*	0.125	0.000*
Member of fraternity	0.024	0.000*	0.024	0.002*
Member of church group	0.088	0.000*	0.105	0.000*
Member of farm organization	0.000	0.291	0.005	0.493
Member of Greek organization	0.000	0.741	0.000	0.973
Member of hobby group	0.010	0.047	0.015	0.044
Member of literary group	0.000	0.797	−0.001	0.931
Member of nationality group	0.000	0.510	0.003	0.722
Member of other group	0.035	0.000*	0.040	0.000*
Member of professional group	0.039	0.000*	0.058	0.000*
Member of school group	0.034	0.000*	0.041	0.000*
Member of service group	0.032	0.000*	0.031	0.000*
Member of sports group	0.024	0.000*	0.038	0.000*
Member of labor union	0.021	0.001*	0.029	0.000*
Member of veterans group	0.007	0.085	0.013	0.079
Member of youth group	0.000	0.883	0.002	0.780

Source: 1972–1998 Cumulative GSS (Davis and Smith 1998).
*Significant at $p < .01$.

organizational membership's influence on civic skills and efficacy and on participation directly, as well as the impact of civic skills and efficacy on political participation. Tables A.7 and A.8 present the results for routine participation and for the measure of difficult participation constructed by Nie, Junn, and Stehlik-Barry (1996). However, the discussion focuses on difficult participation because this measure differentiates among the group types more effectively than routine participation does.

The path diagram allows for a clear presentation of the causal argument: that membership in civic organizations has some effect on political participation, both directly and through two mediating variables. Each path is referred to as p_{xy}, where x is the dependent variable (the outcome to be explained) and y the independent variable (the possible explanation). Paths in a path diagram are additive; that is, the total effect of an independent or mediating variable on a dependent variable is the sum of all paths between the two. The magnitude of a path through one or more mediating variables is the multiplicative product of the individual paths that make up the combined path. For example, in figure A.1,

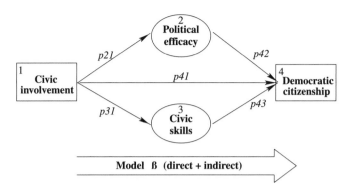

FIGURE A.1. General path model for estimations

the total effect of organizational membership (1) on political participation (4), $p(4 \mid 1)$, for cases in which all paths are statistically significant, is

$$p(4 \mid 1) = p_{41} + (p_{21} \times p_{42}) + (p_{31} \times p_{43}).$$

That is, add the direct path (p_{41}) to the sum of the product of p_{21} and p_{42} and the product of p_{31} and p_{43}.

For cases in which one or more paths are statistically insignificant, these paths are simply dropped from the model.[5] Tables A.7 and A.8 present the path estimates and model β for all organization types; for all models, $p_{42} = 0.169$ and $p_{43} = 0.173$ (table A.4).

The hypothesis that civic participation, in general, increases citizens' likelihood of participating in political life is largely confirmed. Of the eighteen nonpolitical civic organization types listed in the ACPS data, only four (nationality/ethnic groups, senior citizens' organizations, labor unions, and cultural organizations) do *not* significantly predict members' difficult political participation, the type that best approximates active citizenship. These mobilizing organizations run the gamut from such seemingly apolitical organizations as youth groups, literary discussion groups, and sports clubs to groups that are more directly oriented to the public sphere, such as social service organizations and neighborhood associations. Furthermore, no type of organization predicts a significant *decrease* in political activity of its members.

5. For more information on using and interpreting path models, see Fischer (1975); Duncan (1966); and Blalock (1964).

TABLE A.7 **Path estimates for routine political participation**

	p_{41}	$p(H_0)_{41}$	p_{21}	$p(H_0)_{21}$	p_{31}	$p(H_0)_{31}$	Model β
Member of church/synagogue	0.174	0.000*	0.094	0.000*	0.082	0.000*	0.198
Member of a neighborhood or homeowners' association	0.056	0.002*					0.056
Member of a business, professional, or farm group					0.201	0.000*	0.025
Member of a youth group			0.054	0.006*	0.098	0.000*	0.020
Member of an educational institution			0.072	0.001*	0.079	0.000*	0.020
Member of religious group					0.122	0.000*	0.015
Member of group interested in women's issues			0.054	0.006*	0.053	0.001*	0.014
Member of a health or service organization					0.091	0.000*	0.011
Member of service club/fraternity					0.059	0.000*	0.007
Member of a literary/art discussion group					0.061	0.000*	0.007
Member of another organization					0.050	0.002*	0.006
Member of veterans' organization							0.000
Member of nationality/ethnic group							0.000
Member of senior citizens group							0.000
Member of a labor union							0.000
Member of a nonpartisan or civic organization							0.000
Member of a hobby/sports club							0.000
Member of a cultural organization							0.000

Source: ACPS (Verba et al. 1995).
*Significant at $p < .01$.

TABLE A.8 **Path estimates for difficult political participation**

	p_{41}	$p(H_0)_{41}$	p_{21}	$p(H_0)_{21}$	p_{31}	$p(H_0)_{31}$	Model β
Member of a youth group	0.089	0.000*	0.054	0.006*	0.098	0.000*	0.115
Member of a neighborhood or homeowners' association	0.105	0.000*					0.105
Member of an educational institution	0.073	0.000*	0.072	0.001*	0.079	0.000*	0.099
Member of a nonpartisan or civic organization	0.094	0.000*					0.094
Member of a health or service organization	0.074	0.000*			0.091	0.000*	0.090
Member of church/synagogue	0.054	0.002*	0.094	0.000*	0.082	0.000*	0.084
Member of a hobby/sports club	0.072	0.000*					0.072
Member of veterans' organization	0.064	0.000*					0.064
Member of a business, professional, or farm group					0.201	0.000*	0.035
Member of religious group					0.122	0.000*	0.021
Member of group interested in women's issues			0.054	0.006*	0.053	0.001*	0.018
Member of a literary/art discussion group					0.061	0.000*	0.010
Member of service club/fraternity					0.059	0.000*	0.010
Member of another organization					0.050	0.002*	0.009
Member of nationality/ethnic group							0.000
Member of senior citizens group							0.000
Member of a labor union							0.000
Member of a cultural organization							0.000

Source: ACPS (Verba et al. 1995).
*Significant at $p < .01$.

A similar story emerges from the GSS data, with the exception that labor unions show a very small yet significant prediction of political activity (measured as the likelihood of having voted in the most recent presidential election). This finding may result from the fact that some of the GSS data reach further back in time. It is reasonable to expect that, prior to the decline of the labor movement as a political and economic force, unions played a larger role in mobilizing their members. Indeed, the same analysis of the GSS data for surveys taken since 1989 (the year of the ACPS) shows that labor unions' influence on voting is reduced to a very small, although still significant, level in the linear regression model ($\beta = 0.049, p = .007$), and to insignificance in the logistic regression model ($p(H_0) = 0.0173, R = .0340$). Also, since the GSS contains a far greater number of cases, a similar effect may exist in both datasets yet emerge as significant only in the GSS.

The second hypothesis does not fare as well. The idea that different types of civic involvement predict similar amounts of political participation is not supported by these data. On the contrary, the analysis here allows for dividing the organization types in the ACPS into four distinct groups:[6]

1. Those that predict political participation both directly and by predicting civic skills and/or political efficacy (the "general mobilizers"). Members of these groups are more likely to develop civic skills and confidence in the responsiveness of the public realm, and are therefore more likely to participate. In addition, a member of such an organization is more likely to participate than that a nonmember with similar levels of efficacy and civic skills.

2. Those that predict political participation only through their association with civic skills and/or efficacy (the "indirect mobilizers"). Members of these groups are also more likely to have the skills to participate in politics and confidence in the efficacy of their actions. However, membership does not independently increase their likelihood of participation. Such organizations lend their members resources for use in the public realm, but do not directly mobilize them to participate.

3. Those that predict political participation directly, but do not predict civic skills or efficacy (the "direct mobilizers"). These organizations do not increase their members' confidence in their political effectiveness, nor do they foster skills

6. Since the GSS does not allow for measures of civic skills or efficacy, it is impossible to simulate this part of the analysis using the GSS.

for use in the public sphere. Rather, they encourage members to participate *regardless of* their levels of civic skills and efficacy.

4. Those that do not predict political participation (the "nonmobilizers"). Members of these organizations are no more (but no less) likely to participate in political life than are others who have the same demographic and civic profiles.

The four "mobilizing types" and the organizations matching each type appear in chapter 2, table 2.1.

Networks versus Activities

What accounts for these differences in how civic organizations either do or do not mobilize their members? I suggest that there are two main explanations: a theory based on *connections* with other members, and a theory based on the *activities* experienced within an organization. The connection theory (see, e.g., Lin 2001) understands organizational involvement as mostly an opportunity for citizens to meet and interact with each other; what goes on in the organization is secondary to the kinds of people who belong to it. By contrast, the activities theory concentrates on the ideas and experiences a citizen encounters in the organization.

I therefore test the effects of aggregate demographic characteristics in respondents' associational networks to determine whether the role of associations in providing access to others with these characteristics is a substantial part of their mobilizing capacity. In addition, I add individual- and aggregate-level organizational joining, volunteer activities, financial donations, and civic skills to examine whether associational connections with others who are more civically involved are mobilizing factors. These are, of course, not the only characteristics of citizens' associational networks that could play a part in mobilizing them. I use these characteristics because data are available at both individual and aggregate levels and because the individual-level effects of these characteristics are well supported by extant research.

Hypotheses

My primary hypothesis in this section deals with the question of the effects on a person's political participation level of the members encountered in organizations to which that person belongs. The general hypothesis is as follows:

Hypothesis A.3 The aggregate characteristics of other people with whom an individual shares organizational memberships will have an effect on that individual's political participation that is *independent* of the individual's personal characteristics.

As a logical prerequisite to this hypothesis, I expect that the main organizational types to which a person belongs explain some of the differences between the participation levels of that person and others. This is a necessary premise for the argument that anything about group type influences individual participation. Therefore, I test the following:

Hypothesis A.4 The type of organization that an individual labels as her "main" organization will explain some of the difference in political participation between individuals.

In order to test the general hypothesis, the idea that the principal mobilizing effect of organizations arises from connecting members with other members, I look specifically at characteristics of others who may be accessed through group memberships. I test the effects on individual participation of the main members of an individual's main organization, of all members from an individual's main organization, and of all the members encountered in an individual's organizational life. Considering the three different membership groups helps us understand whether more immediate rather than more extended membership groups affect participation level. Therefore, I test three specific variants of the general hypothesis:

Hypothesis A.3a Average aggregate demographic characteristics of the main members of an individual's main organization type will explain some of the difference in political participation between individuals, net of their demographic characteristics.

Hypothesis A.3b Average aggregate demographic and civic characteristics of the members of an individual's main organization will have an effect on that person's level of political activity, net of the person's own demographic characteristics.

Hypothesis A.3c Average aggregate demographic and civic characteristics of the members of all the organizations an individual belongs to will have an effect on that person's level of political activity, net of the persons's own demographic characteristics.

For all the analyses, the outcome of interest is the measure of difficult political participation calculated by Nie, Junn, and Stehlik-Barry (1996). As independent variables, I consider eight individual-level measures—age, income, organizational joining, time spent volunteering, education, donations, civic skills, and efficacy—in addition to their counterparts at the level of organization type. In addition, I consider the respondent's gender and the proportion of members of the organization type who are female.[7]

The nine individual- and aggregate-level independent variables are as follows:

1. Age: The age of the respondent, imputed from year of birth
2. Female sex: The respondent's sex, coded 1 for female, 0 for male. For aggregate analysis, this is the proportion of members of the organization type who are female.
3. Family income: As reported by Nie, Junn, and Stehlik-Barry (1996, 199):

UNDER $10,000	1
$10,000–$19,999	2
$20,000–$29,999	3
$30,000–$39,999	4
$40,000–$49,999	5
$50,000–$59,999	6
$60,000–$79,999	7
$80,000–$99,999	8
$100,000 AND OVER	9

4. Joining tendency: The total number of organizations joined
5. Time spent: Amount of time spent on voluntary activities
6. Education: Years of education
7. Donations: Amount of money donated to church and other organizations
8. Civic skills
9. Efficacy

---

7. Some research suggests that organizational heterogeneity on these factors—exposure to alters who differ on important characteristics—may play a role. Unfortunately, because of the nesting structure of these data, I cannot meaningfully evaluate organizational heterogeneity in this study. Since I am working only with group *types*, not groups themselves, I cannot determine whether a respondent's organization was demographically heterogeneous or, alternatively, if a group type consisted of numerous, individually homogeneous, groups.

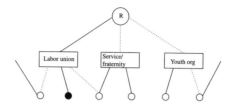

FIGURE A.2. Main Mean model

Respondents were asked which organization they volunteered the most time to, and which one they donated the most money to; they were then asked which of the two was "most important to you." That organization was identified as their "main" organization.

I suspected at the outset that results of this step might be "negative"—that is, that the connection explanation might explain little or none of the variance between organization types. To avoid missing any connection effects, I therefore implement three distinct models. Each one calculates organization-type aggregate measures differently by including different network alters in the calculation:

1. Main Mean: The mean value for those who listed the respondent's main organization type as their main organization type. In figure A.2, a hypothetical respondent is labeled "R." A labor union is her "main" organization (represented by a solid line), and she is also a member of a service/fraternity organization and a youth group (represented by dotted lines). Alters whose characteristics are included in the calculation of the mean are represented as darkened circles; those not included in the calculation are represented as white circles. R's main mean age is set at 40.5, which is the mean age of respondents whose main organization was a labor union. This model tests hypothesis A.3a.

2. Mean: The mean value for *all members* of the organization type labeled by a given respondent as her "main" organization. Extending the previous example, R's organizational mean age is set to 42.2, the mean age for all labor union members (fig. A.3). This model tests hypothesis A.3b.

3. Network Mean: The mean value for all members of all organization types to which the respondent belongs (fig. A.4). For example, R receives a score of

$$\overline{ag}_{lu,sc,yg} = \frac{49.2 + 42.2 + 40.8}{3} = 44.07$$

for *network mean age*. This model tests hypothesis A.3c.

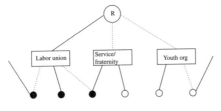

FIGURE A.3. Mean model

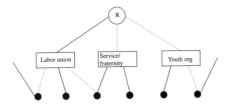

FIGURE A.4. Network Mean model

For the Main Mean model, individual respondents can be appropriately conceived as "nested" within organizations, since we disregard networks arising from memberships in organizations other than the main
one. I therefore use hierarchical linear modeling (HLM; see Raudenbush
and Bryk 2002; Singer 1998) to analyze this model. HLM is a statistical
technique that allows me to determine the extent of the influence of the
groups in which individuals are situated. For example, educational researchers use HLM to determine the importance of classrooms, schools,
and neighborhoods to pupils' educational success (Bryk and Raudenbush
1998; Bryk et al. 1997). I conceptualize individuals as nested within organizations that are, in turn, nested within organization types (fig. A.5).

Because the available data do not include information on the specific
organizations to which respondents belong, I handle individuals as nested
within organizational *types*. I treat individuals as nested only within the
organization type they listed as their main involvement; other memberships are not included. (This assumption is necessary for the construction
of an HLM.) This method allows me to estimate the contribution of organizations to the overall variance in a person's participation.[8] I include
predictors at the level of the individual and the organization type. Individual values are centered on their appropriate group means but remain in

8. Models were run in SAS (Singer 1998) and verified using R (R Development Core
Team 2003; Pinheiro and Bates 2000).

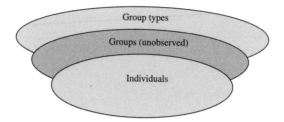

FIGURE A.5. Individuals nested within (unobserved) organizations, nested in turn within organizational types

the original measurement units, following Raudenbush and Bryk (2002, 31–35).

To analyze broader networks—all members of the individual's main organization type (the Mean model) and all members of an individual's potential organizational network (the Network Mean model)—I use more familiar general linear models (GLMs). For these groups, the assumption of strict nesting is untenable. Individuals often belong to more than one organization type, and the number of potential combinations makes HLM solutions to this problem (e.g., Raudenbush and Bryk 2002, 373–98) impractical.

Like the Main Mean model, the Mean and Network Mean models also include individual and aggregate predictors. Essentially, in these models I consider the characteristics of the groups of which individuals are members as individual characteristics. For example, I consider a member of a labor union as belonging to a group with a mean age of 42.2 (Iversen 1991; see also Huckfeldt and Sprague 1993).[9] The Mean and Network Mean models include interaction terms for each individual-aggregate variable pair. These interaction terms allow for the possibility that individual or aggregate characteristics may change the way the others operate. For example, belonging to a generally high-income organization may reduce the impact of an individual's family income on her political participation. If this were true, the effect of the interaction term between individual family income and organizational family income would be significant and negative.

9. Because of the unobserved nesting in the data (fig. A.5), and the fact that the data are nested conceptually and not by sampling design, I do not expect correlated errors to be a significant problem. Since the Mean and Network Mean approaches cannot be captured under the assumption of pure hierarchy required for HLM, and I do not believe correlated error terms to be are a substantial problem, I proceed with GLMs for the remaining analyses.

Do Citizens' Contacts Mobilize Them?

I begin by presenting the results for a preliminary model. This model treats individuals as nested within organization types, as in figure A.5. Unlike the Main Mean model, though, it does not include data for any individual or organizational variables. This allows me to estimate the total variance in political participation attributable to main organization type. I then add information about individual respondents to estimate its effects.

The findings for the Main Mean model show the effect of main organizational type and the effect of the main members of that organization type on participation. Then I turn to the Mean model, which analyzes the effects of all members of the main organization type. Finally, I present results of the Network Mean model, which includes data from all members of all organization types of which the respondent is a member.

The first, preliminary, model is called an "unconditional" model: I do not include any individual or organization-level predictors. This model allows me to test the hypothesis that the type(s) of organization(s) to which citizens belong matters for their participation. The first column of table A.9 presents this model. While most of the difference in level of political activity is due to individual-level differences, an individual's main organization does explain some political participation. Organizational type explains nearly 4 percent of the overall variance in participation in difficult political acts, as is seen in the intraclass correlation (ICC, referred to as ρ) of .038. The ICC represents the proportion of total variance in political participation that can be accounted for by differences between organization types: $0.043/(1.078 + 0.043)$.

Besides the statistical significance ($p = .022$) of the between-organizations random effects, the ICC is a substantively important effect, particularly since organizational *types* are much broader than actual organizations, so we may expect them to incorporate much more variability within the grouping. Overall, hypothesis A.4 is supported, in that some of the difference (4 percent) in political participation level is attributable to organization type.

The next model builds on the first by adding several individual-level variables as predictors of difficult political participation (column 2 of table A.9): age, sex, education, and income. These effects represent individual-level relationships across the organization types.[10] The individual

---

10. This model does not include random slopes, which would provide estimated variance in these coefficients across groups. I ran a model with random slope coefficients, but the

TABLE A.9 **Organization-type and individual effects on difficult political participation (hierarchical linear model)**

	Random intercept model (N = 1,810)	With individual fixed effects (N = 1,783)	With organizational fixed effects (N = 1,783)
Random effects			
Organization	0.043*	0.049*	0.009
	(.022)	(.025)	(.009)
Individual	1.078***	0.994***	0.994***
	(.036)	(.033)	(.033)
ICC (ρ)	0.038	0.047	0.009
Individual demographics			
Age		0.004***	0.004*
		(.002)	(.002)
Female		−0.162***	−0.168***
		(.048)	(.048)
Education		0.070***	0.070***
		(.010)	(.010)
Income		0.071***	0.071***
		(.013)	(.013)
Organization-type demographics			
Age			−0.006
			(.008)
Female			0.791*
			(.320)
Education			0.039
			(.070)
Income			0.180
			(.150)
Intercept	0.878***	0.963	0.958***
	(.060)	(.067)	(.052)

$N_2 = 17$ organization types (nesting units).
* $p < .05$; *** $p < .001$ (two-tailed tests).

characteristics should explain away some of the variation in political participation between individuals within group types. Including these effects does lower the individual-level random effects, that is, the variation in participation due to individual differences. Comparing this conditional model to the previous, unconditional model, we see that the amount of within-organization-type variance in political activity that is explained by the four demographic variables combined is approximately 7.8 percent.

---

variance of all the slopes was zero. Therefore, this model's coefficient estimates are good estimates of the relationship between the individual demographics and difficult political activity for the whole population.

Additionally, each of the individual fixed effects is significant at the $p <$ .001 level. The estimated average β coefficients for the relationship of age, sex, education, and income to difficult political activity are .004, −.162, .070, and .071, respectively. People who are older, more highly educated, and who have higher incomes tend to be more politically active. Women seem less likely to participate, with an average of .162 fewer political acts than men, after controlling for the other variables.

The importance of the main organization type is maintained in this model as well. The organization-level random effects have increased to .049 and remain significant ($p < .05$) in this model, indicating that organization types do differ significantly with regard to their members' average participation in difficult political activity. In fact, an individual's main organizational type explains *more* of the variation in such participation (approaching 5 percent of the variation) once these individual-level predictors are taken into account.

The estimated organization-type mean difficult activity score, controlling for all four individual level variables, is 0.96; individuals engage in, on average, just under one difficult political act across the organizational types, controlling for age, sex, education, and income.

The next model, presented in column three of table A.9, again builds on the random intercept model, but this time I include demographic predictors aggregated at the level of the organization type. Rather than predicting political participation only by individual characteristics, I look for explanations of participation based on the other members encountered through the main organization.

As with the model with individual-level demographics, I expect the added organization-member demographics in this model to account for some of the variation in participation due to organization type. And the between-organization variance does drop markedly, from .043 in the unconditional model to .009 in this model. Almost all of the organization-level variation in difficult political participation is removed by the inclusion of membership characteristics. That these characteristics "explain" the variation is not a definitive conclusion, however. In fact, only one of the organization-level predictors (percentage female) is significant in this model. Overall this model provides weak support for hypothesis A.3a, that organization-level demographics predict difficult political participation.

I now turn to the GLM analyses to estimate the Mean and Network Mean models. For these models, I do not make the assumption of

TABLE A.10 **Predicting political participation: aggregate and individual predictors**

Variable	Main ($N = 1{,}908$) β	Network ($N = 1{,}670$) β
Interaction terms		
R's age × mean age	.001***	.000
R female × percent female	.005	.004
R's income × mean income	−.049	.019
Orgs R joined × Mean orgs joined	.007	.001
Hrs R worked × Mean hours worked	.000	.000
R's education × Mean education	−.052**	−.010*
R's donation × Mean donation	.000*	.000**
R's civic skills × Mean civic skills	−.011	−.008
R's efficacy × Mean efficacy	.001*	.000*
Individual-level predictors		
Age	−.049***	.000
Female	−.300	−.269
Income	.270	−.077
Orgs joined	−.004	.040
Hours worked	.000	.000
Education	.742**	.146*
Money donated	−.000**	.000***
Civic skills	.125	.125**
Efficacy	−.003*	−.004
Organization-level predictors		
Org mean age	−.007***	.022
Org percent female	−.017*	−.004
Org mean income	.498*	.213
Org mean orgs joined	.089	−.094
Org mean hrs worked	.004*	.000
Org mean education	.694**	.003
Org mean donation	−.000	.000
Org mean civic skills	−.186	−.084
Org mean efficacy	−.030	.002
Intercept	−7.569*	−1.080
Adjusted R^2	.217	.201

$^*p < .05;\ ^{**}p < .01;\ ^{***}p < .001.$

straightforward nesting represented in figure A.5. Rather, I consider the fact that many individuals are members of more than one organization type. Results for these models appear in table A.10. The first of these considers the mean values of characteristics of *all members* of the given respondent's main organization (hypothesis A.3b). Interaction terms are included for each individual- and aggregate-level pair. Using the Mean model, six organizational and four interaction terms are significant predictors of political participation. In addition, individual age, education, donations, and political efficacy are significant predictors.

Independent of individual characteristics, several characteristics of organization memberships—including mean age, income, and education, as well as sex distribution—predict members' political participation. Of these, mean age, mean hours worked, and sex distribution have quite small effects. Organizational mean education is significant and strong, as is mean income. Although four interaction terms—age, education, donations, and efficacy—are also significant, their effects are quite small. Interestingly, the interaction between individual and organizational education is *negative*, suggesting that the effect of individual education on participation is reduced by participation in high-education groups. As in most analyses of political participation, individual age and education are significant predictors.

Interestingly, family income drops out of the equation when controlling for interactions between other individual characteristics and organizational characteristics. *Organizational* mean income is a significant predictor of political participation, suggesting that the positive impact of family income on participation may be mediated by participation in higher-income organizations. Organizations of active participants—those who spend more time working on volunteer activities—are also weakly but significantly associated with political participation.

These results provide weak support for hypothesis A.3b. Several aggregate characteristics of organizations are significant predictors of their members' political participation, but few are strong enough to support the theory that organizational networking is the main mechanism for associations' political mobilization.

Finally, I consider the mean values of all organizations in which each respondent is involved (hypothesis A.3c). This analysis takes the broadest approach to capturing all network effects that could play a role in predicting participation. This sensitivity, however, introduces the possibility that specious results will prove statistically significant and also that the influence of significant network access will be "masked" by numerous insignificant network ties. Since all memberships are considered equally, this model cannot discern the relative importance of networks a respondent encounters through different organizational memberships. Including all possible ties arising from memberships appears to mask potentially important main-organization ties, since several significant predictors in the more restricted model lose significance here.

When considering the mean of all organizational memberships, only three non-individual characteristics—and no organizational-level ones—emerge as significant predictors of political participation. These are the interaction terms for education, money donated to organizations, and political efficacy. All three interaction terms, while statistically significant, are very small in magnitude. Most of the other estimates are smaller than their counterparts in the Main Mean model, as is the model's overall R^2. Again, this model provides weak support for hypothesis A.3c.

The Main Mean, Mean, and Network Mean models revealed little evidence that the social networks to which individuals connect through organizations have a significant impact on their political participation (hypotheses A.3a–A.3c). Indeed, no single predictor was significant in all three analyses, and only the interaction term between individual and organizational education was significant in two of the three analyses. No organization-level predictor was significant in more than one analysis.

The Network Mean analysis, which included the widest potential network effects by averaging all organizations of which respondents were members, showed the fewest significant predictors. This suggests that, although many individuals are members of several groups (the mean number of organizations joined is 4.0), the organization to which they feel most closely connected is responsible for most of the effect on participation.

Since so few predictors at the level of the organization type are significant, these data offer little support for the network and social capital explanations that the mobilizing power of civic organizations is principally a matter of the other individuals encountered through such organizations. Because of the relative scarcity of data about individuals encountered, this finding cannot be interpreted as conclusive evidence that networks of individual members are *unimportant*. Further research, with more fine-grained data, is needed to examine the relative importance of individual and organizational pieces of the mobilization puzzle.

Methodology: Focus Group Research

B etween March and June 2000, I conducted focus groups in four civic organizations of each of five types: Presbyterian churches (chosen to represent mainline Protestant churches; see Steensland et al. 2000), Catholic churches, labor unions (one manufacturing union, two service unions, and one white-collar union), business organizations (such as local Chambers of Commerce), and organized sports groups (two bowling leagues, one softball team, and one cycling club). The organizations were all based in southern Alameda County, California.

Unlike typical focus group research (Morgan 1997), mine was intended to measure the effect on political talk of political microcultures *in actually existing groups*. Each focus group therefore contained members of only one specific organization. I recruited participants by contacting the organizations of which they were members and arranging to make an announcement in a meeting or newsletter requesting participants. The announcements offered an "interesting discussion" and promised no sensitive or embarrassing topics. Prospective participants were told no more about the project before they began participation. Although group leaders (e.g., ministers, union officials, etc.) assisted by facilitating the announcements, they were not allowed to recruit for, participate in, or observe the focus groups, so as to minimize the effect of status inequality on group dynamics.

Participants were paid $35 for their involvement and were provided with refreshments. Most (fifteen) of the groups were held in rooms associated with the groups, such as church meeting rooms or union halls. However, in the five cases when groups had no suitable meeting space, the meetings were held in neutral spaces. These arrangements were designed to minimize selection bias; however, selection bias remains an unmeasured source of bias. Participants, that is, may be more interested in discussion in general than are other members of their groups. The payment, easy logistics, and vague recruitment announcement mitigate selection bias by reducing the costs of participation, increasing the benefits, and disconnecting the content of the discussion from the decision process.

For demonstrating this study's central argument—the importance of political microcultures in structuring political talk—these focus groups are an excellent data source. However, given the small number of groups and the possible selection biases, general properties of the group types (characteristics of Presbyterian churches, for example, vis-à-vis labor unions) should be inferred with caution.

I chose the types of organizations for this study based on differences in the kinds and amounts of political activity with which they were associated, as well as their theoretical relevance (see Verba, Schlozman, and Brady 1995 on churches and unions, and Putnam 1995a, 2000 on sports groups). Table B.1 summarizes the demographic breakdown of the focus groups.

I presented each of these focus groups with the same series of four scenarios designed to probe variations in their approaches to political problems. To come up with the four scenarios I eventually used, I generated a list of twenty potential scenarios by searching national newspaper archives. I tested these twenty candidate scenarios by administering a questionnaire about each one to a group of test subjects. In addition to background questions, they were asked to rate each scenario on several dimensions:

- This issue seems interesting to me.
- This issue seems important to me.
- This issue seems too petty for me.
- This issue seems beyond my control.
- This issue affects me personally.
- I could have an impact on this issue.
- I feel I understand the issue.
- How *local* do you consider this situation to be?
- How *big* do you consider the issue to be?

These test subjects answered the questions online and were paid 50 cents per scenario, for a total of up to $10 per subject. I chose four of these scenarios to present to the focus groups, on the basis of the consistency

TABLE B.1 Profile of focus group participants

	Group size	Mean age	Race (%)					Education (%)					Income (%)							Marital status (%)					Mean org types joined
			White	Black	Hispanic	Asian	Other	< High school	High school	Some college	Finished college	Postgraduate education	< $15,000	$15,000–<25,000	$25,000–$40,000	$40,000–$55,000	$55,000–$70,000	$70,000–$100,000	> $100,000	Single	Married	Divorced	Widowed	Remarried	
Business organizations																									
B1	4	55	100							25	25	50			25			25	25		100				3.5
B2	5	52	100							40	40	20			25	25		20	20		80		20		4.4
B3	6	38.8	60	20		20				67	33						60	33	33	33	50	17			2.8
B4	6	51.3	83		17					33	33	33		17	17		17				50	33	17		5.3
Catholic churches																									
C1	7	50.3	29		71				14	57	29				17	50	33				57	29			3.9
C2	5	42.8	80			20		20	20	20	40		25					25		40	40	20			4.0
C3	6	58.5	33	17		50			50	50					33		66				60	20	20		3.7
C4	7	49.9	33		50	17		17	33	17		33	17	17	17		33	17			50	33	17		3.9
Protestant churches																									
P1	9	48.7	89			11				22		88			43	11		22	44	11	56	22			3.7
P2	7	64.4	100						14	29		57			17	29	14	14			60	20	20		6.6
P3	6	58	100							50		50					33	50		17	83				5.0
P4	6	45.8		100						50	17	33		17			17		33		17	67	17		4.0
Sports groups																									
S1	7	61	100					29	43		14	14			66	17		17			86			14	3.1
S2	8	70.1	87	13				13	38	38	13				13	25	13	13			63			38	4.0
S3	13	32.5	54	15	23		8		31	31	23	15			25	17	25	8	25	46	46			8	3.5
S4	8	56.8	86			14			13		38	50			13	38	38	13		13	75		13		4.6
Labor unions																									
U1	9	38.1	44	22	22	11			25	75						33	33	22	11	11	56	33			0.9
U2	7	33.9	57		29	14					14	86			17	17	33	17	17	29	43	29			3.3
U3	10	46.8	70		30				10	80	10				10	20	30	30	10	20	50	30			2.7
U4	7	33.7	14	14	57	14			29	43	29				29	43	14	14		57	43				3.1
Overall	7	48	65	10	16	8	<1	4	17	37	20	22	1	4	16	18	22	17	14	16	55	17	7	2	3.7

Note: Totals may not sum to too 100 percent because of rounding and missing data.

of respondents' answers to the testing survey and on the theoretical relevance of the topics. I looked particularly for scenarios that test subjects rated at the extremes of theoretically important axes ("local" vs. "distant" and "big" vs. "little" issues) and those for which most respondents understood the issue similarly.

Upon their arrival, focus group participants filled out a short questionnaire containing questions about demographics, political ideas, and organizational affiliations. They filled these out individually, before any group discussion began. The group was then gathered at a table or in a meeting room and asked to address the scenarios, first by deciding whether they would want to get involved in the situation and then, if so, by deciding what they would do about it. Groups were asked to try to come to agreement but told that they could move on if they were unable to do so. The following introduction is typical:

MODERATOR: What I'm going to do is give you, as a group, four scenarios that could face your community. They're not scenarios that have faced this community, but they're all ones that have faced other communities elsewhere. . . . What I'd like you to do with these scenarios is discuss among yourselves and decide first of all if it's an issue that you would like to get involved in. . . . And then, if so, what would you want to do about the issue. And I would like you to try to convince one another that your approach to this is right. Either that you think it's not important and they also should think it's not important, or you think that it is important and they also should see it as important. . . . I have a lot more information about each scenario, and so what you should do as well is, as you're deciding is this something you'd like to get involved in and what would you like to do about it, you should ask me questions about the surrounding details and information about the scenario. And I will tell you as much as I can about each one. (P3)

I moderated all focus groups, and I transcribed the proceedings of each focus group into a text file. The files were then parsed using a custom-written program to separate each group conversation into a list of discrete conversational turns (Sacks, Schegloff, and Jefferson 1974; Ford, Fox, and Thompson 1996). In this context, a turn is defined as a contiguous block of speech by a single participant; thus a turn can be as short as a single word or as long as several paragraphs.[1]

---

1. The mean turn was 39.63 words long, with a standard deviation of 56.8, and 90 percent of turns contained 106 words or fewer. The longest turn was 684 words.

I saved the data in a special file using CodeRead (Perrin 2001b). Each turn was then coded for the logics, methods, and resources used in it. The data were exported into a database containing additional information about the speakers and the groups, allowing for each turn to be linked to the person speaking and to the group context in which it was spoken.

Coding Process

In analyzing the focus groups, I paid less attention to what positions participants took on the issues than to what *logics* they used to defend and argue for their positions. I was also interested in what information the groups felt they needed to make decisions. The format of these focus groups closely followed (and was designed to mimic) a common practice in medical settings called "morning report," in which a presenter (often a resident physician) presents a case without all the information. Like my focus groups, "morning report" sessions are designed to elicit discussion about what information is *important* to request instead of assuming an environment of perfect information. When different groups asked the same question, the same answer was provided to insure comparability among the sessions.

Of course, the focus group context was often not the only group context to which participants had access. Focus group participants were members of, on average, 3.7 organizations of different types.[2] This does not include noncivic group contexts such as work, family, and school, from which citizens might derive skills and cognitive resources. If we take seriously the idea that these resources are portable, we cannot ignore this intersection of several civic backgrounds.

However, what individuals say in a group context is likely to be structured as much by what they *expect* to be effective in that context as by the resources they have at their disposal (Calhoun 1999; Goffman 1959, 223). Participants in deliberations, that is, operate within what Ferree et al. (2002, 62) call a "discursive opportunity structure." The relationship between individual participants' resources and the group context is bidirectional: groups gain resources from members' other experiences, but

---

2. This number is significantly higher than the average number of organizations—2.8—to which members belong in the American Civic Participation Survey (Verba et al. 1995). This suggests that the focus group participants had greater access to civic contexts than did average organization members.

they also constrain and structure their members' resources and how they may be used. Hypothetically, any participant might have used a different set of resources, or used them differently, in a different group context. This method, then, captures the political culture of *groups*, not the ideology of the individuals within them. I seek to minimize this concern by including individuals' group memberships in the multivariate models.

For the formal statistical models underlying chapter 7, I broke the pathways down into each of the kinds of outcome variables (codes). For each outcome variable, I considered six separate models. The full models are presented here, including equations representing them:

The Unconditional model contains no specific predictive variables; it is included only to provide an estimate of the proportion of total variance in the model attributable to the individual and group levels. This model is described as follows:[3]

$$g(c_{ijk}) = \beta_0 + v_k + u_{jk} + e_{ijk}. \tag{B.1}$$

where c refers to the distribution of the presence of a given thematic code and i, j, and k reference the first, second, and third levels of the equation—in this case, turns, speakers, and focus groups, respectively. Thus, e_{ijk} is the random intercept for level one (turns), u_{jk} is the random intercept for level two (speakers), and v_k is the random intercept for level three (focus groups). The term β_0 is the combined model's intercept.

The Scenario model adds to equation B.1 by considering the influence of the scenario under discussion at the time of a given turn:

$$g(c_{ijk}) = \beta_0 + \beta_1 \text{AIRPORT}_{ijk} + \beta_2 \text{CHEMCO}_{ijk} + \beta_3 \text{HALFIN}_{ijk}$$
$$+ \beta_4 \text{PROFILE}_{ijk} + v_k + u_{jk} + e_{ijk}. \tag{B.2}$$

The reference case here is the airport scenario. All following models include scenario as a control variable in order to hold constant the influence of the topic of discussion on the style of discussion.

The Demographic model adds several demographic variables—age, minority status, sex, level of education, and household income—about the speaker for each turn. The reference case (at the model's intercept) is a white male of age 0 who has not finished grade school and whose annual

---

3. Because the probit technique involves a transformation of the normal distribution to handle a binary outcome variable, equations are written with the left-hand side as $g(x)$. Where, for example, in a logit equation g would stand for $\log [P_{ijk}/(1 - P_{ijk})]$, in these models g is the probit estimator, sometimes written as F^{-1}.

household income is \$15,000 or less. This further complicates equation B.2; we can describe the situation as shown in equation B.3:

$$g(c_{ijk}) = \beta_0 + \beta_1\text{AIRPORT}_{0ijk} + \beta_2\text{CHEMCO}_{0ijk} + \beta_3\text{HALFIN}_{0ijk}$$
$$+ \beta_4\text{PROFILE}_{0ijk} + \beta_5\text{AGE}_{jk} + \beta_6\text{MINORITY}_{jk} + \beta_7\text{SEX}_{jk}$$
$$+ \beta_8\text{EDUCATION}_{jk} + \beta_9\text{INCOME}_{jk} + v_k + u_{jk} + e_{ijk}. \tag{B.3}$$

The Group Type model extends the Scenario model of equation B.2 by adding a group-level effect for the type of focus group in which the turn occurred, and a speaker-level effect for the speaker's *membership* in each of the four group types (the data do not allow for separating church memberships into Protestant and Catholic, so they are treated as a single variable). The reference case is a business organization group and a speaker with no memberships in any of the four types of groups.

$$g(c_{ijk}) = \beta_0 + \beta_1\text{AIRPORT}_{ijk} + \beta_2\text{CHEMCO}_{ijk} + \beta_3\text{HALFIN}_{ijk}$$
$$+ \beta_4\text{PROFILE}_{ijk} + \beta_{10}\text{PROTMEMB}_{jk} + \beta_{11}\text{CATHMEMB}_{jk}$$
$$+ \beta_{12}\text{UNIONMEMB}_{jk} + \beta_{13}\text{BUSIMEMB}_{jk} + \beta_{14}\text{SPORTSMEMB}_{jk}$$
$$+ \beta_{15}\text{GROUPTYPE}_k + v_k + u_{jk} + e_{ijk}. \tag{B.4}$$

The Full model adds dummy variables for speakers' membership in organization types represented in the focus groups (churches, business organizations, labor unions, and sports groups). The reference case is again a participant in a business organization focus group without memberships in any other of the four group types. This model separates the relative contribution of an individual's group *memberships* from that of the group *context* in which she took a conversational turn.

$$g(c_{ijk}) = \beta_0 + \beta_1\text{AIRPORT}_{ijk} + \beta_2\text{CHEMCO}_{ijk} + \beta_3\text{HALFIN}_{ijk}$$
$$+ \beta_4\text{PROFILE}_{ijk} + \beta_5\text{AGE}_{jk} + \beta_6\text{MINORITY}_{jk} + \beta_7\text{SEX}_{jk}$$
$$+ \beta_8\text{EDUCATION}_{jk} + \beta_9\text{INCOME}_{jk} + \beta_{10}\text{PROTMEMB}_{jk}$$
$$+ \beta_{11}\text{CATHMEMB}_{jk} + \beta_{12}\text{UNIONMEMB}_{jk} + \beta_{13}\text{BUSIMEMB}_{jk}$$
$$+ \beta_{14}\text{SPORTSMEMB}_{jk} + \beta_{15}\text{GROUPTYPE}_k + v_k + u_{jk} + e_{ijk}. \tag{B.5}$$

Group and Scenario Effects

Tables B.2 and B.3 show the scenario and group effects. They summarize in tabular form the analyses by group type and by scenario provided

TABLE B.2 **Conversational elements, by scenario**

	Airport	Chemco	Halfin	Profile	χ^2 $p(H_0)$
Logics ($N = 1,042$)					
Morality	.122	.491	.427	.609	<.001
Interests	.465	.317	.239	.369	<.001
Capacity	.366	.106	.359	.111	<.001
Methods ($N = 599$)					
Public	.765	.817	.316	.604	<.001
Private	.157	.040	.010	.180	<.001
Government	.151	.159	.719	.369	<.001
Resources ($N = 365$)					
Doubt	.000	.221	.071	.028	<.001
Narrative	.976	.640	.536	.695	<.001

TABLE B.3 **Conversational elements, by group type**

	Protestant	Catholic	Business	Union	Sports	χ^2 $p(H_0)$
Logics ($N = 1,042$)						
Morality	.485	.502	.463	.425	.420	<.001
Interests	.400	.295	.360	.306	.379	<.001
Capacity	.146	.196	.229	.244	.208	<.001
Methods ($N = 599$)						
Public	.656	.595	.479	.630	.620	<.001
Private	.104	.037	.085	.138	.093	.052
Government	.323	.429	.479	.326	.333	<.001
Resources ($N = 365$)						
Doubt	.020	.000	.074	.039	.228	<.001
Narrative	.569	.901	.676	.803	.570	<.001

in chapter 7. The tables include chi-square (χ^2) tests of significance for differences between group types and between scenarios on each code. The unit of analysis is the turn, as described in the introductory paragraphs of chapter 7. I make no attempt in this analysis to partition the variance in the use of each conversational element to individuals and groups. Elsewhere, I have used hierarchical linear probit models to do that. Interested readers should see Perrin (2005b) for that analysis.

References

Abelson, Robert P., Elizabeth F. Loftus, and Anthony G. Greenwald. 1992. "Attempts to Improve the Accuracy of Self-Reports of Voting." In *Questions about Questions: Inquiries into the Cognitive Bases of Surveys*, ed. Judith M. Tanur, 138–53. New York: Russell Sage Foundation.

Ackerman, Bruce, and James S. Fishkin. 2004. *Deliberation Day*. New Haven, CT: Yale University Press.

Adorno, Theodor W. 2005. "Opinion Research and Publicness" (*Meinungsforschung und Öffentlichkeit*). Trans. Andrew J. Perrin and Lars Jarkko. *Sociological Theory* 23:116–23. Orig. pub. 1964.

Aldrich, Howard. 1999. *Organizations Evolving*. Thousand Oaks, CA: Sage.

Allen, Danielle S. 2004. *Talking to Strangers: Anxieties of Citizenship since Brown v. Board of Education*. Chicago: University of Chicago Press.

Ansolabehere, Stephen, and Shanto Iyengar. 1995. *Going Negative: How Attack Ads Shrink and Polarize the Electorate*. New York: Free Press.

Arendt, Hannah. 1972. *Crises of the Republic*. New York: Harcourt, Brace, Jovanovich.

Aristotle. 1961. *Poetics*. Trans. S. H. Butcher. New York: Hill and Wang.

Arnold, R. Douglas. 1990. *The Logic of Congressional Action*. New Haven, CT: Yale University Press.

Austin, John Langshaw. 1962. *How to Do Things with Words*. Oxford: Oxford University Press.

Barabas, Jason. 2004. "How Deliberation Affects Policy Opinions." *American Political Science Review* 98:687–701.

Bearman, Peter S., and Katherine Stovel. 2000. "Becoming a Nazi: A Model for Narrative Networks." *Poetics* 27:69–90.

Becker, Howard S. 1974. "Art as Collective Action." *American Sociological Review* 39:767–76.

———. 1982. *Art Worlds*. Berkeley and Los Angeles: University of California Press.

Beem, Christopher. 1999. *The Necessity of Politics: Reclaiming American Public Life*. Chicago: University of Chicago Press.

Belenky, Mary, Blythe Clinchy, Nancy Goldberger, and Jill Tarule. 1996. *Women's Ways of Knowing: The Development of Self, Voice, and Mind*. Tenth anniversary ed. New York: HarperCollins.

Bellah, Robert, Richard Madsen, William M. Sullivan, Ann Swidler, and Steven M. Tipton. 1986. *Habits of the Heart: Individualism and Commitment in American Life*. New York: Harper & Row.

Belsey, Catherine. 1980. *Critical Practice*. London: Routledge.

Benhabib, Seyla. 1992. "Models of Public Space: Hannah Arendt, the Liberal Tradition, and Jürgen Habermas." In Calhoun 1992, 73–98.

———. 2002. *The Claims of Culture: Equality and Diversity in the Global Era*. Princeton, NJ: Princeton University Press.

Berezin, Mabel. 1997. "Politics and Culture: A Less Fissured Terrain." *Annual Review of Sociology* 23:361–83.

Berger, Joseph, Cecilia L. Ridgeway, M. Hamit Fisek, and Robert Z. Norman. 1998. "The Legitimation and Delegitimation of Power and Prestige Orders." *American Sociological Review* 63:379–405.

Berger, Joseph, Cecilia L. Ridgeway, and Morris Zelditch. 2002. "Construction of Status and Referential Structures." *Sociological Theory* 20:157–79.

Biernacki, Richard. 1995. *The Fabrication of Labor: Germany and Britain, 1640–1914*. Berkeley and Los Angeles: University of California Press.

Blalock, Hubert M. 1964. *Causal Inferences in Nonexperimental Research*. Chapel Hill: University of North Carolina Press.

Böhm, Franz. 1955. "Geleitwort" (Introduction). In Pollock 1955, ix–xvii.

Bologh, Gary. 2000. "Learning from Populism: Narrative Analysis and Social Movement Consciousness." Paper presented at the annual meeting of the American Sociological Association, Washington, DC.

Boltanski, Luc, and Laurent Thévenot. 1991. *De La Justification: Les économies de la grandeur*. Paris: Gallimard.

Bourdieu, Pierre. 1979. "Public Opinion Does Not Exist." In *Communication and Class Struggle*. Vol. 1. *Capitalism and Imperialism*, 124–30. 2 vols. New York: International Mass Media Research Center.

———. 1990. *The Logic of Practice*. Stanford, CA: Stanford University Press.

Branch, Taylor. 1988. *Parting the Waters: America in the King Years, 1954–63*. New York: Simon & Schuster.

Brown, Penelope, and Stephen C. Levinson. 1987. *Politeness: Some Universals in Language Use*. Cambridge: Cambridge University Press.

Bryan, Frank M. 2004. *Real Democracy: The New England Town Meeting and How It Works*. Chicago: University of Chicago Press.

Bryk, Anthony S., and Stephen W. Raudenbush. 1998. "Toward a More Appropriate Conceptualization of Research on School Effects: A Three-Level Hierarchical Linear Model." *American Journal of Education* 97:65–108.

Bryk, Anthony S., Y. M. Thum, J. Q. Easton, and S. Luppescu. 1997. "Assessing School Productivity: The Case of Chicago School Reform." *Social Psychology of Education* 2:103–42.

Burns, Nancy, Kay Lehman Schlozman, and Sidney Verba. 2001. *The Private Roots of Public Action: Gender, Equality, and Political Participation.* Cambridge, MA: Harvard University Press.

Calhoun, Craig, ed. 1992. *Habermas and the Public Sphere.* Cambridge, MA: MIT Press.

————.1999. "Nationalism, Political Community and the Representation of Society: Or, Why Feeling at Home is not a Substitute for Public Space." *European Journal of Social Theory* 2:217–31.

Campbell, Andrea Louise. 2003. *How Policies Make Citizens: Senior Political Activism and the American Welfare State.* Princeton, NJ: Princeton University Press.

Cappella, Joseph N., and Kathleen Hall Jamieson. 1997. *Spiral of Cynicism: The Press and the Public Good.* New York: Oxford University Press.

Cartwright, Dorwin, and Alvin Zander. 1968. *Group Dynamics: Research and Theory.* 3rd ed. New York: Harper & Row.

Chaves, Mark. 1999. "Religious Congregations and Welfare Reform: Who Will Take Advantage of 'Charitable Choice'?" *American Sociological Review* 64:836–46.

Chaves, Mark, Mary Ellen Konieczny, Kraig Beyerlein, and Emily Barman. 1999. "The National Congregations Study: Background, Methods, and Selected Results." *Journal for the Scientific Study of Religion* 38:458–76.

Clayman, Steven E. 2004. "Arenas of Interaction in the Mediated Public Sphere." *Poetics* 32:29–49.

Clemens, Elisabeth S. 1997. *The People's Lobby: Organizational Innovation and the Rise of Interest Group Politics in the United States, 1890–1925.* Chicago: University of Chicago Press.

Cohen, Selma Jeanne. 1966. *The Modern Dance: Seven Statements of Belief.* Middletown, CT: Wesleyan University Press.

Conover, Pamela Johnston, Donald D. Searing, and Ivor M. Crewe. 2002. "The Deliberative Potential of Political Discussion." *British Journal of Political Science* 32:21–62.

Coser, Rose Laub. 1991. *In Defense of Modernity: Role Complexity and Individual Autonomy.* Stanford, CA: Stanford University Press.

Csikszentmihalyi, Mihaly. 1996. *Creativity: Flow and the Psychology of Discovery and Invention.* New York: HarperCollins.

Davis, James Allan, and Tom W. Smith. 1998. *General Social Surveys, 1972–1998.* Chicago: National Opinion Research Center [machine-readable data file].

DeBow, Ken, and John C. Syer. 1997. *Power and Politics in California.* 5th ed. Boston, MA: Allyn and Bacon.

Dekker, Paul, and Andries van den Broek. 1998. "Civil Society in Comparative Perspective: Involvement in Voluntary Associations in North America and Western Europe." *Voluntas: International Journal of Voluntary and Nonprofit Organizations* 9:11–38.

Dobbin, Frank. 1994. *Forging Industrial Policy: The United States, Britain, and France in the Railway Age*. New York: Cambridge University Press.

Dodier, Nicolas. 1993. "Review Article: Action as a Combination of 'Common Worlds.'" *Sociological Review* 41:556–71.

Duncan, Otis Dudley. 1966. "Path Analysis: Sociological Examples." *American Journal of Sociology* 72:1–16.

Durkheim, Émile. 1995. *The Elementary Forms of Religious Life*. Trans. Karen Fields. New York: Free Press. Orig. pub. 1912.

Durkheim, Émile, and Marcel Mauss. 1963. *Primitive Classification*. Chicago: University of Chicago Press.

Ehrenhalt, Alan. 1995. *The Lost City: Discovering the Forgotten Virtues of Community in the Chicago of the 1950s*. New York: Basic Books.

Eliasoph, Nina. 1996. "Making a Fragile Public: A Talk-Centered Study of Citizenship and Power." *Sociological Theory* 14:262–89.

———. 1997. "'Close to Home': The Work of Avoiding Politics." *Theory and Society* 26:605–47.

———. 1998. *Avoiding Politics: How Americans Produce Apathy in Everyday Life*. New York: Cambridge University Press.

———. 1999. "What If Good Citizens' Etiquette Requires Silencing Political Conversation in Everyday Life? Notes from the Field." Paper presented at a conference entitled "The Transformation of Civic Life," Middle Tennessee State University, Murfreesboro and Nashville, TN.

Eliasoph, Nina, and Paul Lichterman. 2002. "Culture in Interaction." *American Journal of Sociology* 108:735–94.

Eliot, George. 1885. *The Mill on the Floss*. Chicago: Belford, Clarke.

Emirbayer, Mustafa, and Ann Mische. 1998. "What Is Agency?" *American Journal of Sociology* 103:962–1023.

Erickson, Bonnie H., and T. A. Nosanchuk. 1990. "How an Apolitical Association Politicizes." *Canadian Review of Sociology and Anthropology* 27:206–19.

Fadiman, Anne. 1997. *The Spirit Catches You and You Fall Down: A Hmong Child, Her American Doctors, and the Collision of Two Cultures*. New York: Farrar, Straus, and Giroux.

Ferree, Myra Marx, William Anthony Gamson, Jürgen Gerhards, and Dieter Rucht. 2002. *Shaping Abortion Discourse: Democracy and the Public Sphere in Germany and the United States*. Cambridge: Cambridge University Press.

Fields, Karen E. 1995. "Translator's Introduction: Religion as an Eminently Social Thing." In Durkheim 1995, xvii–liii.

Fiorina, Morris P. 1999. "Extreme Voices: A Dark Side of Civic Engagement." In Skocpol and Fiorina 1999, 395–425.

Fischer, Claude S. 1975. "The City and Political Psychology." *American Political Science Review* 69:559–71.

———. 2005. "Bowling Alone: What's the Score?" *Social Networks* 27:155–67.

Ford, Cecilia E., Barbara A. Fox, and Sandra A. Thompson. 1996. "Practices in the Construction of Turns: the 'TCU' Revisited." *Pragmatics* 6:427–54.

Ford, Cecilia E., and Sandra A. Thompson. 1996. "Interactional Units in Conversation: Syntactic, Intonational, and Pragmatic Resources for the Management of Turns." In *Interaction and Grammar*, ed. Elinor Ochs, Emanuel A. Schegloff, and Sandra A. Thompson, 134–84. Cambridge: Cambridge University Press.

Forsyth, Donelson R. 1999. *Group Dynamics*. 3rd ed. Belmont, MA: Brooks/Cole; Wadsworth.

Frank, Thomas. 2004. *What's the Matter with Kansas? How Conservatives Won the Heart of America*. New York: Metropolitan Books.

Fraser, Nancy. 1989. "What's Critical about Critical Theory? The Case of Habermas and Gender." In *Unruly Practices*, 113–43. Minneapolis: University of Minnesota Press.

———. 1997. "From Redistribution to Recognition?" In *Justice Interruptus: Critical Reflections on the Postsocialist Condition*, 11–41. New York: Routledge.

Fredman, Lionel E. 1968. *The Australian Ballot: The Story of an American Reform*. Lansing: Michigan State University Press.

Friedman, Norman. 1995. "The Developing 'Middle-Position Consensus' about Contemporary American Morality and Religion." *Journal of American Culture* 18:27.

Fukuyama, Francis. 1995. *Trust: The Social Virtues and the Creation of Prosperity*. New York: Free Press.

Gamson, William A. 1992. *Talking Politics*. Cambridge: Cambridge University Press.

———. 2002. "How Storytelling Can be Empowering." In *Culture in Mind: Toward a Sociology of Culture and Cognition*, ed. Karen A. Cerulo, 187–208. New York: Routledge.

Gibson, David R. 2000. "Seizing the Moment: The Problem of Conversational Agency." *Sociological Theory* 18:368–82.

Gilligan, Carol. 1982. *In a Different Voice: Psychological Theory and Women's Development*. Cambridge, MA: Harvard University Press.

Glassner, Barry. 1999. *Culture of Fear: Why Americans Are Afraid of the Wrong Things*. New York: Basic Books.

Goffman, Erving. 1959. *The Presentation of Self in Everyday Life*. New York: Doubleday.

Gordon, C. Wayne, and Nicholas Babchuk. 1959. "A Typology of Voluntary Associations." *American Sociological Review* 24:22–29.

Greenstein, Fred I., and Sidney Tarrow. 1970. *Political Orientations of Children: The Use of a Semi-Projective Technique in Three Nations*. Sage Professional Papers in Comparative Politics, no. 1. Beverly Hills, CA: Sage.

Gruber, Howard E. 1989. "The Evolving Systems Approach to Creative Works." In *Creative People at Work: Twelve Cognitive Case Studies*, ed. Doris B. Wallace and Howard E. Gruber, 3–24. New York: Oxford University Press.

Guinier, Lani. 1994. *The Tyranny of the Majority: Fundamental Fairness in Representative Democracy*. New York: Free Press.

Gumperz, John J. 1982. *Discourse Strategies*. Studies in Interactional Linguistics, no. 1. Cambridge: Cambridge University Press.

Guttmann, Amy. 1998. "Freedom of Association: An Introductory Essay." In *Freedom of Association*, ed. Amy Guttmann, 3–32. Princeton, NJ: Princeton University Press.

Guttmann, Amy, and Dennis Thompson. 1996. *Democracy and Disagreement*. Cambridge, MA: Belknap Press of Harvard University Press.

Habermas, Jürgen. 1989. *The Structural Transformation of the Public Sphere: An Inquiry into a Category of Bourgeois Society*. Cambridge, MA: MIT Press. Orig. pub. 1962.

———. 1998a. *The Inclusion of the Other: Studies in Political Theory*, ed. Ciaran Cronin and Pablo De Greff. Cambridge, MA: MIT Press.

———. 1998b. "Reconciliation through the Public Use of Reason." In Habermas 1998a, 50–73.

Harris-Lacewell, Melissa Victoria. 2004. *Barbershops, Bibles, and BET: Everyday Talk and Black Political Thought*. Princeton, NJ: Princeton University Press.

Hart, Stephen. 2001. *Cultural Dilemmas of Progressive Politics: Styles of Engagement among Grassroots Activists*. Chicago: University of Chicago Press.

Havel, Václav. 1987. "The Power of the Powerless." In *Living in Truth*, 36–122. London: Faber and Faber.

Hendrix, Steve. 1997. "Degrees of Risk." *Backpacker Magazine*, May, 60–64.

Hirschman, Albert O. 1970. *Exit, Voice, and Loyalty: Responses to Decline in Firms, Organizations, and States*. Cambridge, MA: Harvard University Press.

Horkheimer, Max, and Theodor W. Adorno. 1972. *Dialectic of Enlightenment*. Trans. John Cumming. New York: Continuum. Orig. pub. in German in 1944.

Huckfeldt, Robert, Ken'ichi Ikeda, and Franz Urban Pappi. 2005. "Patterns of Disagreement in Democratic Politics: Comparing Germany, Japan, and the United States." *American Journal of Political Science* 49:497–514.

Huckfeldt, Robert, Paul E. Johnson, and John Sprague. 2004. *Political Disagreement: The Survival of Diverse Opinions within Communication Networks*. Cambridge: Cambridge University Press.

Huckfeldt, Robert, and John Sprague. 1993. "Citizens, Contexts, and Politics." In *Political Science: The State of the Discipline II*, ed. Ada W. Finifter, 282–303. Washington, DC: American Political Science Association.

Immigrant Workers Freedom Ride. 2003. http://www.iwfr.org.

Ingram, Helen, and Steven Rathgeb Smith, eds. 1993. *Public Policy for Democracy*. Washington: Brookings Institution Press.

Iversen, Gudmund R. 1991. *Contextual Analysis. Quantitative Applications in the Social Sciences*. Newbury Park, CA: Sage.

Jenkins, Richard. 1992. *Pierre Bourdieu*. London: Routledge.

Jepperson, Ronald L., and Ann Swidler. 1994. "What Properties of Culture Should We Measure?" *Poetics* 22:359–71.

Joas, Hans. 1996. *The Creativity of Action*. Chicago: University of Chicago Press.

Kane, Anne. 2000. "Reconstructing Culture in Historical Explanation: Narratives as Cultural Structure and Practice." *History and Theory* 39:311–30.

Kiousis, Spiro. 2001. "Public Trust or Mistrust? Perceptions of Media Credibility in the Information Age." *Mass Communication and Society* 4:381–403.

Kleinman, Sherryl. 1996. *Opposing Ambitions: Gender and Identity in an Alternative Organization*. Chicago: University of Chicago Press.

Kövecses, Zoltán. 2000. *Metaphor and Emotion: Language, Culture, and Body in Human Feeling*. Cambridge: Cambridge University Press.

Krech, David, Richard S. Crutchfield, and Egerton L. Ballachey. 1962. *Individual in Society: A Textbook of Social Psychology*. New York: McGraw-Hill.

Ladd, Everett Carll. 1999. *The Ladd Report: Startling New Research Shows How an Explosion of Voluntary Groups, Activities, and Charitable Donations Is Transforming Our Towns and Cities*. New York: Free Press.

Lakoff, George. 2002. *Moral Politics: How Liberals and Conservatives Think*. 2nd ed. Chicago: University of Chicago Press.

Lamont, Michèle. 2000a. *The Dignity of Working Men: Morality and the Boundaries of Race, Class, and Immigration*. Cambridge, MA: Harvard University Press.

———. 2000b. "The Rhetorics of Racism and Anti-Racism in France and the United States." In *Rethinking Comparative Cultural Sociology: Repertoires of Evaluation in France and the United States*, ed. Michèle Lamont and Laurent Thévenot, 25–55. Cambridge: Cambridge University Press.

Landy, Marc. 1993. "Public Policy and Citizenship." In Ingram and Smith 1993, 19–44.

Lang, Sabine. 2004. "Local Political Communication: Mobilizing Public Opinion in 'Audience Democracies.'" In *Comparing Political Communication: Theories, Cases, and Challenges*, ed. Frank Esser and Barbara Pfetsch, 151–83. Cambridge: Cambridge University Press.

Lasswell, Harold. 1936. *Politics: Who Gets What, When, How*. New York: Whittlesey House/McGraw-Hill.

Leib, Ethan J. 2004. *Deliberative Democracy in America: A Proposal for a Popular Branch of Government*. University Park: Pennsylvania State University Press.

Leighly, Jan. 1991. "Participation as a Stimulus of Political Conceptualization." *Journal of Politics* 53:198–211.

Lewin, Kurt. 1948. *Resolving Social Conflicts: Selected Papers on Group Dynamics.* New York: Harper.

Lichterman, Paul. 1996. *The Search for Political Community: American Activists Reinventing Commitment.* Cambridge: Cambridge University Press.

Lin, Nan. 2000. "Inequality in Social Capital." *Contemporary Sociology: A Journal of Reviews* 29 (6): 785–95.

———. 2001. *Social Capital: A Theory of Social Structure and Action.* Cambridge: Cambridge University Press.

Mansbridge, Jane. 1980. *Beyond Adversary Democracy.* New York: Basic Books.

Marcus, George E. 2002. *The Sentimental Citizen: Emotion in Democratic Politics.* University Park: Pennsylvania State University Press.

Marcus, George E., W. Russell Neuman, and Michael MacKuen. 2000. *Affective Intelligence and Political Judgment.* Chicago: University of Chicago Press.

Marcuse, Herbert. 1965. "Repressive Tolerance." In *A Critique of Pure Tolerance,* by Robert Paul Wolff, Barrington Moore Jr., and Herbert Marcuse, 81–117. Boston, MA: Beacon Press.

McAdam, Doug. 1982. *Political Process and the Development of Black Insurgency, 1930–1970.* Chicago: University of Chicago Press.

———. 1983. "Tactical Innovation and the Pace of Insurgency." *American Sociological Review* 48:735–54.

McAdam, Doug, Sidney Tarrow, and Charles Tilly. 2001. *Dynamics of Contention.* Cambridge: Cambridge University Press.

Merton, Robert K., Marjorie Fiske, and Patricia L. Kendall. 1956. *The Focused Interview: A Manual of Problems and Procedures.* Glencoe, IL: Free Press.

Meyer, David S. 2000. "Claiming Credit: The Social Construction of Movement Success." Paper presented at the American Sociological Association Annual Meeting, Washington, DC, 14 August.

Meyer, David S., and Nancy Whittier. 1994. "Social Movement Spillover." *Social Problems* 41:277.

Meyer, Leonard B. 1956. *Emotion and Meaning in Music.* Chicago: University of Chicago Press.

Mills, Sara. 2003. *Gender and Politeness.* Studies in Interactional Sociolinguistics, no. 17. Cambridge: Cambridge University Press.

Mische, Ann, and Philippa Pattison. 2000. "Composing a Civic Arena: Publics, Projects, and Social Settings." *Poetics* 27:163–94.

Misztal, Barbara A. 2000. *Informality: Social Theory and Contemporary Practice.* London: Routledge.

Morgan, David L. 1997. *Focus Groups as Qualitative Research.* 2nd ed. Newbury Park, CA: Sage.

Morone, James A. 1990. *The Democratic Wish: Popular Participation and the Limits of American Government.* New York: Basic Books.

Nie, Norman H., Jane Junn, and Kenneth Stehlik-Barry. 1996. *Education and Democratic Citizenship in America*. Chicago: University of Chicago Press.

Olick, Jeffrey K. 2006. "Collective Memory and Nonpublic Opinion: An Historical Note on a Methodological Controversy about a Political Problem." Forthcoming in *Symbolic Interaction*.

Oliver, J. Eric. 2001. *Democracy in Suburbia*. Princeton, NJ: Princeton University Press.

Page, Benjamin I. 1996. *Who Deliberates? Mass Media in Modern Democracy*. Chicago: University of Chicago Press.

Page, Benjamin I., and Robert Y. Shapiro. 1992. *The Rational Public: Fifty Years of Trends in Americans' Policy Preferences*. Chicago: University of Chicago Press.

Parsons, Talcott. 1974. "The Incest Taboo in Relation to Social Structure." In *The Family: Its Structure and Functions*, ed. Rose Laub Coser, 3–12. New York: St. Martin's.

Parsons, Talcott, and Gerald M. Platt. 1982. "American Values and American Society." In *On Institutions and Social Evolution: Selected Writings*, ed. Leon H. Mayhew, 327–38. Heritage of Sociology Series, ed. Don Levine. Chicago: University of Chicago Press.

Passmore, John Arthur. 2000. *The Perfectibility of Man*. 3rd ed. Indianapolis: Liberty Fund.

Perrin, Andrew J. 2001a. *Civil Society and the Democratic Imagination*. PhD diss., Dept. of Sociology, University of California, Berkeley.

———. 2001b. "The CodeRead System: Using Natural Language Processing to Automate Coding of Qualitative Data." *Social Science Computer Review* 19:213–20.

———. 2002. "Making 'Silicon Valley': Culture, Representation, and Technology at the Tech Museum." *Communication Review* 5:65–81.

———. 2005a. "National Threat and Political Culture: Authoritarianism, Anti-Authoritarianism, and the September 11 Attacks." *Political Psychology* 26: 167–94.

———. 2005b. "Political Microcultures: Linking Civic Life and Democratic Discourse." *Social Forces* 84:1049–82.

Perrin, Andrew J., Robin Wagner-Pacifici, Lindsay Hirschfeld, and Susan Wilker. 2006. "Contest Time: Time, Territory, and Representation in the Postmodern Electoral Crisis." Forthcoming in *Theory & Society*.

Persell, Caroline Hodges, Adam Green, and Kurt Seidel. 1998. "Civil Society and Economic Distress: Possible Causes and Consequences of Associational Membership." Paper presented at the annual meeting of the American Sociological Association, San Francisco, August.

Persell, Caroline Hodges, Liena Gurevich, Kurt Seidel, and Adam Green. 1998. "Economic Distress, Civil Society, and Racial Tolerance." Paper presented at the annual meeting of the American Sociological Association, San Francisco, California, August.

Peters, John Durham. 1999. *Speaking Into the Air: A History of the Idea of Communication*. Chicago: University of Chicago Press.

Pinheiro, José C., and Douglas M. Bates. 2000. *Mixed-Effects Models in S and S-Plus*. New York: Springer.

Pitkin, Hanna Fenichel. 1967. *The Concept of Representation*. Berkeley and Los Angeles: University of California Press.

Piven, Frances Fox, and Richard Cloward. 1988. *Why Americans Don't Vote*. New York: Pantheon.

Polletta, Francesca. 2002. *Freedom Is an Endless Meeting: Democracy in American Social Movements*. Chicago: University of Chicago Press.

Pollitt, Katha. 1996. "For Whom the Ball Rolls." *Nation*, 15 April.

Pollock, Friedrich, ed. 1955. *Gruppenexperiment: Ein Studienbericht*. Vol. 2 of *Frankfurter Beiträge zur Soziologie*. Frankfurt: Europäische Verlagsanstalt. Im Auftrag des Instituts für Sozialforschung, herausgegeben von Theodor W. Adorno und Walter Dirks.

Pollock, Philip H. III. 1982. "Organizations as Agents of Mobilization: How Does Group Activity Affect Political Participation?" *American Journal of Political Science* 26:485–503.

Portes, Alejandro. 1998. "Social Capital: Its Origins and Applications in Modern Sociology." *Annual Review of Sociology* 24:1.

Powell, G. Bingham. 1986. "American Voter Turnout in Comparative Perspective." *American Political Science Review* 80:17–43.

Presser, Stanley. 1990. "Can Changes in Context Reduce Vote Overreporting in Surveys?" *Public Opinion Quarterly* 54:586–93.

Putnam, Robert D. 1995a. "Bowling Alone: America's Declining Social Capital." *Journal of Democracy* 6:65–78.

———. 1995b. "Tuning In, Tuning Out: The Strange Disappearance of Social Capital in America." *PS: Political Science and Politics* 28:664–83.

———. 2000. *Bowling Alone: The Collapse and Revival of American Community*. New York: Simon & Schuster.

Raudenbush, Stephen W., and Anthony S. Bryk. 2002. *Hierarchical Linear Models: Applications and Data Analysis Methods*. 2nd ed. Advanced Quantitative Techniques in the Social Sciences, no. 1. Thousand Oaks, CA: Sage.

R Development Core Team. 2003. *R: A Language and Environment for Statistical Computing*. Vienna, Austria: R Foundation for Statistical Computing.

Regnerus, Mark D., David Sikkink, and Christian S. Smith. 1999. "Voting with the Christian Right: Contextual and Individual Patterns of Electoral Influence." *Social Forces* 77:1375–1401.

Ridgeway, Cecilia, and Chris Bourg. 2004. "Gender as Status: An Expectation States Approach." In *Psychology of Gender*, 217–41. 2nd ed. New York: Guilford Press.

Riesman, David, Nathan Glazer, and Reuel Denney. 1950. *The Lonely Crowd: A Study of the Changing American Character.* New Haven, CT: Yale University Press.

Rosenstone, Steven J., and John Mark Hansen. 1993. *Mobilization, Participation, and Democracy in America.* New York: Macmillan.

Rothbell, Gladys. 1991. "'Just a Housewife': Role-Image and the Stigma of the Single Role." In *Social Roles and Social Institutions: Essays in Honor of Rose Laub Coser,* ed. Judith Blau and Norman Goodman, 21–36. Boulder, CO: Westview Press.

Rushdie, Salman. 1990. *Haroun and the Sea of Stories.* London: Granta Books.

Sacks, Harvey, Emanuel Schegloff, and Gail Jefferson. 1974. "A Simplest Systematics for the Organization of Turn-Taking for Conversation." *Language* 50:696–735.

Samuelson, Robert J. 1996. "Join the Club." *Washington Post National Weekly Edition,* 15–21 April.

Sandman, Peter. 1986. "Explaining Environmental Risk." Washington: U.S. Environmental Protection Agency, Office of Toxic Substances. Available online at http://www.psandman.com.

Sarfatti-Larson, Magali, and Robin Wagner-Pacifici. 2001. "The Dubious Place of Virtue: Reflections on the Impeachment of William Jefferson Clinton and the Death of the Political Event in America." *Theory and Society* 30:735–74.

Scarry, Elaine. 1985. *The Body in Pain: The Making and Unmaking of the World.* Oxford: Oxford University Press.

Schattschneider, E. E. 1960. *The Semi-Sovereign People: A Realist's View of Democracy in America.* New York: Holt, Rinehart, and Winston.

Schlozman, Kay Lehman. 1994. "Voluntary Organizations in Politics: Who Gets Involved?" In *Representing Interest Groups and Interest Group Representation,* ed. William Crotty, Mildred A Schwartz, and John C Green, 67–83. Lanham, MD: University Press of America.

Schlozman, Kay Lehman, and Sidney Verba. 1979. *Injury to Insult: Unemployment, Class, and Political Response.* Cambridge, MA: Harvard University Press.

Schudson, Michael. 1992a. "Was There Ever a Public Sphere? If So, When? Reflections on the American Case." In Calhoun 1992, 143–63.

———. 1992b. *Watergate in American Memory: How We Remember, Forget, and Reconstruct the Past.* New York: Basic Books.

———. 1995. "The Politics of Narrative Form." In *The Power of News,* 53–71. Cambridge, MA: Harvard University Press.

———. 1996. "What If Civic Life Didn't Die?" *American Prospect* 25:17–20.

———. 1998. *The Good Citizen: A History of American Civic Life.* New York: Free Press.

Sewell, William H., Jr. 1992. "A Theory of Structure: Duality, Agency, and Transformation." *American Journal of Sociology* 98:1–29.

Shefter, Martin. 1994. *Political Parties and the State: The American Historical Experience*. Princeton, NJ: Princeton University Press.

Silber, Ilana Friedrich. 2003. "Pragmatic Sociology as Cultural Sociology: Beyond Repertoire Theory?" *European Journal of Social Theory* 6:427–49.

Silver, Brian D., Barbara A. Anderson, and Paul R. Abramson. 1986. "Who Overreports Voting?" *American Political Science Review* 80:613–24.

Simmel, Georg. 1910. "Sociability." In *On Individuality and Social Forms*, ed. Don Levine, 127–40. Chicago: University of Chicago Press.

———. 1950. "On the Significance of Numbers for Social Life." In *The Sociology of Georg Simmel*, ed. Kurt Wolff, 87–99. Glencoe, IL: Free Press.

Singer, Judith D. 1998. "Using SAS PROC MIXED to Fit Multilevel Models, Hierarchical Models, and Individual Growth Models." *Journal of Educational and Behavioral Statistics* 24:323–55.

Skocpol, Theda. 1996. "Unravelling from Above." *American Prospect* 25:20–25.

———. 1999. "How Americans Became Civic." In Skocpol and Fiorina 1999, 27–80. With the assistance of Marshall Ganz, Ziad Munson, Bayliss Camp, Michele Swers, and Jennifer Oser.

———. 2003. *Diminished Democracy: From Membership to Management in American Civic Life*. Norman: University of Oklahoma Press.

Skocpol, Theda, and Morris P. Fiorina, eds. 1999. *Civic Engagement in American Democracy*. Washington: Brookings Institution Press.

Smith, Christian S. 1998. *American Evangelicalism: Embattled and Thriving*. Chicago: University of Chicago Press.

———. 2003. *Moral, Believing Animals: Human Personhood and Culture*. Oxford: Oxford University Press.

Smith, Steven Rathgeb, and Helen Ingram. 1993. "Public Policy and Democracy." In Ingram and Smith 1993, 1–14.

Sobieraj, Sarah, and Deborah White. 2004. "Taxing Political Life: Reevaluating the Relationship between Voluntary Association Membership, Political Engagement, and the State." *Sociological Quarterly* 45:739–64.

Steensland, Brian, Jerry Z. Park, Mark D. Regnerus, Lynn D. Robinson, W. Bradford Wilcox, and Robert D. Woodberry. 2000. "The Measure of American Religion: Toward Improving the State of the Art." *Social Forces* 79:291–318.

Stivers, Richard. 1994. *The Culture of Cynicism: American Morality in Decline*. Oxford: Blackwell.

Swidler, Ann. 1986. "Culture in Action: Symbols and Strategies." *American Sociological Review* 51:273–86.

———. 1992. "Inequality and American Culture: The Persistence of Voluntarism." *American Behavioral Scientist* 35:606–29.

———. 2001. *Talk of Love: How Culture Matters*. Chicago: University of Chicago Press.

Swidler, Ann, and Ronald L. Jepperson. 1995. "Interpretation, Explanation, and Theories of Meaning." Paper presented at the annual meeting of the American Sociological Association, Los Angeles, California.

Tannen, Deborah. 1990. *You Just Don't Understand: Women and Men in Conversation*. New York: Morrow.

———. 1998. *The Argument Culture: Stopping America's War of Words*. New York: Ballantine.

Taylor, Charles. 2002. "Modern Social Imaginaries." *Public Culture* 14:91–124.

Taylor, Lynne. 1996. "Food Riots Revisited." *Journal of Social History* 30:483.

Teixeira, Ruy A. 1987. *Why Americans Don't Vote: Turnout Decline in the United States 1960–1984*. Westport, CT: Greenwood.

———. 1988. "Will the Real Nonvoter Please Stand Up?" *Public Opinion* 2:41–44, 59.

———. 1989. "Registration and Turnout." *Public Opinion* 12/13:56–58.

Tenn, Steven. 2005. "An Alternative Measure of Relative Education to Explain Voter Turnout." *Journal of Politics* 67:271.

Tilly, Charles. 1978. *From Mobilization to Revolution*. Reading, MA: Addison-Wesley.

———. 1992. "How to Detect, Describe, and Explain Repertoires of Contention." Center for Studies of Social Change Working Paper Series, no. 150, New School for Social Research, New York.

———. 1995. *Popular Contention in Great Britain, 1758–1834*. Cambridge, MA: Harvard University Press.

———. 1999. "The Trouble with Stories." In *The Social Worlds of Higher Education: Handbook for Teaching in a New Century*, ed. Bernice A. Pescosolido and Ronald Aminzade, 256–70. Thousand Oaks, CA: Pine Forge Press.

———. 2004. *Contention and Democracy in Europe, 1650–2000*. Cambridge: Cambridge University Press.

Tocqueville, Alexis de. 1969. *Democracy in America*. New York: Harper & Row.

Tsfati, Yariv. 2003. "Media Skepticism and Climate of Opinion Perception." *International Journal of Public Opinion Research* 15:65–82.

Turner, Victor. 1980. "Social Dramas and Stories about Them." *Critical Inquiry* 7:141–68.

Tversky, Amos, and Daniel Kahneman. 1974. "Judgment under Uncertainty: Heuristics and Biases." *Science* 185:1124–31.

U.S. Department of Health and Human Services. 2000a. *Healthy People 2010: Understanding and Improving Health*. 2nd ed. Washington, DC: U.S. Government Printing Office. Available online at http://www.healthypeople.gov/Document/pdf/uih/2010uih.pdf.

———. 2000b. *Healthy People 2010. With Understanding and Improving Health and Objectives for Improving Health*. 2nd ed. Washington, DC: U.S.

Government Printing Office. Available online at http://www.healthypeople.
gov/Document/tableofcontents.htm.

Valelly, Richard M. 1990. "Vanishing Voters." *American Prospect* 1:140–50.

———. 1993. "Public Policy for Reconnected Citizenship." In Ingram and Smith
1993, 241–66.

Verba, Sidney, Kay Lehman Schlozman, and Henry E. Brady. 1995. *Voice and
Equality: Civic Voluntarism in American Politics*. Cambridge, MA: Harvard
University Press.

Verba, Sidney, Kay Lehman Schlozman, Henry E. Brady, and Norman H. Nie.
1995. "American Citizen Participation Study." [Computer file.] Available from
Inter-University Consortium for Political and Social Research, study no. 6635.

Vidich, Arthur J. 1958. *Small Town in Mass Society*. New York: Doubleday.

Voss, Kim. 1996. "The Collapse of a Social Movement: The Interplay of Mobilizing Structures, Framing, and Political Opportunities in the Knights of Labor." In *Comparative Perspectives on Social Movements: Political Opportunities, Mobilizing Structures, and Cultural Framings*, ed. Doug McAdam, John
D. McCarthy, and Mayer N. Zald, 227–59. Cambridge: Cambridge University
Press.

Voss, Kim, and Rachel Sherman. 2000. "Breaking the Iron Law of Oligarchy:
Union Revitalization in the American Labor Movement." *American Journal
of Sociology* 106:303–49.

Wagner-Pacifici, Robin Erica. 1986. *The Moro Morality Play: Terrorism as Social
Drama*. Chicago: University of Chicago Press.

Walker, Jack L. 1991. *Mobilizing Interest Groups in America: Patrons, Professions,
and Social Movements*. Ann Arbor: University of Michigan Press.

Walsh, Katherine Cramer. 2004. *Talking About Politics: Informal Groups and Social Identity in American Life*. Chicago: University of Chicago Press.

Walters, Barbara R. 2003. *The Politics of Aesthetic Judgment*. Dallas, TX: University Press of America.

Walzer, Michael. 1983. *Spheres of Justice: A Defense of Pluralism and Equality*.
New York: Basic Books.

———. 2004. *Passion and Politics: Toward a More Egalitarian Liberalism*. New
Haven, CT: Yale University Press.

Warner, Michael. 1992. "The Mass Public and the Mass Subject." In Calhoun 1992,
377–401.

———. 2002. "Publics and Counterpublics." *Public Culture* 14:49–90.

Warren, Mark E. 2001. *Democracy and Association*. Princeton, NJ: Princeton University Press.

Warren, Mark R. 2001. *Dry Bones Rattling: Community Building to Revitalize
American Democracy*. Princeton, NJ: Princeton University Press.

Wedeen, Lisa. 1999. *Ambiguities of Domination: Politics, Rhetoric, and Symbols in
Contemporary Syria*. Chicago: University of Chicago Press.

―――. 2002. "Conceptualizing Culture: Possibilities for Political Science." *American Political Science Review* 96:713–28.

White, Hayden. 1987. *The Content of the Form: Narrative Discourse and Historical Representation*. Baltimore, MD: Johns Hopkins University Press.

Whyte, L. B., and S. M. Shaw. 1994. "Women's Leisure: An Exploratory Study of Fear of Violence as a Leisure Constraint." *Journal of Applied Recreation Research* 19:5–21.

Whyte, William Hollingsworth. 1956. *The Organization Man*. New York: Simon & Schuster.

Wilson, John, and Marc Musick. 1997. "Who Cares? Toward an Integrated Theory of Volunteer Work." *American Sociological Review* 62:694–713.

Wolfinger, Raymond E., and Steven J. Rosenstone. 1980. *Who Votes?* New Haven, CT: Yale University Press.

Wood, Richard L. 2002. *Faith in Action: Religion, Race, and Democratic Organizing in America*. Chicago: University of Chicago Press.

Woodberry, Robert D., and Christian S. Smith. 1998. "Fundamentalism et al.: Conservative Protestants in America." *Annual Review of Sociology* 24:25–56.

Wuthnow, Robert. 1998a. "Inequality and Civic Involvement." Paper presented at the annual meeting of the American Sociological Association, San Francisco, California, August.

―――. 1998b. *Loose Connections: Joining Together in America's Fragmented Communities*. Cambridge, MA: Harvard University Press.

Wyatt, Robert O., Elihu Katz, and Joohan Kim. 2000. "Bridging the Spheres: Political and Personal Conversation in Public and Private Spaces." *Journal of Communication* 50:71–92.

Young, Iris Marion. 2000. *Inclusion and Democracy*. Oxford: Oxford University Press.

Index